Praise for

NICE GIRLS DON'T GET
THE CORNER OFFICE

"Good advice...The pointers work equally well for men and women."
—*New York Times*

"Check out Frankel's career-damaging mistakes to get yourself to the top of your professional game!"
—*Complete Woman*

"Girlfriends, follow the recommendations in this important book and you will be more admired, respected, and important in your career. This book will help you become appropriately assertive, responsible, courageous, adult, and proficient in important people skills."
—Dr. Laura Schlessinger

"Whether you're at entry-level or you already occupy the corner office, you need to know which 'nice girl' mistakes are affecting, or sabotaging, your career and your life. As you're reading NICE GIRLS DON'T GET THE CORNER OFFICE you'll instantly recognize some of your own errors, and Lois will give you common sense solutions on how to avoid them."
—Karen Finerman, CEO, Metropolitan Capital Advisors, Inc., CNBC's "The Chairwoman," and author of *Finerman's Rules*

"Every page of this book is filled with something you or one of your friends does every day...A simple, quick guide to presenting ourselves as the strong and bold women v
—Gail Evans, author of *She Win*

"A frank career primer that can help us eliminate habits that hold us back in the workplace."
—*Essence*

"A must-have book for any woman looking to get ahead. Follow Lois Frankel's advice and you'll be sure to avoid the pitfalls women often make in their careers."
—Barbara Stanny, author of *Secrets of Six-Figure Women* and
Overcoming Underearning

"Excellent...This is a superb learning tool, I can't recommend it enough."
—*Kingston Observer* (Kingston, MA)

"A very intelligent book...these tips can help you succeed in business without really trying."
—*ShelfLife*

"Dr. Lois Frankel's advice is critical for any woman who wants to keep her balance on 'the thin pink line,' the narrow band of acceptable behavior for women in the workplace. This new edition is out just in time for a new generation of women entering the radically changed post-recession employment environment. Even if you read the previous edition, you need this new one. If somehow you missed reading it, correct your mistake!"
—Carol Frohlinger, principal, Negotiating Women, Inc., and
coauthor of *Her Place at the Table*

"A game changer. NICE GIRLS DON'T GET THE CORNER OFFICE is a blueprint for career success, and more importantly, career introspection."
—Jen Haley, coordinating producer, Bloomberg US Television

"This is the book every woman (diva or otherwise) needs on her desk. Like a fine wine, the anniversary edition has only gotten better over time."
—Josh Berman, creator, *Drop Dead Diva*

NICE GIRLS DON'T GET THE CORNER OFFICE

Also by Lois P. Frankel, PhD

Nice Girls Don't Get Rich

See Jane Lead

Stop Sabotaging Your Career

Women, Anger, and Depression

Nice Girls Just Don't Get It

Revised and Updated

NICE GIRLS DON'T GET THE CORNER OFFICE

Unconscious Mistakes
Women Make
That Sabotage Their Careers

Lois P. Frankel, PhD

GRAND CENTRAL
PUBLISHING

NEW YORK   BOSTON

Grand Central Publishing
Hachette Book Group
1290 Avenue of the Americas
New York, NY 10104

www.HachetteBookGroup.com

Printed in the United States of America

LSC-C

First Revised Edition: February 2014
11

Grand Central Publishing is a division of Hachette Book Group, Inc.
The Grand Central Publishing name and logo are trademarks of Hachette Book Group, Inc.

The Hachette Speakers Bureau provides a wide range of authors for speaking events. To find out more, go to www.hachettespeakersbureau.com or call (866) 376-6591.

The publisher is not responsible for websites (or their content) that are not owned by the publisher.

Library of Congress Cataloging-in-Publication Data
Frankel, Lois P., 1951–
    Nice girls don't get the corner office : unconscious mistakes women make that sabotage their careers / Lois P. Frankel. — First revised edition.
        pages cm. — (A nice girls book)
    Summary: "The New York Times bestseller, which has become a must-have for women in business, is now revised and updated in celebration of its tenth anniversary. Internationally recognized executive coach Dr. Lois P. Frankel teaches women how to eliminate unconscious mistakes that could be holding them back, and gives invaluable coaching tips that can easily be incorporated into social and business skills. The results are career opportunities women never thought possible and the power and know-how to occupy the corner office! Stop making 'nice girl' mistakes such as: -Mistake #13: Avoiding office politics -Mistake #21: Multi-tasking -Mistake #54: Failure to negotiate -Mistake #82: Asking permission -Mistake #100: Smiling inappropriately. These and other behaviors are why NICE GIRLS DON'T GET THE CORNER OFFICE."—Provided by publisher.
    Includes bibliographical references.
    ISBN 978-1-4555-4604-6 (pbk.) — ISBN 978-1-4789-2539-2 (audio download) — ISBN 978-1-4789-2538-5 (audiobook)   1. Women—Psychology.   2. Achievement motivation in women.   3. Self-actualization (Psychology)   4. Success—Psychological aspects.   5. Attitude (Psychology)   I. Title.
    HQ1206.F68 2014
    155.3'33—dc23
                                                                            2013021641

This book is dedicated to Bob Silverstein.
With his passing the world lost
one of its few male feminists . . . and I lost
not only a great literary agent
but also a dear friend.

Contents

Chapter 4: *How You Think*   126

Chapter 5: *How You Brand and Market Yourself*   173

Chapter 7: *How You Look*   262

Chapter 8: *How You Respond*   293

Acknowledgments

First and foremost I must thank you, the readers from every corner of the globe who propelled the *Nice Girls* series of books to popularity, shared them with friends, bought them for your sisters and daughters, read them in book clubs, sent me e-mails with questions and comments, and invited me to speak in your organizations. I am grateful for the many ways in which you let me know how my books touched and changed your lives. You have certainly influenced mine.

Thank you to the many women who pointed out issues that I overlooked in the first edition and offered suggestions for what to include in this one. I tried my best to use *all* of them.

Diana Baroni, thank you for always pushing me to deliver only the best, giving me the opportunity to write this book the first time, and then welcoming the idea to update it on the tenth anniversary of its initial publication. Your foresight has made a difference in the lives of countless women.

Thank you to the entire staff at Grand Central Publishing, both past and present, who are consummate professionals at editing, designing, promoting, advertising, and everything in between that goes into producing and launching a best seller.

I am grateful to my fellow sister-authors, including Anne Fisher, Carol Frohlinger, Pamela Mitchell, Barbara Stanny, Liz Cornish,

Carolyn Kepcher, and Liz Weston, for your friendship, support, and encouragement.

And finally, I thank my family and friends for your encouragement, support, and patience. You know who you are, and I love each of you.

Introduction

In the intervening years since *Nice Girls Don't Get the Corner Office* was first published, the United States elected its first African American president, the world was introduced to the concept of social networking, the Arab Spring deposed male rulers from nearly two dozen countries, and baby boomers began their mass exodus from the world of work. Despite these changes of a huge magnitude, progress for women has remained relatively flat. There's no denying that there has been some movement, but it has been at glacial speed, and the numbers remain largely unchanged and bleak. As of this writing:

- Women total 3.8 percent of Fortune 500 CEOs.
- Worldwide, 8 percent of top executives are female.
- Women make up 23.7 percent of US legislators.
- There are twenty women heads of state worldwide.
- Women account for 20.3 percent of elected parliamentarians around the globe (kudos to Nordic countries with 40 percent women!).
- Globally, the differences in earnings between men and women vary, with Japan and Korea seeing the largest disparity of 28 percent and 39 percent, respectively (Hungary is the lowest with only a 4 percent difference in earnings between men and women).
- On average in the United States, Caucasian women earn 77 percent of what men earn for doing the same jobs, but African

American women earn only 69 cents on the dollar and Latinas only 58 cents on the dollar.

- Within just one year of completing college, women are earning 8 percent less than the men with whom they graduated, and by mid-career that number increases to more than 20 percent.

Frankly, I wish I didn't have to write an updated and revised tenth-anniversary edition of this book. It's not that I have better things to do or that I don't want to spend the time on it. It's that I wish there was no need for it because in the decade since it was first published, women have made more progress at work, in politics, and at home. Whereas in many instances women have broken through the glass ceiling, there remains a *glass tree house*—that place where the upper tier of senior executives and directors of companies reside. Although there are notable exceptions (Marissa Mayer, Christine Lagarde, Sheryl Sandberg, Indra Nooyi, and Meg Whitman among them), the vast majority of women are left peering in from the outside. This happens despite the fact that data from the research organization Catalyst and consulting firm McKinsey & Co., Inc., reveal that having more women in leadership roles is correlated with stronger financial returns.

If you're not persuaded by the numbers and instead believe that society embraces the concept of equality for women, let me dissuade you of this notion by sharing just a few of the comments I've heard from women just like you around the world. These are women who read the first edition of this book and then wrote to me or who came up to speak with me after one of my *Nice Girls Don't Get the Corner Office* presentations.

- Janice from Colorado said that despite the fact that she instills in her four-year-old daughter the notion that she is equal to anyone else, and dresses her in sneakers and overalls so that she can run and climb on the playground, her child came home from preschool and announced, "Mommy, my teacher said you should dress me more like a girl."

- Ingrid from Copenhagen was surprised when her boss told her he was promoting her, because there were several men in the company with more tenure. He told her the change would take place within a month or so. In the interim, Ingrid learned she was pregnant and shared this with her boss. When the promotion seemed to be lagging, she asked him what was happening. The boss feigned surprise, pretended the conversation about the promotion never took place, and suggested she must have misunderstood him.

- Rosa from Miami is an attorney working for an immigration law firm. Her boss continually makes demeaning remarks to the women in the office about their appearance. If he doesn't like a certain hairstyle, he'll say, "Did you lose your comb?" Or if he thinks a woman's skirt is too short, he'll remark, "Did your grandmother run out of yarn before she finished making that?"

- Fiona from Sydney changed her major in college to engineering. Her mother's response upon hearing this was "Oh great. Now you'll *never* get married."

- Allison, from a small town in West Virginia, had to send her letter to me via US mail because her emotionally abusive husband reads all her e-mails. She wanted to know what she should do about the fact that she wants to go back to work now that her children are grown so that she can gain some financial independence, but her source of primary emotional support, her mother, told her, "Just don't make any waves. You're lucky to have a husband making a good living who provides for you."

- Farah is an Iranian Jewish physician who dreads going to Friday-night dinner with her parents because all they want to know is when will she give up this crazy idea of being a professional woman and get married and have babies.

There's one more reason why I'm writing this book: The workplace has changed in the past ten years. The biggest economic decline since the Great Depression has caused it to become increasingly competitive, social networking wasn't even a blip on the radar screen a decade ago but is now a must-do, work-life integration is an even greater challenge as women in need of the income work more hours, and educated women are entering the workforce at higher percentages than ever before. Given these new issues, I want to provide additional coaching tips for how you can get and keep the job you want.

These statistics, comments, social changes, and the women themselves make me realize my work is far from over. In the last decade I have been fortunate to travel around the world talking about women's issues. I have learned that women from native villages in Alaska share common challenges with women from South Africa. Despite what we are telling our daughters (and sons) at home about the capabilities of women, we cannot protect them from the external messages that continue to minimize the roles of women in society. And, perhaps most important, I learned that the advice provided in this book has made a difference in the lives of readers.

The mistakes described in each chapter are real, as are the accompanying examples (although the identities have been altered to maintain confidentiality). Many come from more than two decades of interacting with women and men as an executive coach. The coaching tips that follow each mistake work. I know this because my clients and readers have told me that when they follow them, they get the promotions they want, the confidence they need, and the respect they deserve. I measure my own effectiveness through *their* success stories and am delighted whenever an unsolicited e-mail appears in my in-box, or letters from as far as the Ukraine arrive at my office, telling me, "Your book made a difference in my life."

But you should know from the outset—this book isn't for everyone. Many women have found ways to overcome the stereotypes they learned in childhood and act in empowered ways most of the time (it's nearly impossible to act empowered *all* the time). Whether it's by honing your own unique style of communication and behavior or adopting and modifying more stereotypically masculine behaviors, you may be one of those women who is satisfied with the degree of professional success you've achieved. If that's the case, then you may find some additional tips in this book to help you further develop your unique style or to use with coaching and mentoring others. To you I say, "You go, girl!" Other women may find they've tried to do the same, only to be criticized by men and women alike for their strident or atypical behaviors. If you fall into this category, this book will seem the antithesis of all you've worked toward and, therefore, will be difficult for you to relate to. Not to worry, though. There are plenty of other books out there written just for you.

How do you know if this book will help *you*? Simple. First read through the following list of twelve characteristics and check those that you can honestly say are typical of you *most* of the time:

_____ I make decisions without being overly concerned with what others will say.

_____ I have created a unique personal brand that distinguishes me from others.

_____ I use social networking cautiously and appropriately.

_____ I negotiate effectively for what I want or need.

_____ I exhibit the courage to speak to the unspoken.

_____ I leverage workplace relationships to my advantage.

_____ Others describe me as articulate and persuasive.

_____ When it comes to playing workplace politics, I'm definitely in the game.

_____ My middle name is self-confident.

_____ I market myself effectively.

_____ I compete to win.

_____ I actively advocate for other women.

If you've checked all twelve items, it's time for you to write your own book. On the other hand, if you checked zero through only eight items, this book was written for you. Keep in mind that the corner office is simply a metaphor for achieving the career success you want. You may not aspire to be a senior executive, but you might want a promotion, more pay, or other perks. Not only are the characteristics above critical for success (for women *and* men), but I have also found that they are the development areas most frequently addressed in coaching engagements with women. The majority of women I coach don't have to work on all twelve areas (although I've known a few who do), but rather identify two or three as requiring development if they are to achieve their career goals.

From the therapy room to the conference room, for more than twenty-five years I have listened to women tell stories of how they were overlooked for promotions and placated when they expressed their ideas. I have observed women in hundreds of meetings. The thread common to those who were ignored was how they acted in and reacted to their situations. I could hear and see the ways in which they unknowingly undermined their credibility and sabotaged their own careers. No one had to do it for them.

I was trained at the University of Southern California as an existential clinician. The title sounds fancy, but all it really means is that it's the therapist's job to illuminate for the client the array of choices available. No matter what hand life deals us, we are ultimately left with the dilemma of how we choose to respond. That is where our control lies. It doesn't lie in the hand that's already been dealt. It doesn't lie in trying to change others—that's an illusion. It lies in the actions we choose to take in response to our particular situations. And when it comes to being women in the workplace, we can choose to behave in ways consistent with what others want and expect or we can choose another course—empowerment.

I am fully aware that there are those who say the term *empowerment* is outdated and overdone. I strongly disagree. The people who think it's overdone are those who possess the most power. Easy for them to say! They don't really want anyone to have the same power and influence that they enjoy, and so they downplay empowerment's importance in the employment and social arenas. It's a classic case of the desire to maintain the status quo. Those who have power don't really want to share it, so they minimize the need for others to share it. Without embarrassment or apology I say, *This book is about empowerment.*

Unlike other books that help you identify potential areas for development or point out critical success factors, this book doesn't stop there. Raising awareness is only the first step. Next, you need concrete suggestions for behavioral change that are *proven* to be effective in moving women forward in their careers. Behaviors that were appropriate in girlhood, but not in womanhood, may be contributing to your career's stagnating, plateauing, or even derailing from its career path. Success comes not from acting more like a man, as some might lead you to believe, but by acting more like a *woman* instead of a girl. Even if you select only 10 percent of the hundreds of coaching tips provided in this book and incorporate them into your skill set, your investment will pay off.

How to Get the Most from This Book

The book contains 133 typical mistakes women make at work due to their socialization. Keep in mind, most women don't make all 133 mistakes—but they do make more than one. I've found through my practice and experience that the more mistakes you make, the less likely you are to achieve your full career potential. I suggest you begin by completing the self-assessment in chapter 1. It will help you identify the self-defeating behaviors in which you most often engage.

After you've completed the self-assessment, you can go directly to those specific behaviors that get in your way most often. After each mistake, you will find tips for counteracting the mistake. As I said earlier, these are the same tips I give to my own clients when they come for coaching, so I know they work. But like a diet, they work only if you commit to them fully and apply them consistently.

At the bottom of each page of coaching tips you'll find an Action Item box. Put a check mark on the page of tips that you commit to using as a way of overcoming self-defeating behavior. Once you've finished the book, take these checked items and complete the personal development plan contained in the last chapter. Don't make it more complex than it needs to be. Choose just one behavior a week and focus on it. What you will find is that by focusing on the behavior, you'll become increasingly aware of when and how you sabotage yourself. The next step is to replace the self-defeating behavior with more effective action. You *can* do it. It's *your* choice. All it takes is acting more like the woman you are capable of becoming than like the girl you were taught to be. There's an A.A. Milne quote I've always enjoyed that I'd like you to keep in mind as you read this book: "There is something you must always remember. You are braver than you believe, stronger than you seem, and smarter than you think."

NICE GIRLS DON'T GET THE CORNER OFFICE

Chapter 1

Getting Started

Here's your first coaching tip: Don't begin reading this book until you've learned how to use it to your advantage. You'll only end up thinking everything applies to you in equal proportions when in fact you're probably doing better than you think. I'm always surprised when a woman tells me, "I make every mistake you list in the book!" You know how we women can be—more critical of ourselves than necessary and reluctant to take credit where it's due. When I coach women, I often tell them that changing behavior is much easier if they can understand where it comes from and what purpose it serves. All behavior serves a purpose—take a few minutes now to understand what purpose yours serves.

From the outset I want you to know and, even more important, believe that *the mistakes impeding you from reaching your career goals or potential don't happen because you're stupid or incompetent* (although others might want to make you think so). You are simply acting in ways consistent with your socialization or in response to cultural expectations. Beyond girlhood, no one ever *tells* us that acting differently is an option—and so we don't. Whether it's because we are explicitly discouraged from doing so, because social messages inform our behavior, or because we are unaware of the alternatives, we often fail to develop a repertoire of woman-appropriate behaviors.

Why do smart, capable women act in ways detrimental to their career mobility (not to mention mental health)? During my career, working with literally thousands of professional men and women and comparing their behaviors, I found the answer to that question through inquiry and study: *From early childhood, girls are taught that their well-being and ultimate success are contingent upon acting in certain stereotypical ways, such as being polite, soft-spoken, compliant, and relationship-oriented.* Throughout their lifetimes, this is reinforced through media, family, and social messages. It's not that women *consciously* act in self-sabotaging ways; they simply act in ways consistent with their learning experiences.

Even women who proclaim to have gotten "the right" messages in childhood from parents who encouraged them to achieve their full potential by becoming anything they want to be find that when they enter the real world, all bets are off. This is particularly true for many African American women who grew up with strong mothers (something I address in Mistake 3). Whether by example or encouragement, if a woman exhibits confidence and courage on a par with a man, she is often accused of being that dreaded "b-word."

Attempts to act counter to social stereotypes are frequently met with ridicule, disapproval, and scorn. Whether it was Mom's message—"Boys don't like girls who are too loud"—or, in response to an angry outburst, a spouse's message—"What's the matter? Is it that time of the month?"—women are continually bombarded with negative reinforcement for acting in any manner contrary to what they were taught in girlhood. As a result, they learn that acting like a "nice girl" is less painful than assuming behaviors more appropriate for adult women (and totally acceptable for boys and adult men). In short, women wind up acting like little girls, even after they're grown up.

Now, is this to say gender bias no longer exists in the workplace? Not at all. The statistics at the beginning of this introduction speak for themselves. Additionally, women are more likely to be overlooked for developmental assignments and promotions to senior levels of an organization. Research shows that on performance evaluation ratings, women consistently score less favorably than men. These are the realities. But after all these years I continue to go to the place of "So what?" We can rationalize, defend, and bemoan these facts, or we can acknowledge that these are the realities within which we must work. Rationalizing, defending, and bemoaning won't get us where we want to be. They become excuses for staying where we are.

Although there are plenty of mistakes made by both men and women that hold them back, there are a unique set of mistakes made predominantly by women. Whether I'm working in Jakarta, Oslo, Prague, Frankfurt, Trinidad, or Houston, I'm amazed to watch women across cultures make the same mistakes at work. They may be more exaggerated in Hong Kong than in Los Angeles, but they're variations on the same theme. And I know these are mistakes because once women address them and begin to act differently, their career paths take wonderful turns they never thought possible.

So why *do* women stay in the place of girlhood long after it's productive for them? One reason is because we've been taught that acting like a nice girl—even when we're grown up—isn't such a bad thing. Girls get taken care of in ways boys don't. Girls aren't expected to fend for or take care of themselves—others do that for them. Sugar and spice and everything nice—that's what little girls are made of. Who doesn't want to be everything nice? People like girls. Men want to protect you. Cuddly or sweet, tall or tan, girls don't ask for much. They're nice to be around and they're nice to have around—sort of like pets.

Being a girl is certainly easier than being a woman. Girls don't have to take responsibility for their destiny. Their choices are limited by a narrowly defined scope of expectations. And here's another reason why we continue to exhibit the behaviors learned in childhood even when at some level we know they're holding us back: *We can't see beyond the boundaries that have traditionally circumscribed the parameters of our influence.* It's dangerous to go out-of-bounds. When you do, you get accused of trying to act like a man or being "bitchy." All in all, it's easier to behave in socially acceptable ways.

This might also be a good time to dispel the myth that overcoming the *nice girl syndrome* means you have to be mean and nasty. It's the question I am asked most often in interviews. Some women have even told me they didn't buy the book because they assumed from the title that it must contain suggestions for how to be more like a man. Nothing could be further from the truth. If I've said it once, I've said it literally five hundred times in the last ten years: *Nice is necessary for success; it's simply not sufficient.* If you overrely on being nice to the exclusion of developing complementary behaviors, you'll never achieve your adult goals. This book will help you to expand your tool kit so that you have a wider variety of responses on which to draw.

When we live lives circumscribed by the expectations of others, we live limited lives. What does it really mean to live our lives as girls rather than women? It means we choose behaviors consistent with those that are expected of us rather than those that move us toward fulfillment and self-actualization. Rather than live consciously, we live reactively. Although we mature physically, we never really mature emotionally. And while this may allow us momentary relief from real-world dilemmas, it never allows us to be fully in control of our destinies.

Missed opportunities for career-furthering assignments or promotions arise from acting like the nice little girl you were taught to be in childhood: being reluctant to showcase your capabilities, feeling hesitant to speak in meetings, and working so hard that you forget to build the relationships necessary for long-term success. I've observed these behaviors magnified in workshops at which men *and* women are the participants. My work in corporations has allowed me to facilitate both workshops for only women and leadership development programs for mixed groups within the same company. Even women whom I've seen act assertively in a group of other women become more passive, compliant, and reticent to speak in a mixed group. When men are around, we dumb down or try to become invisible so as not to incur their wrath.

The Case of Susan

Let me give you an example of a woman with whom I worked who wondered why she wasn't reaching her full potential. Susan was a procurement manager for a Fortune 100 oil company. She'd been with this firm for more than twelve years when she expressed frustration over not moving as far or as fast as male colleagues who'd commenced employment at the same time she did. Although Susan thought there might be gender bias at play, she never considered how she contributed to her own career plateauing. Before Susan and I met one-on-one in a coaching session, I had the opportunity to observe her in meetings with her peers.

At the first meeting I noticed this attractive woman with long blond hair, a diminutive figure, and deep blue eyes. Being from Texas, she spoke with a delicate Southern accent and had an alluring way of cocking her head and smiling as she listened to others. She was a pleasure to have in the room, but she reminded me of a cheerleader—attractive, vivacious, warm, and supportive. As others spoke, she nodded her head and smiled. When she did speak, she used equivocating phrases like "Perhaps we should consider..."; "Maybe it's because..."; and "What if we..." Because of these behaviors no one would ever accuse Susan of being offensive, but neither would they consider her executive material.

After several more meetings at which I observed her behavior vis-à-vis her peers, Susan and I met privately to explore her career aspirations. Based on her looks, demeanor, and what I had heard her say in meetings, I assumed she was perhaps thirty to thirty-five years old. I was floored when she told me she was forty-seven, with nearly twenty years' experience in the area of procurement. I had no clue she had that kind of history and experience—and if I didn't, no one else did either. Without realizing it, Susan was acting in ways consistent with her socialization. She had received so much positive reinforcement for these behaviors that she'd come to believe they were the only ways she could act and still be successful. Susan bought into the stereotype of being a nice girl.

Truth be told, the behaviors she exhibited in meetings did contribute to her early career success. The problem was that they would not contribute to reaching future goals and aspirations. Her managers, peers, and direct reports acknowledged she was a delight to work with, but they didn't seriously consider her for more senior positions or high-visibility projects. Susan acted like a girl and, accordingly, was treated like one. Although she knew she had to do some things differently if she were to have any chance of reaching her potential, she didn't have a clue what those things would be.

I eventually came to learn Susan was the youngest of four children and the only girl in the family. She was the apple of Daddy's eye and protected by her brothers. She learned early on that being a girl was a good thing. She used it to her advantage. And as Susan grew up, she continued to rely on the stereotypically feminine behaviors that resulted in getting her needs met. She was the student teachers loved having in class, the classmate with whom everyone wanted to be friends, and the cheerleader everyone admired. Susan had no reference for alternative ways of acting that would bring her closer to her dream of being promoted to a vice presidential position.

We're All Girls at Heart

Although Susan is an extreme example of how being a girl can pay huge dividends, most of us have some Susan in us. We behave in ways consistent with the roles we were socialized to play, thereby never completely moving from girlhood to womanhood. As nurturers, supporters, or helpmates, we are more invested in seeing others get their needs met than in ensuring that our needs are acknowledged. And there's another catch. When we *do* try to break out of those roles and act in more mature, self-actualizing ways, we are often met with subtle—and not-so-subtle—resistance designed to keep us in a girl role. Comments like "You're so cute when you're angry," "What's the matter? Are you on the rag?" or "Why can't you be satisfied with where you are?" are designed to keep us in the role of a girl.

When others question our femininity or the validity of our feelings, our typical response is to back off rather than make waves. We question the veracity of our experience. If it's fight or flight, we often flee. Every time we do, we take a step back into girlhood and question our self-worth. In this way we collude with others to remain girls rather than become women. And here is where we must begin to accept responsibility for not getting our needs met or never reaching our full potential. Eleanor Roosevelt was right when she said, "No one can make you feel inferior without your consent." Stop consenting. Stop colluding. Stop being that nice little girl you were taught to be in childhood!

Self-Assessment

Now it's time to assess where you need the most work. The inventory on the next few pages is designed to help you identify the specific behaviors that may impede your career movement. You'll find there are areas you've already worked to address and that no longer present obstacles to you. If you're like most women, you'll also find a few areas that still require your attention. Take time now to complete the inventory. When you're finished, there are some guidelines for how to apply your score to what you read. You may not even need to read the entire book. Imagine that! Your first lesson in working smarter, not harder.

NICE GIRLS SELF-ASSESSMENT

Using the scale provided, indicate the degree to which each statement is true of you. Be honest—this is a tool to help you move from nice girl to winning woman.

> 1 = Rarely true *or* I'm not sure
> 2 = Sometimes true

3 = Usually true
4 = Almost always true

1. _____ I can tell you the unwritten rules for success in my company.
2. _____ I prepare in advance for social events by creating a list of possible topics to discuss.
3. _____ I'm comfortable questioning those in authority when their expectations or requests don't make sense.
4. _____ My elevator speech rolls off the tip of my tongue.
5. _____ My communications are crisp, clear, and concise.
6. _____ My hair and makeup augment my verbal messages for maximum credibility.
7. _____ I do not express negative opinions about others in online public forums.
8. _____ I engage in social networking via Facebook and/or LinkedIn.
9. _____ The need to be liked does not preclude me from saying things others might not like to hear.
10. _____ When given an assignment with too little time or too few resources to complete it, I negotiate for what I need to make it more reasonable to accomplish.
11. _____ When asked what I do, I describe my work in terms of achievements and the way in which I add value to my company.
12. _____ I present my ideas as statements rather than couching them as questions.
13. _____ My nonverbal communications enhance my verbal ones.
14. _____ When someone hurts my feelings, I let it go and move on.
15. _____ I use office politics to my advantage.
16. _____ I rarely bring food to the office to share with others.
17. _____ My focus is more on adding value than on doing my job.
18. _____ I seek high-profile assignments that will stretch my skills and let others see what I'm capable of.
19. _____ It's unusual for me to apologize.
20. _____ I dress for success.
21. _____ I believe I'm as smart if not smarter than the next person.

22. _____ I capitalize on the professional relationships I make.

23. _____ I don't multitask as a steady diet.

24. _____ I'm an effective negotiator.

25. _____ There's nothing on my social media sites that I wouldn't want a prospective employer to see.

26. _____ I speak slowly and clearly.

27. _____ I don't engage in public grooming such as applying makeup, fixing my hair, et cetera.

28. _____ I am powerful.

29. _____ I have one or more mentors who I know will advocate for me when opportunities arise for which I am qualified.

30. _____ When I'm bullied, I let the other person know how I feel about it.

31. _____ I devote time each week to building and maintaining my network.

32. _____ I effectively toot my own horn.

33. _____ Others describe me as articulate.

34. _____ I have no obvious tattoos or multiple piercings.

35. _____ I speak early and often in meetings.

36. _____ I actively seek to understand the needs of others so that I can better serve them.

37. _____ My office decor underscores my professionalism.

38. _____ I don't aim for perfection.

39. _____ I regularly solicit feedback that will help me build my personal brand.

40. _____ I vary my communication style to influence others to accept my ideas and proposals.

41. _____ When seated at a conference table, I put my hands on the table and lean in.

42. _____ When others act inappropriately toward me, I address it directly with them rather than hold it in or complain to friends.

43. _____ I don't wait to be given what I want, need, or deserve—I ask for it.

44. _____ I'll ask a question even if I fear it might sound stupid.
45. _____ I tend not to be hard on myself when things go wrong.
46. _____ I use meetings to market my personal brand.
47. _____ I present ideas using influential business language.
48. _____ I know how to accessorize outfits to make a statement.
49. _____ When given critical feedback, I take it in stride rather than perseverate over it.

SELF-ASSESSMENT SCORE SHEET

INSTRUCTIONS

1. Transfer your answers to the score sheet below.
2. Add your scores down by column for a total in each category.
3. Add your category total scores across for an overall total.

How You Play the Game	How You Act	How You Think	How You Brand & Market Yourself	How You Sound	How You Look	How You Respond	
1.	2.	3.	4.	5.	6.	7.	
8.	9.	10.	11.	12.	13.	14.	
15.	16.	17.	18.	19.	20.	21.	
22.	23.	24.	25.	26.	27.	28.	
29.	30.	31.	32.	33.	34.	35.	
36.	37.	38.	39.	40.	41.	42.	
43.	44.	45.	46.	47.	48.	49.	
Category Total	Category Total	Category Total	Category Total	Category Total	Category Total	Category Total	Overall Total

INTERPRETATION OF YOUR SCORES

Overall Score of 159–196 or **A Category Score of 22–28**	You go, girl! Your score indicates you must already have the corner office or are well on your way to getting it. To stay on track, focus on those questions where you rated yourself "1" or "2." Also, remember to pay it forward by mentoring other women.
Overall Score of 110–158 or **A Category Score of 14–21**	Fine-tuning is the name of your game! Although you often engage in behaviors worthy of a winning woman, there are times when you don't get your due because you get caught up in nice girl syndrome. First read the chapters that correspond with your lowest category scores, then go back and read the rest as a refresher course.
Overall Score of 49–109 or **A Category Score of 7–13**	Danger! You are falling into the trap of acting like the nice little girl you were taught to be in childhood. You frequently wonder why you're not achieving the success you've worked so hard for. This book was written for *you*, so take out your pen and start making notations for what you commit to doing differently.

Unconscious Competence

See? I told you your behavior wasn't as bad as you thought. To help you further understand the process of self-assessment, I want to introduce you to a model used in coaching for helping people develop new behaviors. It's called "Unconscious Competence." The following chart illustrates how it works.

UNCONSCIOUS COMPETENCE

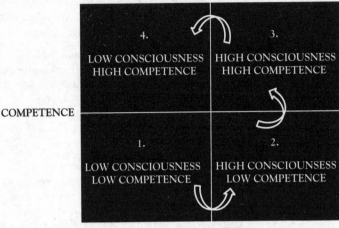

COMPETENCE

4.	3.
LOW CONSCIOUSNESS HIGH COMPETENCE	HIGH CONSCIOUSNESS HIGH COMPETENCE
1.	2.
LOW CONSCIOUSNESS LOW COMPETENCE	HIGH CONSCIOUNSESS LOW COMPETENCE

CONSCIOUSNESS

Your challenge is to move from Box 1 to Box 4 *over a period of time.* You begin in Box 1—unaware that you're even doing anything wrong, so you can't possibly have competence in that area (low consciousness and low competence).

After taking the self-assessment and reading the mistakes described in this book, you'll be more aware of your self-defeating behaviors, but you still won't know what to do to change them. You've moved to Box 2—still low competence but now high consciousness.

By actually practicing the coaching tips presented after each mistake, you'll move to Box 3—high consciousness and high competence. If you've ever learned to play a sport or a musical instrument, you're familiar with how this works. You'll become increasingly capable of incorporating these behaviors into your regular repertoire of skills, not even thinking about when you do them (Box 4—high competence and low consciousness). Although this is the goal, don't be discouraged if in some cases it doesn't come naturally. Whether it's a golf swing or a piano piece, you know you can do it, but you may have to concentrate on doing it well. That's Box 3.

As when you're learning to acquire any new skill, for a while you'll be self-conscious about how you're acting. Finally, after a period of practice and success, you'll incorporate these behaviors without thinking. In some areas, however, you may never quite get there. Socialization can make it difficult—no, change that to *impossible*—to engage in certain behaviors without having to think about it first. There's nothing wrong with this. As long as you act consciously and purposefully, you'll be fine.

Managing Your Anxiety

I can see by the looks on women's faces, and from their comments, that anxiety and confusion are part of the process for becoming more confident, competent, and courageous. When the suggestion is made to embrace their power, women reject the notion for fear of being perceived as too masculine, aggressive, or uncooperative. When I ask a group of hundreds of women to raise their hands if they're powerful, people tend to look around at one another. Then only a few hands go up. Then a few more. Rarely does every woman in the room raise her hand. Ask a group of men and women the same question, and nearly every male hand goes up immediately. It is so counter to our socialization that women prematurely dismiss the notion of being powerful. The belief that we must be for others rather than for ourselves is implanted so strongly that we are reluctant to explore the alternative.

The irony is that women act powerfully all the time, but in ways different from men. Relying on our "girlish charm" can be just as influential, but less direct and less confrontational. In other words, we wield power less directly than men. We've learned to be less direct so we will not be perceived as taking too much power away from men.

This is at the core of our difficulties with gaining increased influence skills, negotiation capabilities, and organizational visibility.

Each time a woman *directly* asserts herself, however, she is essentially saying to the men in her life (whether they are husbands, sons, bosses, or other male authority figures), "I want something from you. I want what is rightfully mine. I expect my needs to be met, too." With each assertion we frequently feel guilty. We equate taking control *back* with taking something *away* from someone else. More than simply getting what we need, deserve, or want, we are forcing others to give back what we have been giving away for so long. The reactions we get are difficult to cope with. Others don't really want the situation to change—*they* already have everything *they* need, so why should they change?

Resistance to change is normal. It is to be expected. Like the alcoholic in recovery who finds others colluding to bring him or her back to a place of intoxication, the girl who moves toward womanhood will find herself faced with people who want to continue to infantilize her. This is what you must keep in mind if you want to achieve your goals.

What's a Girl to Do?

Here are some specific coaching tips—a prelude of what is to follow. Take them one at a time. Don't try to do them all at once—you'll only set yourself up for frustration. Choose one or two on which to work, then come back for more.

• **Give yourself permission to move from nice girl to adult woman.** It may seem like a simple idea, but it's one that is often resisted for all the reasons mentioned above. Have a good, long talk with yourself. Tell yourself that you are not only allowed but *entitled* to act in ways that move you toward goal attainment. Try the mantra "I am entitled to have *my* needs met, too."

- **Visualize yourself as you want to be.** If you can see it, you can be it. Picture yourself in the role to which you aspire. If it's in the corner office, see yourself at the desk with the accoutrements that go along with it. Consider the behaviors in which you will engage to warrant this position and the ways in which you will act. Bring them into your reality.

- **Talk back to the fearful voice inside your head.** This may sound crazy at first, but you must counter the old messages and replace them with new ones. If your fearful girl's voice says, *But no one will like me if I change,* let your woman's voice respond with *That's an old message. Let's create a new, more empowered one.*

- **Surround yourself with a Plexiglas shield.** The Plexiglas shield is designed to allow you to see what is going on around you, but not be punctured by the negativity of others. I suggested this to a client, who later told me she thought it sounded a little crazy but decided to try it—only to find that it worked! In difficult situations she would picture herself encapsulated in a Plexiglas bubble that protected her from the disparaging remarks of others and allowed her to remain in a grounded, adult position.

- **Create the word on the street.** There's a word on the street about all of us. It's what people say about us when we leave a room. A routine exercise we do in leadership classes is to ask participants to write a twenty-five-word statement of how they want to be described, then list the behaviors needed to get them there. You can do the same. Write down what you want others to be saying about you, then follow it up with specific actions to make it happen. In short, accept the responsibility of adulthood.

- **Recognize resistance and put a name to it.** When you find others resisting your efforts to be more direct and empowered, consider first that their responses are designed to keep you in a less powerful place. Rather than acquiesce, question it. Say something like "It seems you don't agree with what I'm saying. Let me give you the rationale for my position, and then perhaps you can tell me what it is you take issue with." Others may be so invested in having you remain the same that they can't engage in an objective dialogue about your needs. If this is the case, you may want to get professional help to learn how to deal with their resistance in a healthy and productive way.

• **Ask for feedback.** If you're worried that you are in some way acting inappropriately, ask a trusted friend or colleague for feedback. Avoid asking a yes or no question (such as "Did you think I was out of line?"). Try asking an open-ended question that will give you insight into how you are perceived (such as "Tell me what I did in that meeting that helped me or hindered me from achieving my goals").

• **Don't aim for perfection.** Even *I* don't engage in all the behaviors described in this book. There are some that are just so counter to my personality, I don't even try; there are others that, no matter how hard I try, I don't do well. As I often tell women, "I'm a recovering nice girl." The important thing is to do a few really well and allow the rest to fall into place.

Next Steps

You'll be on your own in just a minute. I suggest you begin by reading the two chapters that coincide with your *lowest* scores. This is where you need the most help. Not every mistake in those chapters will apply to you, so don't get carried away and make every coaching tip a goal. Instead, check the box at the bottom of the pages that contain those tips you think will make the biggest difference and commit to taking action on those. Avoid the tendency to ignore the tips that seem hard. That's probably where you can get the greatest leverage in changes to your behavior.

After you've read the sections that correspond with your lowest scores, go back and review the remaining mistakes. All 133 mistakes are real mistakes made by real women. They were accumulated as the result of my own work as a coach, soliciting input from men and women in companies I've worked with around the world, contributions made from women who attended my Nice Girls Don't Get the Corner Office workshops and keynote presentations, and women who wrote to me after reading this book when it was first published.

As for the coaching tips, most are suggestions I've provided to women for years and gotten feedback confirming that even small changes have a big impact on how they are perceived. Others were provided by my colleagues, many of whom are on the consulting team at Corporate Coaching International and who are subject-matter experts in various coaching areas, including communications, strategic career planning, and work-life integration. As you read the tips, you'll find I make reference to books or classes. The appendix provides you with two important things: a summary of these references and a personal development plan template. If you're serious about achieving your personal and professional best, I urge you to complete the plan soon after reading the book. It will help to keep you on track and allow you to chart your own progress. Now it's up to you. Go get your corner office!

Chapter 2

How You Play the Game

A friend and I were discussing the Olympics soon after the closing ceremony. I remarked that I loved seeing people achieving the goals they had strived for their entire lives and performing at the top of their games. She, on the other hand, said she didn't like how competitive it was, with constant reminders of how many medals each country had won. "It's the Olympics!" I blurted out in disbelief. "They're *supposed* to be competitive."

A few days later I was playing online Scrabble and my opponent got two bingos in a row (a bingo is when you use all your letters to get bonus points), which is somewhat unusual at my level of play. The person typed, "I'm sorry." I immediately typed back, "May I ask if you're a man or a woman?" The reply didn't surprise me; of course it was a woman. I've never had a man apologize for legitimately gaining an advantage.

Many women—especially those who grew up in the 1960s and 1970s—never had the opportunity to participate in competitive sports. Until relatively recently, few of us served in the armed forces, attended military academies, or participated in other activities that required us to play to win. As a result, we don't know how to play the game, let alone play within bounds but at the edge (which will be explored further a little later in this chapter), and play to win without feeling apologetic or guilty. Worse yet, many women view the whole idea of the game of business as something unpleasant, dirty, and to be avoided at all costs.

Let's start with the most important lesson: Business *is* a game, and you *can* win it. As a matter of fact, women are born to win this game. I spend half of my time working with men, teaching them to be more like women. Of course, I don't put it quite that way, or I would be out of business. I coined the term *feminization of leadership* to describe the ways in which today's workforce responds more positively to stereotypically feminine behaviors than to masculine ones. I talk to men about the importance of things like listening, collaborating, motivating, and seeing the human side of their staff. These factors contribute to what's known as EQ (emotional quotient), and EQ is the sine qua non for workplace success. On top of that, it's been shown that women exceed men in four out of five EQ factors, including self-awareness, self-regulation, empathy, and social skills. Women and men are equal on the fifth factor, self-motivation. Whether women do these things because they've been taught the behaviors and have had a lot of practice at them or because they come naturally really doesn't matter. To win the game of business, you need to capitalize on your high EQ.

The areas in which women often aren't quite as skilled as men include knowing where the imaginary boundaries of the workplace playing field are, getting into the game, and understanding the unspoken rules for winning the game. Of all the coaching tips in this book, the following are the most difficult for women to incorporate into their corporate skill set. Many of the suggestions are counter to everything we learned growing up. Resist the urge to skip the hard stuff. If you don't play, you can't win.

Mistake 1

Pretending It Isn't a Game

*T*he workplace is exactly that—a game. It has rules, boundaries, strategies, winners, and losers. Women tend to approach work more like an event (picnic, concert, fund-raiser), where everyone comes together for the day to play together nicely. In our desire to create win-win situations, we unknowingly create win-lose ones—where we're the losers. Playing the game of business doesn't mean you're out to cause others to fail, but it is competitive. It means you are aware of the rules and develop strategies for making them work to your advantage.

An interesting scenario played out that underscores this uniquely feminine phenomenon. The women's softball teams of Western Oregon University and Central Washington University were competing toward the end of the season, when a senior who had never hit a home run during her college career came up to bat and smacked it over the fence. As she was running toward first base, she tore a ligament in her leg and could no longer run. Knowing her situation, and not wanting to deprive her of one last chance for a homer, players from the opposing team carried her around the field to touch each base, allowing her to have officially hit a home run. When was the last time you heard this happen in *any* sport where men were playing? To the contrary. As a male Nestlé executive said to me, "When a man's friend wins, a little piece of him dies."

Although I think it was a nice thing to do—and maybe even the right thing to do under the circumstances—women also need to understand when playing to win is more important than being nice and putting the needs of others first. The ability to differentiate when collaboration that will yield maximum results is needed from when going flat out to win should be employed moves you from nice girl to winning woman.

Barbara is a workplace example of someone who didn't understand the game. She worked as a director of marketing in the banking industry for many years. She reached the point in her career where she was so successful that she was sought after for senior positions by a number of companies. She selected one, in the specialty chemicals business, where she entered as a vice president. When she was referred to me for coaching, she could not understand why she was foundering. Everything that had worked for her in banking failed her in her new position. Her polite, laid-back way of managing and interacting with others was now seen as weak and indecisive. Not understanding that this was a new ball game, Barbara played the new game by the old rules—and found herself facing the possibility of failure for the first time in her career. In a more competitive business, or when working for someone who values competition, you've got to play to win, or you'll soon find yourself on the bench.

Not only is business a game, but the rules of the game change from organization to organization and from department to department *within* an organization. What works with one boss may not work with the next one. Keeping your eye on the ball is essential when it comes to winning the game of business.

COACHING TIPS

- Learn to play chess. It will help you develop a more strategic mind when it comes to winning games.
- Make a list of the rules of the game at your workplace. Remember, these are usually unspoken expectations for how fast-trackers should behave. Rather than completing it in one sitting, you may have to compile the list gradually as you observe interactions, memos, and meetings in a different way than you have in the past. Examples of rules in some workplaces include "Don't disagree with the boss"; "Everyone works at least ten hours of overtime"; "Being polite is more important than being right"; "Deadlines must be met no matter what the circumstance"; "Budgets are strictly adhered to"; "The customer always comes first," and so on. As you make your list, begin thinking about how your behavior compares with the expectations.
- Read *Hardball for Women: Winning at the Game of Business* (revised edition), by Pat Heim, PhD, and Susan Golant. It will help you better understand the male business culture and how to use it to your advantage. Among the tips provided are ways to be assertive without being obnoxious, how to engage in smart self-promotion, and methods to display confidence even when you may feel powerless.
- Identify a mentor—someone who is successful at playing the game and with whom you can openly discuss the rules in your organization. It's often helpful to have both a man and a woman as mentors, as each will have invaluable guidance for success.
- If you don't currently play a sport—start. It doesn't matter whether it's tennis, kickboxing, softball, or golf. Playing sports helps you learn the language of the game.

ACTION ITEM ☐

Mistake 2

Playing the Game Safely and Within Bounds

$\mathcal{A}$s an avid but quite average tennis player, I used to hit the ball squarely within bounds for fear of going out and losing the point. In an effort to play safely, I artificially narrowed my playing field. After a while, it occurred to me that I would never win the game playing that way. I had to learn to hit the ball toward the edges of, yet within, bounds if I ever hoped to win. So I started going outside my comfort zone and found that I actually won more games.

In any game, points aren't won in the middle of the field, they're won at the edge. Taking calculated risks might sometimes cause you to go out-of-bounds, but as long as you win the majority of points, you won't lose the game. It's important to get yourself out of the women's safe zone and toward the edge of the field where the winners are playing.

I had the opportunity to use this analogy with a client who was recently promoted to supervisor and getting feedback that she wasn't "proactive" enough. "How can I be accused of not being proactive?" she wondered. "I do everything I'm supposed to without being asked." Doing everything you're supposed to isn't being proactive. It's only doing what you're supposed to. At her new level, management expected her to take more responsibility and make decisions independently. When I suggested this to her, she said she didn't want to overstep her authority, so she ran most important decisions by her supervisor first.

I asked the woman if she played tennis, and, fortunately, she did. Within moments of using the analogy of playing it safe in tennis, she

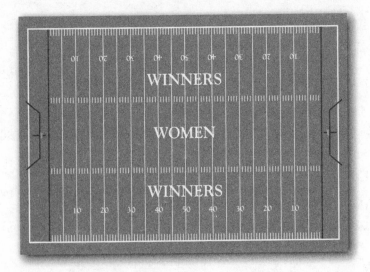

got it. She could understand how she wasn't using all the court available to her. By making assumptions about what would and wouldn't be acceptable to her management, she narrowed her playing field. Rather than risk hitting the ball out-of-bounds, she engaged only in behaviors she knew would land the ball squarely within the court. It wasn't enough for the woman's manager, who wanted her team members to take calculated risks and go beyond what was asked of them.

This same phenomenon plays out in the workplace all the time. Even when a woman knows the workplace is a game, she has the tendency to play safe rather than play smart. She obeys all the rules to the letter and expects others to as well. If the policy says don't do it, then it can't be done. If it might upset someone, she doesn't do it. You never want to act unethically, but it *is* a game—and one you want to win. To do so, you have to use the entire field available to you.

In my client's case, she followed my suggestion to ask her manager to help her define her scope of authority so that she would feel more comfortable taking risks. The manager called me several weeks later and, during the course of conversation about another matter, mentioned that the woman was now showing more initiative and meeting her performance objectives.

COACHING TIPS

• Play the game within bounds, but at the edges. If you're not sure where the edges of your company's playing field are, look at the women in your workplace who are winning the game. Consider what they're doing that you should be doing, too.

• Write down two rules you interpret narrowly and always follow. Have you seen other people bend these rules? If so, what's happened to them? If nothing, then take the risk of stretching the bounds by broadly, rather than narrowly, interpreting the rules.

• If you're not sure something is *fair*, do it anyway. If you're not sure something is *ethical*, ask.

• If you're called out, don't take it personally—and by all means don't revert to playing safe. Look at it as an opportunity to learn where the edge of the boundary is and how to play to it.

ACTION ITEM

Mistake 3

Assuming the Rules, Boundaries, and Strategies Are the Same for Everyone

*T*his is by far the most controversial issue I discuss in my keynote presentations. I intentionally left it out of the first edition because I wasn't sure how readers would respond. I chose to play it safe. Now, after receiving so much positive feedback from groups that I've spoken to (along with some pushback from those finding it patently unfair), I feel I not only should but must include it, because to do otherwise would be an egregious oversight.

If you've ever wondered why when you say something in the exact same way a male counterpart says it you get called a bitch and he gets called assertive, it's because the rules, boundaries, and strategies are different for men and women and for people of color and Caucasians. I don't think it's fair or right, but it does explain why people are treated and evaluated differently at work. The playing field diagram is useful in understanding these differences.

Using the example of assertiveness, you can see from the following illustration that the boundaries are practically nonexistent for men. The more assertive, direct, and straightforward they are, the better. Now let's take a look at the same playing field for women (page 28).

Notice how the boundaries come in, making the field narrower. The narrower the boundaries, the easier it is to go out-of-bounds. Women can't play by the same rules as men and expect to win the game. Right or wrong, we live in a society where we don't like men who act like women and we don't like women who act like men. Imagine if Warren Buffett cried during an earnings call! People would think the "Oracle from Omaha" had completely lost it. Simi-

THE ASSERTIVE PLAYING FIELD: MEN

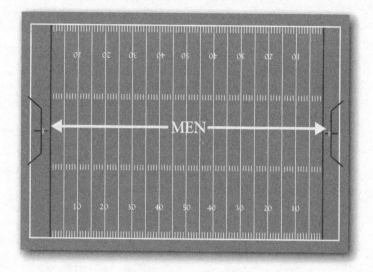

larly, when women exceed the boundaries of acceptability for assertiveness in their corporate culture, they risk getting called out, called
names, or called on the carpet.

Finally, let's look at the assertive playing field for women of color
(page 29). The boundaries are even narrower! As a Caucasian
woman, I can say things in a more assertive manner without going
out-of-bounds than can a woman of color. When women of color, particularly African American women, are assertive, they are wrongly
accused of being "angry." Cultural issues that go into understanding the strength of their messages (such as having strong female role
models and the acceptability of louder communications) are ignored,
and they are categorized in a way that disinclines them from speaking
their minds in the future—which just might be the purpose of the
accusation to begin with!

Renata was just such a woman. As the CIO (chief information
officer) at a multinational women's clothing firm, she was smart,

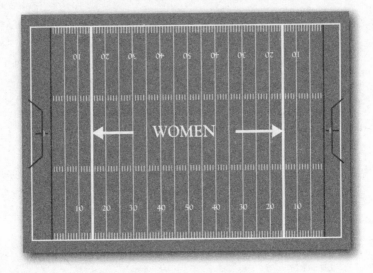

no-nonsense, articulate, hardworking, and quick on her feet. If she were a man, she'd be envied. But because she was an African American woman, she was feared. When she was referred to me for coaching, I conducted interviews with her peers, her management, and people who reported to her. In the vaguest terms they described her as capable but not in sync with their corporate culture. This is usually code for "She goes out-of-bounds."

Personally, I liked Renata and saw that she had a lot of value to add to her employer, but their playing field was so narrowly defined that she would have to turn herself into a pretzel to conform to it. This was an unfortunate circumstance where, despite my best efforts to help her see it wasn't her but the culture that needed changing and there was nothing either of us could do about that, she refused to adjust her behavior. Instead, she continued acting and communicating in ways that were most comfortable for *her*, but not for those around her. In the best of all worlds I would have liked her to find a

THE ASSERTIVE PLAYING FIELD: WOMEN OF COLOR

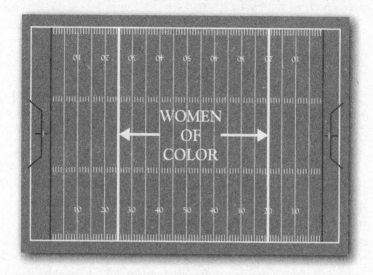

bigger playing field where she could simultaneously be herself and be appreciated, but instead her intransigence around change caused her to ultimately be terminated.

One additional thing to remember is that the rules, boundaries, and strategies don't only change for women and people of color, they change from company to company and boss to boss. What makes you successful in one company or with one boss won't always hold true in a different company or with a different boss. Each corporate culture has its own unique rules of engagement.

I was talking about the playing field concept to a group of women at a defense contractor. Instead of using assertiveness to illustrate my point, I used creativity. After explaining that the boundaries for creativity in the entertainment industry are almost nonexistent, whereas the boundaries for creativity in the defense industry are narrower (wacky ideas aren't embraced in quite the same way as in entertainment), a woman raised her hand and said, "That explains everything." It turns out she had recently transferred to this company from a film studio, and, as she put it, "Whereas I could do nothing wrong in my last job, I can do nothing right in my current one."

COACHING TIPS

- Size up the playing field in your organization and identify the rules and boundaries for various behaviors. This in turn will help you to create strategies for successfully maneuvering the field within bounds but at the edge.

- Consciously decide if it's you or the size of the field that's holding you back. Sometimes we receive feedback that would be true on any field—in which case it's best to take it to heart and act on it. At other times the feedback is unique to the situation or company. If in every job you've had you've heard that you don't communicate crisply enough, then it's time to do something about it.

- Understand that it is unlikely that you will change the size of the playing field to suit your needs. Playing your game at the edge can help to stretch the boundaries, but if it's too narrowly defined for you, start looking for a bigger field.

- When transferring to a new company or a different boss, don't overrely on past strengths to build your credibility. They may or may not work. If you find yourself challenged by the transition, assess the new playing field by observing the behaviors of the people who seem to be winning the game. You might need to add some of their actions to your tool kit.

- If you're a manager or business owner, focus on making the playing field equal for everyone by avoiding stereotyped judgments, proactively valuing and capitalizing on diversity, and holding people accountable for treating everyone equitably.

ACTION ITEM

Mistake 4

Dancing Around Pregnancy

*W*hat should be the happiest moment of your life becomes one of the scariest when you realize you're going to have to tell the boss about it. You obsess over the right time to do it, how to do it, and whether it will cause him or her to treat you differently. You try to hide it, avoid it, or play it down when what you really want to do is shout it loud: "I'm pregnant and proud!"

I know there are many pundits who suggest that you keep your pregnancy on the DL (down low) for as long as possible, but I'm not one of them. Men don't keep the impending births of their children a secret (at least not intentionally), and you shouldn't have to either. The difference, of course, is that it's not expected that a man's performance will be impacted by the birth of his child, but it's expected that a woman's performance will be. Like everything else that you do with your career, this presents yet another opportunity for you to be strategic.

Marissa Mayer made a splash when, on the same day the company announced her appointment as CEO of Yahoo!, she announced that she was six months pregnant. I have no doubt that she told the board of directors before accepting the offer. I also have no doubt that she assured them she was up for the challenge, pregnant or not. Her promotion despite her pregnancy was touted as a win for women in the workplace. But not so fast.

Another situation that was compared with Mayer's was that of Jennifer Christiansen, an associate director of consumer marketing at the pharmaceutical company Bayer (a client of mine and a company that I consider to be a great place for women to work). A major difference, however, was that the pregnant Christiansen asked if she could participate in the company's job sharing program. Despite the fact that she had a history of outstanding performance, her boss refused to allow her to take advantage of the program and supposedly said, "I need to stop hiring women of reproductive age." While on maternity leave Christiansen was terminated and is now part of a $100 million class-action suit against the company.

There's no doubt about it—if you're pregnant in the workplace, you're between a rock and a hard place. When you hide your pregnancy for fear of what others will think, you wind up looking less than honest and perhaps even deceptive. If you announce it sooner than later, others may make judgments about your capabilities or commitment. I believe the only thing your employer really cares about at the end of the day is that you get your job done. Whereas Mayer made her pregnancy a nonissue, Christiansen asked for more flexible working hours. Regardless of what policies are in place that provide consideration for pregnancy, by assuring your management that you're not going to miss a beat, you appear more confident and in control of things when you belly up to the bar early on this one (pun intended).

One more thing to note while I'm on the subject of working moms is taking advantage of other company policies, such as flextime and telecommuting. After the birth of her third child, I asked a woman who works in publishing (a field dominated by women) if she was working flex hours. Without hesitation she said no, to do so would be the kiss of death. Consequently, I've consulted with other women to get their input, and it's been the same. Their strategy, and I think it's a wise one, is to simply take time off or work from home when a family situation requires them to do so. As each woman implied, it doesn't matter if you're a man or a woman—formally requesting flextime as a steady diet contributes to the opinion that you're less than committed to the job.

Before you start sending me irate letters and e-mail, let me say I'm a huge proponent of creating avenues for women to be able to work while still meeting the expectation that they will be the primary caretakers for their children. It's an unfair burden that is placed on women in society. Although savvy companies are addressing the issue in an effort to retain talented women, and the fact that there are laws to protect pregnant women, it remains a hot-button topic. So hot, in fact, that when Google's Marissa Mayer abolished telecommuting soon after assuming the position of CEO, she was accused of being sexist and having no concern for women without the same resources and stature that she has. I disagree with the critics. Mayer defended her position by saying that people are more creative and innovative when working collaboratively and that is best achieved in the office. It was a business decision based on the needs of the company at the time.

COACHING TIPS

- Announce your pregnancy when *you're* ready. For a variety of reasons, it does not have to be the moment it's confirmed by your doctor. You're entitled to your privacy. Decide on a time that makes the most sense to you and your significant other.

- Accompany your announcement with a clear and definitive statement of what can be expected of you during the pregnancy and after. In no uncertain terms, inform your management that you will continue to perform at the level you always have, will prepare for your absence so that nothing slips between the cracks, and will return to work fit for resuming your duties.

- Handle pregnancy-related issues (morning sickness, doctor's appointments, etc.) on a case-by-case basis in the same manner you handle all other personal issues. If you need to miss work, don't go into graphic detail about why. Simply inform whoever needs to be informed that you'll be late or out and offer assurance that the projects you're working on are on track for completion.

- Give yourself permission to change your mind about your priorities. For Marissa Mayer, it was business as usual before and after the birth of her son. If at any point you realize that for health or personal reasons you can't work at the same pace or the same hours as you have in the past, then honor your values. Be clear about your priorities and live your life in a way that reflects your commitment to them. This is *your* life—no one else's. Starting a family may significantly change your perspective about the importance of work or family. No one will take away your card to the sacred women's club because you choose to focus more on one or the other.

ACTION ITEM

Mistake 5

Sitting Out the Social Network Game

$\mathcal{R}$emember how your parents used to tell you that just because everyone else was doing something that didn't mean you should? When it comes to social networking, they were wrong. I'm the first to admit that social networking can be a nuisance. I have more important things to do than check my Facebook page or be interrupted by an incoming feed that tells me where someone is having lunch today. One tech-savvy friend went so far as to call me a Luddite (I had to look that one up!).

Yet, like it or not, we live in an age where social networking is not a "nice-to" but rather a "must-do" if we want to be considered in the know. Even I grudgingly have to agree that when used properly, the advantages of social networking include that it

- makes you appear as if you belong in the twenty-first century;
- allows you to market yourself;
- enables you to engage in my number one rule for success: "Build strong 360-degree relationships";
- gives you access to what the competition is up to;
- provides you with a forum to exchange ideas or solicit opinions;
- enhances your credibility as a subject-matter expert; and
- can be a fun and efficient way to keep up with colleagues.

The key phrase here is *used properly*. Unfortunately, many women don't realize the web footprint they leave with their Facebook pages, LinkedIn accounts, and tweeting. As a result, they do more potential damage to their reputations and credibility than they do good.

I'll talk more about that in the chapter on personal branding, but for now suffice it to say that if you're not engaged in social networking, it's time to buy a front-row seat to this game.

COACHING TIPS

• Set up a Facebook page and use it for business purposes only. In subsequent Mistakes you'll find coaching tips for how to maximize its value to you and how to avoid common pitfalls when engaging in social networking.

• Join LinkedIn, the social networking site for professionals. By nature, it limits what you can post and whom you can communicate with (and vice versa). It's designed to showcase you professionally and enable you to network with people with whom you have colleagues in common.

• Create your own personal website. It's an inexpensive way to market your brand while having control over content (although not necessarily over who visits the site). Check out weebly.com for an inexpensive place to establish numerous websites and blogs.

ACTION ITEM

Mistake 6

Overlooking the Importance of Mentors and Sponsors/Advocates

The September 2010 issue of *Harvard Business Review* contained an article titled "Why Men Still Get More Promotions Than Women," by Herminia Ibarra, Nancy M. Carter, and Christine Silva. The premise of the piece is that women receive fewer promotions than men because they are less likely to have mentors who are also advocates for them. The authors found through their research:

> There is a special kind of relationship—called sponsorship—in which the mentor goes beyond giving feedback and advice and uses his or her influence with senior executives to advocate for the mentee. Our interviews and surveys alike suggest that high-potential women are overmentored and undersponsored relative to their male peers—and that they are not advancing in their organizations. Furthermore, without sponsorship, women not only are less likely than men to be appointed to top roles but may also be more reluctant to go for them.

The difference between mentoring and advocacy (or sponsorship) is the level of active involvement in helping you with your career. Mentors offer advice and guidance that help you to grow in your career, in your field, and within your company. Advocates, on the other hand, speak up for you on your behalf in your absence, introduce you to people who might be able to help you (and vice versa), and put you on the radar screens of people who can help further your career.

As I mentioned previously, mentors can also help you to learn the rules of the road and find the edge of the playing field. Yet many women are reluctant to ask someone to mentor them because they fear it's an imposition, they don't feel connected enough to the people who could mentor them, or they don't know whom to ask to be a mentor. The following tips will help you overcome these and other challenges and increase the likelihood of getting both mentorship and sponsorship.

COACHING TIPS

• Find out if your company has a formal or informal mentoring program. If so, this is the place to identify a few people who could potentially mentor you. Again, it's not a bad idea to have a male and a female mentor, because each will have unique experiences that will add to your understanding of how to play the game to win on your corporate field.

• If your company does not have a mentoring program, look to the edge of the playing field. That's where the people who are winning the game are playing. Identify a few people you admire and ask if they would be willing to spend thirty minutes to one hour a month or even a quarter with you to answer questions you have about career issues. Be specific about the amount of time you are asking for so that they don't think this is going to take an inordinate amount of time. Also, make it clear that you will be responsible for getting on their calendars and for driving the agenda. The easier you make it for the person, the more likely they are to agree to mentor you.

• Go to the website mentoringgroup.com and order *The Mentor's Guide* and *The Mentee's Guide*. These two pamphlets are extraordinarily helpful in establishing roles and responsibilities in mentoring. During your first meeting with your mentor, give him or her *The Mentor's Guide*, explain what you've learned from your own guide, and use it to discuss the terms of engagement for your relationship.

• Ask for situation-specific advocacy from people in positions to provide it. These people might include your mentors, but possibly also individuals who do not mentor you yet are familiar with your work and are in positions to provide you with visibility or recommendations. "Situation-specific" means asking for advocacy related to a particular opportunity, not simply asking the person to keep you in mind when a good opportunity arises. For example, ask an advocate to write a letter of recommendation for a promotion you're up for or to recommend you for a committee that will get high visibility from executive management. The more specific you are, the more likely the person is to take action.

• Join the appropriate "affinity group" within your company. Many companies have initiated groups for people with common workplace challenges as a means of providing support for them. Find out if your company has such a group for women (and/or for people of color), and if so, join it. You'll often find senior women involved in these groups who want to mentor younger or less senior women, making your task of asking for a mentor that much less daunting.

ACTION ITEM

Mistake 7

Working Hard

There's a popular saying: "Women have to work twice as hard to be considered half as good." As a result, women are like little ants—working, working, working. They complain that they do more than everyone else, and they do! It's a myth that people get ahead because they work hard. The truth is, no one ever got promoted purely because of hard work. Likability, strategic thinking, networking, and being a team player are but a few of the other factors that go into crafting a successful career.

In every organization there's a baseline for hard work. In some organizations that baseline is higher than in others. I work with a lot of professional and financial services firms where working hard is not only expected, it's required. Women, however, take it to the extreme, working far harder than their male colleagues. When you consistently go over that baseline you aren't always recognized, but you usually are given more work to do—because you've shown you can and will do it.

Sometimes I think women work hard because it's easier to do what they know best, rather than to engage in behaviors that seem foreign to them. One woman complained to me about the guys she worked with who, every Monday morning during football season, spent the first half hour of the day rehashing Sunday's games with the boss.

"What a waste of time. Here I am working away, and they're talking about football!" she lamented. What bothered her even more was the fact that these same guys were being tapped for prime assignments. Whereas women see it as "wasting the company's money" to do anything other than focus on the task at hand between 8 a.m.

and 5 p.m., men know that whether it's talking about football or last weekend's golf scores, they're building relationships that will later work for them. In this situation her male coworkers were bonding with the boss in a way that allowed him to better know these team members. As a result, when growth opportunities became available, he picked them because he was familiar and comfortable with them.

And herein lies one of business's best-kept secrets. People aren't hired and promoted simply because they work hard. It happens because the decision maker knows the *character* of the person and feels confident about his or her ability not only to do the job, but also to do it in a way that promotes collegial team relationships. By keeping her nose to the grindstone, the woman was actually acting in a way detrimental to getting what she most wanted—more interesting work and an opportunity to show she was capable of doing more.

COACHING TIPS

• Give yourself permission to "waste" a little time. If you're not spending 5 percent of your day building relationships, you're doing something wrong.

• Define your work hours and stick with them. Remember Parkinson's Law: "Work expands to fill the time available." This isn't to say there won't be times when you must work overtime, but if you're consistently the last one left at the office, there's something wrong with that picture.

• At the beginning of each day, define what you want to accomplish. You can avoid the tendency to take on whatever comes across your desk during the course of the day by deliberately scheduling it for a later time.

ACTION ITEM

Mistake 8

Doing the Work of Others

*W*hen Harry S. Truman said, "The buck stops here," surely he was thinking of a woman. Our tendency to take responsibility for not only our own work but also the work of others is yet another self-defeating behavior. Yes, you have a responsibility to your employer to ensure the delivery of a high-quality product or service, but it is not your responsibility alone. Women have a nasty habit of saying, "Well, if I don't do it, no one else will." This only ensures that you'll be doing it—and for a l-o-n-g time.

And there's another problem associated with taking too much responsibility. While women are doing the grunt work, men are building their careers. They're no fools. Promotions are rewards for getting the job done, not necessarily doing the job. I had a boss once who told me there are two kinds of people in the world: careerists and achievers. Achievers keep busy by doing the work. Careerists spend their time managing their careers. Truth be known, you've got to be a little of both to get ahead.

COACHING TIPS

- Stop volunteering for low-profile, low-impact assignments. If necessary, sit on your hand rather than raise it.
- Recognize when people delegate inappropriately to you. Practice saying unapologetically, "You know, I'd love to help you out with this, but I'm just swamped." Then stop talking. Avoid the inclination to want to solve the problem for them. It's *their* problem, not yours.
- If you're a manager or supervisor, don't let people delegate up. This most often happens when people reporting to you claim to be unable to perform a task or say they don't have the time. Avoid the tendency to take it over because it will be faster if you do it yourself. Instead, suggest that they ask a coworker for technical assistance, or, if you have the time, use it as a teaching opportunity.
- Use self-talk to replace feeling guilty about saying no. Try saying something like "I don't have to feel guilty about seeing that my needs are met."

ACTION ITEM

Mistake 9

Working Without a Break

*T*here's certainly truth to the adage "If you need something done, give it to a woman." Women will work *nonstop* to crank out a project. Working without a break is not only damaging to your health, but actually impedes optimum performance as well. Productivity experts suggest that a break every ninety minutes is required to maintain maximum levels of concentration and accuracy. "From a productivity standpoint, there are diminishing marginal returns when you ask your brain to exert constant effort through an eight-hour day," says Dr. Janet Scarborough Civitelli, a workplace psychologist at VocationVillage.com.

Working without a break also contributes to the impression that you're flustered or inefficient. One executive told me that a female vice president reporting to him made him feel "uncomfortable" because she always looked like she was overworked and *harried* (a word you *rarely* hear used to describe a man). Working through lunch hours or without coming up for air won't get you ahead. Giving the impression you are always up to your ears in alligators could hinder being given special projects or assignments that could later bring you recognition.

And if you're not convinced yet, according to self-proclaimed time management ninja Craig Jarrow, there are five more good reasons why you should take breaks:

1. **Gain Perspective**—If your head is down in your work, you aren't aware of your surrounding environment. Priorities may have changed since you started your project. A break can let you zoom in and out again.

2. **Recharge**—Everyone needs to "fill their tanks," or eventually their energy reserves will reach zero. Rest is needed to let the body and the mind recharge.
3. **Refocus**—It is easy to get distracted and pulled off task. Taking a break can let you address those distractions and then refocus your energy on the more important tasks.
4. **Get Advice**—No one can operate entirely independently. Seeking advice from others can save you much time and effort. Maybe they have previously done what you are doing and can provide time-saving tips.
5. **Take Care of Yourself**—Life is a marathon, not a sprint. You can't keep going at 100 percent without burning yourself out. Even top-notch machines will burn out if they are not maintained. Make sure you are maintaining yourself.

COACHING TIPS

• Get in the habit of getting up from your desk for a stretch break at least once every ninety minutes.

• At the beginning of each week, make it a point to schedule at least one lunch meeting.

• Schedule times throughout the day to drop by a colleague's office for a few minutes of casual conversation. When someone drops by yours, stop what you're doing and invite him or her in.

• Use the alarm function on your computer to remind you of your break (and when it goes off...take your break).

• Use the lunch hour to your advantage. Join a Toastmasters club, run an errand that will allow you to get home earlier after work, or just take a walk and refresh yourself for your afternoon activities.

• If about now you're thinking, *I don't have time for this*, then you're definitely doing too much at work.

ACTION ITEM

Mistake 10

Being Naive

*W*omen may not have the market on naïveté, but we certainly do our fair share of taking what people say at face value. The dynamic behind this is interesting. We often don't probe deeply to determine the veracity of what we're told, either because we don't want to embarrass the other person or because we want to see only the good in people. By busily focusing on the work itself, we often miss the more obvious behaviors that lie on the periphery.

Lisa was someone whose naïveté got her into trouble. She was the director of development for a nationally known nonprofit agency. Her department was efficient, there was a good sense of teamwork and camaraderie among the staff, and every year that Lisa was at the helm they surpassed their fund-raising goals—until she hired Adam, that is. He was the son of one of the board members, and her colleagues at the agency warned her it was not a good idea to hire him. Lisa was sure that if she established ground rules and kept the lines of communication open with Adam, it would work out just fine.

Within a few months the team began to falter. Morale was spiraling down. Team members weren't hitting their monthly targets. Several team members confided in Lisa that Adam was bad-mouthing her behind her back and spreading lies about her. Lisa's manager called her into his office several times to discuss the unrest on her team. For the first time in her career, she was seen as a less-than-capable leader.

When she openly discussed the problem with Adam, he denied doing anything to undermine her authority. She wanted to believe him and reiterated her expectations of him. The problem only went from bad to worse. Board members were beginning to question the head of the agency about problems that kept surfacing. Finally, Lisa left the agency for a better position, but not one she would have considered before Adam had come along.

When we see naïveté in another person, we often find it refreshing. Sometimes young people just beginning their careers benefit from it by making others want to mentor them or show them the rules of the road. When we see it in a more seasoned professional, however, we use it to discredit them. A woman's expression of naïveté underscores her inability to read a situation appropriately or learn from her experience.

COACHING TIPS

- If something doesn't make sense to you, ask for an explanation. If someone downplays your need for an explanation, be suspicious.
- Without assuming the worst, get in the habit of asking yourself what a person's motives might be.
- Don't rely on just one person's expertise when making major decisions. Solicit input from several reliable sources.
- If you find yourself the only person in the room who disagrees with the consensus that it can't be done, and you think, *But I could make it happen*, an alarm should go off that you're being naive.
- Trust your instincts. If it looks like a duck, sounds like a duck, and walks like a duck—it's a duck.
- Read *Spy the Lie* by Phillip Houston, Michael Floyd, and Susan Carnicero. Former CIA agents help you to identify deceptive behaviors before you fall prey to them.

ACTION ITEM

Mistake 11

Pinching Company Pennies

$\mathcal{A}$ccustomed to having to account for how they spend their money, it seems even women who aren't hesitant to spend their own money on themselves fall into the trap of pinching company pennies. They allow themselves to be inconvenienced, or deny themselves the smallest item, for fear of spending a few extra dollars of the company's money on legitimate business expenses. Some women wear their savings as a badge of honor—when in most cases the amount of money they save is rounding off numbers for their corporation.

I was reminded of the folly of this when a woman executive told me about being delayed in Los Angeles for a flight to JFK. She was originally going to take a train to her hometown where her husband would pick her up, but, with the delay, it would be too late to catch the last train. She struggled with how to get home in the most economical way possible—she even considered asking her husband to pick her up at 2 a.m. to save cab fare. Now, *that's* a mistake! A man wouldn't hesitate to call a car company or take a cab at that hour—regardless of the expense.

As someone who travels quite a bit for clients who pay my expenses, I pride myself on treating their money the same as I would my own—frugally. Recently I had a discussion with a male colleague about the increasing cost of airfare tickets and how much I hated to charge back these high prices to my clients. He was amused at my concern for the bottom lines of these behemoth corporations. "I don't treat myself the same as if I were writing the check," he said. "I treat myself better. If they want me to arrive refreshed, eager to work, and delighted to be there, then I'm going to fly business class no matter what the cost. They know the cost of doing business and you should too." Hmmmm...my inner nice girl flinched, but I knew he was right.

In another scenario, the assistant to a female executive at a major manufacturing company was retiring after twenty-two years of service. The executive, notorious for her frugality, arranged a potluck going-away party. Thinking that she must be saving the money for a nice retirement gift, several employees asked if she would like help in purchasing it. Without hesitation or embarrassment, the executive said she thought the party was enough. As you can imagine, the word on the street about this executive was that she was cheap and thoughtless. It would be one thing if the company was experiencing financial difficulties, but this was far from the case. In fact, the male executives in the same company were known for quite lavish send-offs for long-term loyal employees.

When you pinch pennies, you're wasting time and energy on meaningless matters. Additionally, you're more likely to be viewed as someone who isn't ready to play in the big leagues, and you definitely aren't taking care of the company's greatest assets—you and others.

COACHING TIPS

• When considering an expenditure, look at the big picture and how much difference the expense will really make in the larger scheme of things.

• If you have a budget—use it. Few companies reward, let alone notice, employees for being frugal.

• Consider the payoffs for spending small amounts of money on employees. Paying for a lunch or a floral arrangement to a staff member in the hospital won't break the budget, but it will reap dividends in terms of goodwill and loyalty.

• Unless you're directed otherwise, never ask permission to spend money. Instead, expect you'll be told if there's a problem...and if there is, don't apologize. Simply acknowledge your understanding of the message and ask for clarification around spending authority.

• When the voice comes into your head that says, *I'm not sure I should spend this money,* talk back to it by asking, *What's the cost [in terms of time, resources, goodwill, or money] of not spending it?*

ACTION ITEM

Mistake 12

Waiting to Be Given What You Want

I frequently hear women express disappointment over not having their needs met without having to ask. I don't get it. Ever hear the saying "The squeaky wheel gets the grease"? On the other hand, if you're one of those people who, no matter what they're given, it isn't enough, you might find people resisting your constant requests. Still, more often women are made to feel like they're asking for too much when, in fact, they're not. If you won't ask, you don't risk hearing no, but you also won't get what you want.

The most obvious examples of this come when women finally get up the nerve to ask for a raise. They're frequently made to feel they're doing something wrong or have no right to ask for what is rightfully theirs. Having worked in human resources for many years, I know that men take care of their own needs but will often minimize what women are worth or owed. As of this writing, on average, full-time working women earn $36,931 compared to men's $47,715. As mentioned earlier, the figures are even bleaker for African American women and Latinas. Although part of this discrepancy is clearly due to discrimination, and another reason is the fact that women gravitate toward lower-paying jobs, it's largely true because disenfranchised groups are less likely to *ask* for what they want.

A client once called to tell me that she hadn't received the same signing bonus everyone else had already gotten as the result of transferring to a newly formed department. I inquired as to why she thought this happened. As people often do when confronted with a situation they don't understand, she made up a story in her head that it must have something to do with not being respected or just treating her as if she were invisible. It bothered her so much that she was losing sleep over it. Obviously, she needed to do something about it, but she was hesitant to "rock the boat."

After much discussion, we scripted out what she could say to her human resource manager to find out about the missing bonus. The way she *wanted* to put it was to ask whether she was entitled to a bonus. Typical girl behavior—never assume you're entitled to something you've been promised! My tip to her was not to ask, but to assume she was entitled to the bonus and find out why she hadn't received it. Essentially, she went in and said, "My signing bonus wasn't in my check for the past two pay periods, and I'm wondering when I can expect to receive it."

Lo and behold, it had nothing at all to do with respect or being a woman. He had made a mistake. Of all the people who had transferred over, she was the only one who was due a performance review and annual raise within the next several weeks. He decided to wait on giving her the bonus so that he could do all the paperwork at one time. When her performance review was postponed because of the new assignment, though, he had forgotten to put in for the bonus. If she hadn't asked, she would have continued to be distracted by and lose sleep over this apparent slight.

The lesson for her was twofold: First, rather than make up a negative story, get the facts. Second, don't wait to be given what's owed to you—ask for it.

COACHING TIPS

• Mentally prepare requests in advance. Think about what you want and why you want it. When asking, be direct, straightforward, and accompany each request with two or three legitimate reasons why you should be given what you've requested. Try using the DESCript method provided under Mistake 91.

• Consider the value of using the negotiation technique of fait accompli. That is, couch your request in the form of a statement. For example, rather than say, "I'd like to ask for an additional ten thousand dollars for next year's training budget," say, "I've added ten thousand dollars to the training budget. Additional staff and new technology account for the increase."

• Read *Her Place at the Table: A Woman's Guide to Negotiating Five Key Challenges to Leadership Success,* by Deborah Kolb, Judith Williams, and Carol Frohlinger. The authors describe common negotiation problems encountered by women and give realistic suggestions for how to overcome them. The book also illuminates some of the hidden agendas that often accompany trying to get what you want.

• Separate being liked and getting what you deserve. If you ask for what you deserve in an appropriate way, and you're suddenly not liked because of it, someone is just yanking your chain and hoping you'll acquiesce to his or her expression of displeasure.

• Carefully choose your times for asking for what you want or deserve. Asking for a raise after layoffs is not a good idea. Nor is asking for a transfer to another department in the middle of a crucial project—it will make it look like you're trying to get out of work. Timing is everything in life—make sure you time your requests.

ACTION ITEM

Mistake 13

Avoiding Office Politics

*R*epeat after me: "*Politics* is not a four-letter word." Trying to avoid office politics is like trying to avoid the weather. Like it or not, it is what it is. Politics is how things get done—in the workplace, in government, in professional organizations. If you're not involved in office politics, you're not playing the game, and if you're not playing the game, you can't possibly win.

The business of politics is simply the business of relationships and understanding the quid pro quo (something in exchange for something else) inherent to every relationship. The film *Lincoln*, starring Daniel Day-Lewis as Honest Abe, portrays this beautifully. He was so committed to ensuring passage of the Thirteenth Amendment to the Constitution abolishing slavery that he sent his allies out to cut deals with lawmakers in Congress in exchange for their votes. Did the end justify the means? You bet it did. It changed the course of history and the lives of countless indentured servants.

Interestingly, a female friend I went with to see the movie thought this was the low point of the film—and I think most women are equally uncomfortable with this kind of brokering of deals because they find it a little smarmy. Men, on the other hand, get the concept of one hand washing the other, or "You scratch my back, and I'll scratch yours." In fact, an article I read about the movie (authored by a man) praised Lincoln for his political prowess in achieving his vision that all men are created equal (it took a little while longer for women to be created equal).

A successful workplace relationship, whether with a boss or a coworker, is one in which you clearly define what you have to offer and what you need or want from the other person. It happens all the time without putting a name to it. Consider your relationship with your best friend. You may need counsel from her or you may want company, a racquetball partner, or a variety of other things. If she gives you those, you're more likely to want to give her what she needs or wants. It may never be discussed, but the trade is implicit in the relationship. Workplace politics is no different. Each time you go out of your way for someone or give them what they need, you've earned a figurative "chip" that you can later cash in for something you need.

COACHING TIPS

• Approach political situations as you would any negotiation. Take time to find out what the other person needs, what you have to offer, and how you can facilitate a win-win situation.

• Remember: The quid pro quo of politics is *something in exchange for something else*. Don't just give in; think about what you want in exchange. Don't be afraid to cash in your chips.

• You can often win in the long run by giving up the smaller, less important points. When you do, you bank currency to be used at a later time.

• Don't avoid what you perceive to be a political problem. People will only go around you. Work through political situations in a way that allows others to see you as a problem *solver*, not a problem.

• Read *Survival of the Savvy: High-Integrity Political Tactics for Career and Company Success*, by Rick Brandon and Marty Seldman. Although some people feel as if the authors are preaching inauthenticity, I believe they speak the hard truth about a difficult subject. Even if you use only half of their suggestions, you'll most likely be twice as far along as you are currently when it comes to workplace politics.

ACTION ITEM ☐

Mistake 14

Being the Conscience

CIO magazine claims that women who report organizational malfeasance are more likely to experience retaliation than men who do the same. Whereas you might think that being higher in the organization would protect you from retaliation, this held true for men in the study; but for women? Not so much.

The terrorist attacks of September 11 and the spate of shady corporate financial dealings in the early 2000s gave us three extreme examples of women being the conscience—only to find they were ignored, stonewalled, or crucified. First, Enron's global finance vice president, Sherron Watkins, warned the company's president, the late Kenneth Lay, about her discomfort with the firm's accounting practices long before the company's demise. In August 2001 she had written a memo to Lay complaining about a "veil of secrecy" surrounding private investment partnerships at the firm. "I am incredibly nervous that we will implode in a wave of accounting scandals," wrote Watkins. "We are under too much scrutiny and there are probably one or two disgruntled 'redeployed' employees who know enough about the 'funny' accounting to get us in trouble." Unfortunately for Lay, and thousands of other Enron employees, he didn't heed her warning.

Cynthia Cooper, formerly with the now-defunct WorldCom's financial auditing department, felt she had no choice but to go to the board of directors to report the misappropriation of massive amounts of money when her management told her to ignore inappropriate accounting procedures. This, of course, was the beginning of the end for the prestigious conglomerate. Although she received praise from strangers for her courage, coworkers blamed and shunned her.

Then there was former FBI staff attorney Coleen Rowley, who became the conscience of the agency after coming forward to speak the truth about inappropriate handling of evidence of terrorist activity prior to the attacks of September 11. Even though the public lauded her and in 2002 *Time* magazine named her one of three "Persons of the Year" (along with Watkins and Cooper), she was treated as a pariah by fellow FBI staffers, unable to win a congressional seat for which she ran, and denied the opportunity to sit on the 9/11 Commission, a position for which she was nominated.

Is this to say women shouldn't act in concert with their consciences and, at times, moral and ethical standards? Not at all. But women are far more likely than men to point out variance between company policy and practice. Most men have no difficulty with bending the rules as needed and when it's a case of "no harm, no foul."

Let me give you an example. Claudette was an executive assistant for the vice president of consumer relations at a large entertainment company. Her boss routinely arrived late for work and expected that Claudette would cover for him. When the division president would call at nine-thirty, she would feel uncomfortable saying that her boss was "in a meeting" or had "stepped away from his desk." In her mind, the company start time was nine o'clock, and he should have been there on time. Similarly, if he was tardy in completing the required weekly expense report, he would change the dates to the current week so that he could be reimbursed for expenses incurred earlier in the week or month.

At first she would remind the boss of the rules, and he would cajole her into stretching them. After working for this boss a short time, Claudette went to human resources to complain. She felt the boss was asking her to compromise her values and ethics through these actions. Human resources, on the other hand, understood that the norms for this particular company were not very stringent and that she should be more cooperative with her boss if she wanted to build a successful relationship with him.

Unable to shift from her rigid interpretations, she finally asked for a transfer to another boss. Human resources was happy to oblige, but knew that Claudette would encounter the same problem with most of the executives at the company. What her boss asked her to do wasn't that unusual—nor was it unethical or immoral. Although she was eventually transferred to another boss who was known to be more of a straight arrow, human resources had by then branded her as somewhat of a prude and was aware of the limitations they would encounter in promoting or transferring her in the future.

The point of the story is, you need to weigh the benefit of pointing out minor infractions in company policy or procedure in light of the potential consequences. Sherron Watkins, Cynthia Cooper, and Coleen Rowley are to be admired for acting in concert with their consciences. In their cases the consequences were enormous for the company, the country, and them. Most of us, however, simply need to understand the realities of the workplace.

COACHING TIPS

- The workplace isn't a platform. Don't use it to further your cause.
- If you are being asked to do something illegal, unethical, or immoral, consider alternatives that will protect you from liability and extricate you from the situation without being labeled a whistleblower.
- Don't equate doing *good* with doing *right* for yourself. Taking a controversial position on an issue may make you feel better—but except in unique situations it's not likely to get you ahead.
- Choose your battles carefully. Ask yourself if the risk of being the conscience is worth the potential profit. There will definitely be times when it is worth the risk—make it a calculated one.

ACTION ITEM

Mistake 15

Protecting Jerks

I don't know what it is about women and jerks. We're like jerk flypaper. Not only do we attract them more than men do, but we also tolerate them longer. In our usual attempts to avoid making others feel bad, we let them take up more of our time than we should, shoulder the blame for their mistakes, and make excuses for their behavior. Men seem to have a much better detection device when it comes to jerks. They smell them a mile away—and avoid them at all costs.

Greta is a good example of how women protect jerks. She works as a regulatory specialist on Wall Street. Her job is to ensure that trades are lawful and within the guidelines established by her nationally known firm. Greta reports to a jerk. He knows nothing about the regulations, but that doesn't stop him from continually telling her how to do her job—and often giving her and others wrong information that could create substantial liability for the company. Despite Greta's attempts to tell him he's wrong, he insists that she follow his directives.

When the department vice president asked why so many errors were made on several recent trades, she refused to say she was simply following the instructions of her boss. As a result, her performance review moved her down a notch on the rating scale, her pay was reduced accordingly, and the promotion she was up for was postponed for another year. Greta's efforts to protect her boss not only backfired on her, but also put the company in jeopardy of being fined for regulatory violations.

COACHING TIPS

- Trust your instincts. When you think someone is a jerk, he or she probably is.
- Distance yourself from jerks. Don't be found guilty by association.
- Politely but firmly tell a jerk to take a hike (more on this under Mistake 120).
- When you get blamed for the actions of some jerk, don't hesitate to redirect your accuser to the real source (which is what Greta should have done). Try saying something like "I can see why you would be upset over this. Why don't you speak with Chris about it to find out why he wanted it done that way?"
- When the jerk is your boss, it's time to look for another job. Research conducted by the Center for Creative Leadership reveals that trying to change your boss is a waste of time. Employees don't change bosses' behaviors. So stop wishing he or she will change and put your own needs first.

ACTION ITEM

Mistake 16

Holding Your Tongue

Fearful of hearing the accusation that we're too aggressive or pushy, women will often avoid saying things that should legitimately be said. How many times have you withheld a comment, only to have a male colleague be applauded for saying exactly what you were thinking? Keep in mind that the accusations of being too pushy are *designed* to keep you quiet. They're ploys to make you feel bad about having an opinion or alternative viewpoint. Holding your tongue only serves to make you frustrated and appear less willing than you really are to speak up for what you believe.

Take Marilyn, for example. She was embroiled in an e-mail war with a colleague who had a reputation for being Teflon-like. Nothing stuck to him because he was so busy pointing the finger at others. For a while she spent most of her time placating him so she wouldn't be blamed, but he eventually got around to her. When I asked her why she didn't just tell him she felt the blaming wasn't doing any good and they should focus on the problem instead, she said she didn't want to fuel the fire any further. My suggestion to her was that the next time he started pointing the finger, she should turn it into a problem-solving discussion. She could say something neutral, such as "Blaming won't get us anywhere, Joe. Let's talk about how we can fix the problem of communication between our two departments." Even if his retort is "I'm not blaming, I'm just looking for the cause of the problem," she can be a broken record and say, "Be that as it may, I'm ready to move into the problem-solving phase."

An interesting aside to this situation is the fact that Marilyn is a fifty-year-old Italian woman from a very traditional Brooklyn background and married to a man significantly older than she. As we explored what got in the way of her coming up with this solution herself, it became clear that her traditional socialization caused her to acquiesce to "macho" men. I pointed out to her that the name of the game is *When in Rome, do as the Romans do.* In other words, it may be appropriate to back off at home with her husband or with her father because that is the rule of her family, but at work the rules are different.

COACHING TIPS

- Disagree without being disagreeable. You can do this by first acknowledging what the other person said, then giving your opinion. It sounds like this: "If I understand you correctly, you think we should put Joe on the Stanford account. I propose we consider several other more qualified staff." Be prepared to back this up with two or three good reasons.

- Take more risks with giving your opinions at meetings. Practice giving your opinion at least once during every meeting. It gets easier every time you do it.

- Don't disregard the customs and traditions of your ancestors, but be more selective about how, when, and where you apply them.

- To counterbalance the feeling of being too aggressive, after you've expressed your opinion you could add an inquiry. For example, "That's how I see it. I'm curious to know what others think."

ACTION ITEM

Mistake 17

Unwillingness to Capitalize on Relationships

$\mathcal{A}$ woman consultant was having difficulty selling her idea for a new book to a publisher. As we talked about how she might go about getting the attention of a particular editor, she mentioned that her father, an internationally known leader in his field, had a good relationship with this man. When I asked why in the world she didn't mention this to the editor, she said that she didn't want to capitalize on her father's name. This is yet another way women play differently than men. Men rely on relationships to open doors for them; they don't view it as taking advantage of anyone. For Pete's sake, it's why they build relationships in the first place!

There's a difference between name-dropping and using a relationship to help open a door. It's a reality that relationships sell everything from cars to consulting services. We do business with, and trust the judgments of, people we like. As opposed to guilt by association, it's success by affiliation. Don't be afraid to connect the dots among people in your network.

COACHING TIPS

- Ask permission to use a colleague's name when you're trying to get the attention of someone. For example, "I saw on LinkedIn that you're connected with Ellen Torres. I'm trying to schedule a meeting with her and wonder if it would be all right to mention that I know you."

- Ask for introductions. If there's someone you'd like to know at a meeting or party, ask the person organizing the event to make an introduction.

- Introduce people with like interests or needs. Doing so models the behavior you would like returned in kind.

- Ask for referrals. If you're looking for a job or just information, ask people if they know someone to whom they can refer you and if you can use their name when making the call.

ACTION ITEM

Mistake 18

Not Understanding the Needs of Your Constituents

*F*ormer British prime minister Margaret Thatcher was raised by a father who always told her to think for herself and not be swayed by the opinions of others. She learned this lesson so well that it earned her the nickname of Iron Lady. This strength became her ultimate downfall, however, when she found herself embroiled in controversy after she proposed a tax on everyone who voted. Despite every indication that her constituents strongly opposed the tax, Thatcher told advisers who urged her to reconsider her position, "You turn if you want to. The Lady's not for turning."

Although we're not all politicians in the truest sense of the word, we all have constituents. They're the people we serve. Whether we serve them through our services or our products, we must know what they need and expect if we're to be perceived as adding value. The trap many women fall into is thinking they know what's best for their constituents and therefore not asking the right questions on the front end.

Take Belinda, a technical consultant to engineering firms. Belinda is as bright as they come—sharp as a whip. She knows her business inside and out. Other consultants go to *her* for consultation. Several years ago Belinda found that her business wasn't as successful as she wanted it to be. She would sell an initial project to a company, only to find that she didn't get repeat business.

One day a client with whom Belinda had developed somewhat of a friendship asked if he could give her some feedback. When he told her that his company appreciated her expertise but not her rigidity, she was shocked. She thought she was offering the best advice possible and always had the best interests of the client in the forefront of her mind. Instead, she found that her unwillingness to listen to clients' practical needs and applications was impeding her from being seen as adding value to a company. She was viewed as intractable and difficult to work with.

It was difficult for her to hear, but Belinda was also smart enough to know that the feedback was a gift. If this man's firm felt this way, others must, too, but without telling her. Instead, like most dissatisfied clients, they'd just stopped using her services. This was why she hadn't been able to grow her business the way she wanted to.

With one simple change, Belinda was able to turn the situation around. Following the initial diagnosis of client needs and presentation of her ideas and recommendations, she would stop and ask for input. If her ideas were met with skepticism, rather than seeing this as client ignorance of the "right" way to do things (and selling her ideas harder), she would shift to listening and asking more questions. She discovered that initial resistance was often due to miscommunication; further discussion helped bridge that gap. In some cases she found that although the client wanted to implement her ideas in a manner different from the way she envisioned it, the changes actually worked and were ones she could later use with other clients.

Belinda is a terrific example of someone who, aware of her own intelligence and capability, could be contemptuous of others who may not have been as talented. The lesson here is that there's often more than one way to skin a cat. You must take care not to be a victim of your own success.

COACHING TIPS

- Read *The Trusted Advisor*, by David Maister. I also mention this book later in Mistake 64 related to the importance of consultative skills, but it is such a good book that I thought mentioning it twice can't hurt. Maister talks about ways to build trust with your constituents that serves both you and them well. There is even a workbook that accompanies the book, which I've included on the reading list.

- Be more concerned with doing the right thing than doing things right. It's not a sign of weakness to change your mind when data collected dictates it's the right thing to do.

- Be acutely aware of the needs of your constituents. If you don't know what they are—ask. Keep in mind the quid pro quo inherent to every relationship—one thing in exchange for another.

- Differentiate polling from understanding the needs of your constituents. Polling is what you do when you can't make a decision independently. (See Mistake 24 for more on polling.) Understanding the needs of others is information you may or may not use to make decisions that impact them.

- When met with resistance avoid the urge to oversell, which usually results in polarizing factions or creating win-lose situations. Instead, let resistance be your cue to back off and shift to active listening.

ACTION ITEM

Chapter 3

How You Act

In the play *As You Like It*, William Shakespeare reminds us:

> *All the world's a stage and all the men and women are merely players. They have their exits and their entrances and one man in his time plays many parts.*

Success in the world of business depends on your ability to know your part and how to play it. It may sound as if I'm suggesting that you be phony or false, but that's not it at all. Just as actors and actresses are judged by how well they play their roles, we are judged by whether we understand the nuances of what it means to *act* professionally.

It could be argued that the behaviors described in every chapter constitute *how you act*. This chapter is somewhat different in that it focuses on the subtle, stereotypical ways in which women behave that contribute to an overall impression of their being less competent than they really are. People do not know and judge us by our intentions; they know and judge us by our actions.

Too many women mistakenly assume that they have to act like men to get ahead. These are often the same ones who fail to understand the rules of the playing and that there are different rules for men and women. As I'll discuss shortly, the goal isn't to strive to be a poor imitation of a man, but rather to act as an adult woman and not the nice little girl you were taught to be in childhood.

Let me remind you that any one of the behaviors described in this book taken alone would not be a deal buster—but put several of them together and they can divulge a woman's underlying naïveté, need for approval, and lack of self-confidence. And the truth is, most of us engage in more than just one of these mistakes.

Mistake 19

Difficulty Transitioning from Nice Girl to Winning Woman

*W*hen Carol Frohlinger and I wrote *Nice Girls Just Don't Get It*, we wanted to make it clear that the opposite of a nice girl isn't a bitch—it's a winning woman. The difference is that a nice girl acts in ways that are designed to make others like her, and a winning woman acts in ways that ensure her goals are met by knowing what she wants, having clarity about where she's headed, and achieving both through high likability and emotional intelligence. The following chart illuminates the behaviors in which you must engage to make it a reality.

The difficulty comes when you make a conscious decision to make the transition from being that nice little girl you were taught to be in childhood to being the adult woman you are now. You begin with the best of intentions but are waylaid when you get resistance from those around you. Carol and I wrote:

> Nice girls find that others will try to make them feel guilty, selfish, or uncaring when they try to change things up and put their needs first. Whereas the nice girl wants to change, other people want to maintain status quo because it works for them. Winning women look at resistance as a necessary part of building relationships.

The problem for many women is in choosing to take the path of least resistance, thereby avoiding the kinds of intense discussions

that can accompany change. Most forms of resistance can be overcome. That's the good news. It simply requires tenacity, regrouping, and employing a tactical approach to countering what at first seem like insurmountable obstacles.

COACHING TIPS

- If you get resistance, you're on the right track. It means you are asserting yourself and advocating for your needs. Depending on the situation, some measure of resistance is inevitable. Don't be discouraged by it, but rather use it to further your goals.

- Practice countering resistance in low-risk situations. Select situations that won't make a huge difference in your life as a place to begin to advocate for yourself. Transactional situations such as insisting on returning an item you purchased or returning a restaurant meal that wasn't prepared properly are ideal. You can then apply what you've learned when the stakes are higher.

- Use questions to get at the real reason for the resistance. It's not enough to know that people don't want you to change; you need to know why. When you encounter resistance, don't just take it at face value, but ask questions to clarify. From there, you can often move into negotiating a win-win outcome.

ACTION ITEM

Mistake 20

Failure to Prepare for Social Interactions

*T*he best piece of advice I ever got in school was from a seventh-grade science teacher who preached, "Chance favors the prepared mind." This, of course, requires forethought—which nice girls are capable of, but often overlook due to a focus on getting as many things done in the *present* as possible. This, then, renders them at a disadvantage when it comes to being able to think on their feet, lobby for support for projects or ideas, and make the most of social situations.

This is precisely what happened to Deeana when she was at a holiday party for her company. She had a good relationship with the department vice president, so it was natural for her to go up and speak with him at the event. He welcomed her with a big smile and immediately started talking about his son, who was about to go off to the same college that Deeana's daughter attended. They exchanged pleasantries, with Deeana all the while wishing she could transition the discussion to a big project she was working on and for which she needed his blessing.

Before she could turn it around, a male peer of hers walked up and joined them. He began the conversation talking about some of the company's challenges and achievements over the past year. The vice president, having said about all he could on the subject of his son, turned his attention to the man and they continued chatting about business issues. As Deeana said, "I'm glad I have good relationships with these executives, but I want them to see me as more than just a mother or a woman who will listen to them."

This is one of the pitfalls of high emotional intelligence for nice girls. We make others feel comfortable with us, but, as was already discussed, we don't always capitalize on that comfort by preparing for perfect opportunities to discuss business during social interactions or casual conversations.

COACHING TIPS

- Prepare for every social event that you attend. Assume that opportunities will present themselves to discuss business matters of importance to you—or to others. Knowing in advance who is attending will help you to identify key issues, challenges, or projects for which you want support or have support to offer.

- Preparation will help you to guide discussions in the direction you want them to go. In Deeana's case, had she gone to the party with at least one hot topic in mind, she could have easily segued the conversation toward it with a simple statement, such as "I'm delighted that your son is going to be attending what I consider to be one of the top engineering schools in the country, and I would be happy to help by providing whatever information I can. I'm also delighted to have a few minutes of your time to talk about how the sales training program is progressing."

- Get the agenda for both formal and informal meetings in advance. Each meeting provides you with an opportunity to build your brand by letting others know you show up for every game suited up. Do your homework around the agenda items and come prepared to add value rather than just be a seat warmer.

- Attend the Dale Carnegie Course on Effective Communications and Human Relations/Skills for Success. This course focuses on strengthening your interpersonal relationships, being a persuasive communicator, and developing a take-charge attitude initiated with confidence and enthusiasm.

ACTION ITEM

Mistake 21

Multitasking

*I*t's a proven fact of biology that women are better multitaskers than men. Without getting too technical, we know that the corpus callosum (the nerve connections between the right and left hemispheres of the brain) is 30 percent more highly developed in the female brain than in the male brain. This allows information to flow more easily from one side of the brain to the other, allowing a woman to focus on more than one thing at a time. Oh, joy. Now we're expected to not only do *more* than men, we're expected to do more *at the same time* than men.

As a psychiatrist friend once said to me, "Just because you *can* do something, doesn't mean you *should* do it." This is certainly true in the case of multitasking. Dr. Jeremy Hunter, an expert in workplace productivity and professor at the prestigious Drucker School of Management, has found that multitasking not only makes you less efficient and less effective, but, over time, stresses and even damages the brain. Splitting attention between two tasks decreases the limited amount of brainpower a person can devote to each task. The result? Neither task is done particularly well.

Additionally, says, Hunter, the short-term costs of inefficiency and ineffectiveness are compounded by long-term costs of chronically stressing the brain. This leads to a neurochemical cascade that inhibits memory, reduces concentration, and impairs decision making and learning. Chronic stress can lead to depression, anxiety disorders, heart disease, infertility, and suppressed immune response. All of which could be avoided if you'd just learn to focus on one thing at a time.

COACHING TIPS

• Ask for help. We often multitask because we simply have too much on our plates. Whether at work or at home, ask for help with routine tasks that don't necessarily have to be done by only you.

• Identify three to five times during the day when you commit to *not* multitasking. These might include when you're getting ready for work in the morning, driving to work, having a meal with family or friends, exercising, playing with the kids, attending a concert or play, or sitting in a meeting. By being more conscious of when you are multitasking, you can take proactive measures to reduce it.

• Turn the e-mail alert off on your computer so that you're not distracted each time new mail arrives.

• Turn your cell phone off when working on a project.

• Most important, focus on whatever you're doing or whom you're with in the moment. Remember, we are human beings, not human doings.

ACTION ITEM

Mistake 22

Ragging on Other Women

 *O*ne of the questions I'm asked in about half of the presentations I make isn't really a question at all. When someone asks, "What do you think about the fact that women don't support one another and are always trying to cut down other women?," I know that they're really expressing their own perceptions of the sometimes difficult relationships between women in the workplace. My own personal experience is quite different. Sure, there have been women who would stab me in the back in a nanosecond, but there have been equal numbers of men who would do the same. Backstabbing is gender-blind.

I believe there are a number of reasons why women react so strongly to the insensitivity of other women but overlook it in men:

- We expect women to treat us better than men treat us, and when this doesn't happen it creates "cognitive dissonance" or discomfort with the expectation versus the reality.
- It's more socially acceptable to point out the foibles of women than to do the same with men. Men do it to women all the time, so the less enlightened woman follows suit.
- There is increased competition among women for opportunities for upward mobility given that these opportunities are fewer and farther between than for men. Therefore, women on upwardly mobile paths may mistakenly view other women as the real competition.

Regardless of the rationale for either treating other women less respectfully than you would a man or perpetuating the myth that we are one another's worst enemies, it's a huge mistake. Not only because it's wrong to treat anyone disrespectfully, but also because it's just plain stupid. What happens when that woman who heard you dissing her in the ladies' room is promoted to the head of your division? Or when you leave the company to start your own business and that same woman is the one who makes decisions about bringing in outside vendors. Do you really think she's not going to remember?

COACHING TIPS

- Replace ragging with raving. Look for opportunities to build up the reputations of your female colleagues. Compliment them publicly. When necessary, provide constructive feedback only in private.
- Recommend women for promotions or high-profile assignments without fear that you'll be accused of doing so only because it's a woman. That kind of remark is a ploy used by men to get you to stop doing it!
- If you don't already have one, start a women's affinity group in your company. To learn more about these groups, google and read the article "Affinity Networks: Building Organizations Stronger Than Their Parts," published by the Network of Executive Women (NEW).
- Disengage from conversations where women are gossiping about other women. You can simply walk away, or you can show even more courage by saying you think you all should be supporting, not ragging on, women in the office.

ACTION ITEM

Mistake 23

Being Too Thin-Skinned

*R*emember this scene from the movie *A League of Their Own* where Jimmy Dugan (played by Tom Hanks), coach of the women's baseball team the Rockford Peaches, gives his player some tough-love feedback (and if you haven't seen the movie you must rent it because the support these women show for one another is really inspiring)?

> **Jimmy Dugan:** Evelyn, could you come here for a second? Which team do you play for?
>
> **Evelyn Gardner:** Well, I'm a Peach.
>
> **Jimmy Dugan:** Well I was just wonderin' why you would throw home when we got a two-run lead. You let the tying run get on second base and we lost the lead because of you. Start using your head. That's the lump that's three feet above your ass.
>
> [Evelyn starts to cry.]
>
> **Jimmy Dugan:** Are you crying? Are you crying? ARE YOU CRYING? There's no crying! **THERE'S NO CRYING IN BASEBALL!**

Crying is just one way women show that they're thin-skinned, and I'll address this specific mistake a little later. Withholding information, the silent treatment, and passive aggressiveness are but a few other ways women reveal their thin skin. I'm sure you've noticed that men can argue and fight with one another and then go out for a beer afterward as if nothing happened. That's because to them, nothing did happen other than an open and honest disagreement. We women, on the other hand, can hang on to a grudge like nobody's business. One small slight, and a relationship of even years can be irreparably damaged.

If you fall into the category of being overly sensitive, I have only three words for you: *Get over it.* In her book *The Male Factor: The Unwritten Rules, Misperceptions, and Secret Beliefs of Men in the Workplace,* Shaunti Feldhahn cites this as one of the top pet peeves men have about women. Men are simply not wired to take things as personally as do women. To them, work is just business; it's not personal. If women want to be seen as having the stamina to play in the big leagues, then they need to take personal out of the equation—especially when it comes to receiving feedback.

COACHING TIPS

• Assume the best of intentions rather than the worst. Most people don't start off the day with a fervent desire to hurt your feelings. Shit happens. Before stewing on a comment or action that offended you to the point where it has you boiling over, consider the other person's intent. Yes, an offhanded comment made in a hurry or in the heat of the moment can be hurtful, but you don't have to let it become a festering wound.

• Use your words. Rather than act out your feelings, put words to them and engage in a dialogue with the offender. Usually, having this kind of discussion releases some of the intense feelings around the issue.

• When given feedback, resist the tendency to become defensive. Instead, ask questions that will help you to understand it, thank the person for taking the time to give the feedback to you, and think about whether or not it has some validity. If so, take action. If not, *let it go.*

ACTION ITEM

Mistake 24

Polling Before Making a Decision

$\mathcal{J}$ennifer is a lead auditor with a Wharton MBA and just over five years' experience working for a Fortune 500 company. Her performance is acknowledged as superb. When a promotional opportunity became available, her name was one of those considered on a short list of candidates. The word on the street about her, however, was that she was unwilling or unable to make a move without first getting input from everyone around her. As a result, she wasn't viewed as someone who could take quick and decisive action. Making her a manager was out of the question. In other words, Jennifer was one of those women who had to conduct a poll before she would take action.

Participative decision making is a good thing. The inability to act without knowing what everyone thinks and if they approve isn't. It's a technique nice girls use to avoid later confrontation. If they can get approval on the front end, no one can criticize them on the back end. The fine line you walk is between being seen as a lone ranger who acts independently, without regard for the opinions of others, and someone who can't make her own decisions or isn't confident enough to act without external input. The ideal is to act interdependently, recognizing the value of alternative input.

COACHING TIPS

• Take more risks by acting without first getting input from your supervisor. Begin with small, low-profile decisions. It helps to factor in the combination of data and feelings when taking a risk. If you have all the data you need and you feel really good about it, it isn't really a risk at all. On the other hand, if you have little data and you're not feeling so hot about it, then it's a foolish risk. You've got to have some of both (data and good feelings) to take a good risk.

• Ask yourself what you have to lose by acting in an independent manner. Try to explore the internal mechanism that keeps you tied into approval. Once you know, you can tape over the old message.

• Don't let the pendulum swing entirely in the other direction. There are times when it's appropriate to seek extensive input and/or approval. These tend to center on high-profile decisions where significant cost or potential loss is involved.

ACTION ITEM

Mistake 25

Needing to Be Liked

I can't deny the fact you like me! Right now, you like me!" There is no better example of how the need to be liked can impede success than this exclamation from Sally Field upon winning the 1984 Best Actress Oscar for her work in *Places in the Heart*. Up until that time, Ms. Field's body of work included the likes of *Gidget*, *The Flying Nun*, and Burt Reynolds's sidekick in *Smokey and the Bandit*. This acceptance-speech gaffe marked a turning point for her. From that point on she assumed more serious roles, moved into film directing and production, and changed how she communicated with the public.

Your LQ (likeability quotient) is a critical factor in your success. People get promoted, demoted, hired, and fired based on how likable they are. In our office we have a very scientific test we use to determine likability. It's called the Beer Test. When we meet a client for the first time we ask ourselves, *Is this someone I would like to go out and have a beer or a cup of coffee with?* If the answer is no, we know we have our work cut out for us.

The desire to be liked is so strongly ingrained in some nice girls that it becomes nearly impossible for them to act in any alternative manner. They become immobilized at the thought of disappointing someone. It's critical to understand the difference between being liked and being respected. If you're concerned only with being liked, you will most likely miss the opportunity to be respected. Your need to be liked will preclude you from taking the kinds of risks taken by those who are respected. Conversely, if you're concerned only with being respected and not liked, you lose the support of people you may need in your camp. Paradoxically, it's the people who are liked and respected who are most successful in the workplace.

Carol Frohlinger, JD, an expert in how women negotiate, taught me a valuable distinction when we were working on our book *Nice Girls Just Don't Get It*. Not all relationships are created equal. There are transactional relationships, those with people I am doing business with or encountering only once; and personal relationships, those that are ongoing. Women tend to treat both relationships the same, and wind up wasting time and energy (not to mention feeling used or taken advantage of) by not differentiating the two.

Let's take for example the person sitting next to you on the airplane who wants to chat it up with you. You've had a long week of meetings, and all you want to do on the flight is relax and listen to music. Acting like a nice girl, you talk to the person because he or she wants you to. Acting like an adult woman, you politely tell the person that you enjoyed speaking with them, and are going to put your earphones on now so that you can relax. This is a transactional relationship—you most likely will never again see that person. It doesn't give you permission to be rude, but it does give you permission to not put as much energy into the relationship as you might with one that is more important to you. It doesn't really matter if this person likes you or not.

If, in the same scenario, you're sitting next to a colleague with whom you've been working all week and who wants to talk about a personal issue that arose on the trip, you have a harder decision to make. This is not a transactional but rather a personal relationship—one that you anticipate will continue for some period of time. It's not about wanting the colleague to like you; it's about wanting to maintain a good working relationship.

There's a little girl in most of us who wants to be liked—and there's nothing wrong with that. It's when the needs of the little girl overshadow the rational, adult woman that we get into trouble. Nice is necessary for success for both men and women. It's simply not sufficient.

COACHING TIPS

• Read *Nice Girls Just Don't Get It: 99 Ways to Win the Respect You Deserve, the Success You've Earned, and the Life You Want,* by yours truly and Carol Frohlinger, JD. Carol, an attorney with expertise in negotiation, and I teamed up to write this book to help readers learn how to establish boundaries and negotiate for what's important to them in all aspects of their lives, not just work.

• Use self-talk to counter the need to have everyone like you all the time. That's an impossibility. Replace the thought *But people won't like me if . . .* with *People might get upset with me, but at least I will be acting in accordance with my values.*

• Ask yourself where the inordinate need to be liked comes from. Questions such as *What am I afraid of happening if I'm just myself?* or *What was I taught in childhood about the importance of being liked?* can help you pinpoint what purpose the need to be liked serves in your life. If you can find the answer to these and similar questions, you're more likely to be able to overcome this need.

• Balance your inclination to serve others' needs with serving your own. Before agreeing to something you may not want to, ask yourself how much it will matter if the other person is a little annoyed. When people get angry or annoyed with us, it's often for the purpose of getting us to do what they want. Don't fall for the ploy.

• Differentiate transactional relationships from personal ones and act accordingly.

ACTION ITEM

Mistake 26

Not Needing to Be Liked

*N*o, your eyes aren't playing tricks on you. For many women, this mistake is the inverse to the need to be liked. Fear of being perceived as a pushover causes some women to adopt the attitude of *I'm not here to win a popularity contest*. Well—I'm here to tell you that yes, you are. Look at what happened to Hillary Clinton in the 2008 election. I don't think she lost the nomination because the United States wasn't ready for a woman president, I believe her likeability quotient wasn't as high as Barack Obama's (and it's certainly nowhere near Bill Clinton's LQ). If she is to make a bid for the presidency in 2016, I'd coach her to work on her LQ.

Dr. Sharon Mass, director of social services at Cedars-Sinai Medical Center, is another example of someone who didn't care whether or not people liked her. She has graciously allowed me to use her name and situation as an example of how this phenomenon can get in your way of achieving your career goals.

Sharon has a heart of gold. She genuinely cares about people. She also happens to be brilliant and the best at what she does. Her problem when we first met was that people didn't know any of this. They viewed her as a perfectionistic taskmaster, focused on getting the job done rather than on the needs of her staff. An underlying fear was that if anyone saw how warm and empathic she really was, they might take advantage of those traits. As a result, she compensated by going in the opposite direction. Like many women, Sharon had to learn how to allow her human, more stereotypically feminine side to emerge while at the same time capitalizing on the best of her more stereotypically masculine style of management.

COACHING TIPS

• Read *The Power of Nice: How to Conquer the Business World with Kindness*, by Linda Kaplan Thaler and Robin Koval. When their book first came out we were often pitted against one another in interviews, but the fact is we're very much in agreement. Nasty will never get you as far as nice—as long as you don't act like the little girl you were taught to be in childhood.

• Disabuse yourself of the notion that familiarity breeds contempt. By learning to set boundaries, you need never worry about someone taking advantage of you.

• Every single day, take time to build or strengthen a relationship. When you need a relationship, it's too late to build it. Listen to someone who needs an ear, learn what's important to your colleagues or customers, and don't follow the Golden Rule (treat others as you want them to treat you); rather, follow the Platinum Rule: Treat others as *they* want to be treated.

• Follow Mary Kay Ash's motto for success: "Treat everyone as if they are wearing a sign that reads 'Make me feel important.'"

ACTION ITEM

Mistake 27

Not Asking Questions for Fear of Sounding Stupid

*H*ow many times do we have to be told, "There are no stupid questions," before we believe it? The problem is that we've come to rely on the old adage "It's better to keep your mouth shut and look like a fool than to open it and confirm it." Well, I disagree. There are so many ways in which women remain silent that we don't need to find any more. Asking a legitimate question (as opposed to making a statement couched as a question, which I'll talk about later) to ensure understanding is a sign more of confidence than of ignorance. If nearly three decades of working inside corporations has taught me anything, it's that if I don't understand something, most likely no one else does, either.

Nice girls sometimes don't ask questions because they don't want to waste the group's time. Asking yourself the simple question *Will the answer apply to only me?* should help you decide whether you should ask it. If the answer is yes, and you know you will have the chance to ask it following the meeting, then wait to ask your question off-line. If the answer is no, or you know you won't have the opportunity to ask again (the participants won't get together again or the speaker won't be available), then ask away. Do, however, be sensitive to the needs of the other participants in the meeting. If you've already asked several questions and you notice people are getting fidgety or the meeting is running late, consider how critical it is that you get the answer just then.

COACHING TIPS

• If you don't understand, ask. It's far better than going off in the wrong direction.

• Observe people in meetings and you'll notice when others are confused or not understanding the message. Use this as an opportunity to help the group by saying something like "I can tell by the looks on people's faces that this is not quite clear. Can you give us some examples or state it in other words?"

• Trust your instincts. If it doesn't seem clear, it's probably not.

• Use simple paraphrases as a way of gaining clarification. For example, "Do I understand you correctly that we're being given six months to complete phase one of the project, three months to complete phase two, and six months to complete phase three?" If you're wrong, you'll be told so; if not, you've gotten the information you need.

• If people make you feel stupid over a question you've asked, you can assume it's their problem, not yours. If they do it consistently, ask them point-blank why they feel the need to put you down just because you've asked a question.

ACTION ITEM

Mistake 28

Acting Like a Man

*T*he emphasis in this mistake is on *acting*. Many women possess stereotypically male characteristics and behave accordingly. These women aren't acting; they're just being themselves. It can work for them, especially when it's authentic. If you're not one of these people, don't start now. You'll never play the role of a man as well as you will a woman who plays her role well. At this point I hope you've gotten the idea that this book is about having a full arsenal of tactics and techniques at your disposal that are consistent with being a woman, not acting like a man.

Acting like a man in the workplace will inevitably get you into trouble. Just as we expect men to act in certain ways, we expect the same of women. When they don't, it creates a kind of dissonance. If behaviors don't match expectations, we tend to mistrust people or think they're not playing their roles appropriately. Instead, you must play the role that's expected—while also widening the boundaries of the stage.

Being different from men isn't something to change or hide. We may be made to feel there's something wrong with how we act, but that's simply another ploy that's used to keep us in our places. Don't buy into it. Women bring a unique set of behaviors to the workplace that are needed, especially in today's climate. Our tendencies to collaborate rather than compete, listen more than talk, and use relationships rather than muscle to influence are the very same behaviors I coach men to acquire. But it's all about balance. Just as men can overuse their stereotypical characteristics, so can women.

A caveat of which to be aware is that behavioral norms for men and women vary among corporate cultures. One company I consult with has a strong norm that women and men must always act like ladies and gentlemen. I discovered this when I gave feedback to a woman that, if she wanted to be taken seriously, she needed to speak more loudly and be a bit more assertive when expressing her ideas. She responded—and other women in the meeting affirmed—that the company president didn't like aggressive women and she would be out of a job if she acted any differently. This particular woman had no problem conforming to the expectation because it was consistent with her character.

If by magic we plucked this woman up and set her down in another company—say, one where the norm is that everyone has to be aggressive to be heard—her behavior would not conform, and she would likely not experience the same success she currently enjoys. She would then have to decide whether she wanted to expand her behavioral skill set or find a culture more consistent with her natural tendencies where no changes would be needed. In most companies, however, the norm is a little less rigidly defined, and women have to find ways to expand the boundaries without being called out.

COACHING TIPS

• Continue to learn about your style, what works, where you get stuck, and ways you can complement your natural strengths with new behaviors. You can do this by asking for feedback, videotaping yourself in a meeting or giving a presentation, or taking a workshop on personal development. The appendix includes several resources for workshops that I recommend.

• If you tend to be more aggressive and it's not working for you, read Jean Hollands's book *Same Game, Different Rules: How to Get Ahead Without Being a Bully Broad, Ice Queen, or "Ms. Understood."* It can be difficult to find the book, but try online booksellers that may have a used one in stock. The book points out that women often can't get away with the same behavior as men—and pretending that you can could ruin your career. You may have to decide whether it's more important to you to further your career or take on the system. I often hear women lament over this double standard, but it does exist and it is real.

• Modify the rules to meet your needs and others' expectations. Pounding the table and speaking loudly may not be acceptable, but being a broken record (saying the same thing again and again in different ways) can accomplish the same end.

• Be conscious of the fact that behavioral expectations vary among corporate cultures. What works in one company may not work in another. Be sure to observe the cultural norms and modify your style accordingly. If you can't bring yourself to act in a way that is acceptable, your best bet is to find a work environment that complements your natural style.

ACTION ITEM

Mistake 29

Trying to Be One of the Guys

This is a variation on the theme of acting like a man. It's a situation I'm often asked about by women who work in predominantly male fields such as construction, paramilitary operations like the fire or police departments, and certain kinds of engineering. The problem is exacerbated when you're a young woman working with older guys who tend to want to treat you like a daughter rather than as a coworker.

A woman in these situations might frequently find herself the only woman in a meeting or at an event. Too often, women revert to trying to be just like one of the guys by swearing like a sailor, laughing at (or telling) off-color jokes, or closing the bar down with the guys. It might work in the short term to alleviate some of the tension around being the only woman in the room, but it's not a good long-term strategy. As I said in the previous mistake, unless you truly are one of those women who can pull off being one of the guys with authenticity, men ultimately aren't going to trust you.

Does this mean you should go to the other extreme and be a femme fatale or damsel in distress who bats her eyelashes to get men to accept her? Absolutely not! That's not authentic either. The real secret to successfully maneuvering these scenarios is to be yourself and emphasize your professionalism, the value that you add, and your ability to handle the guys with grace, aplomb, and a little bit of humor.

COACHING TIPS

- Allow boys to be boys—up to a point. For some reason that I have yet to figure out, when you get a bunch of guys together in one place they revert to behavior usually saved for frat houses. It's not your responsibility to clean up their acts, but neither is it your responsibility to tolerate abuse. If a guy swears then looks at you and apologizes, make light of it by saying something like "I've heard it before. No problem." On the other hand, if you find feces in your hard hat (which actually happened to one woman working in a refinery), you have to let the guys know you'll let it go this one time, but twice will be too many and you'll do whatever is necessary to make it stop.

- Don't confuse the men at work with your brothers, father, grandfathers, or husband. Women often project onto men characteristics associated with the men in their families. The norms for interacting with family members are not likely the same ones that should be used with coworkers. Assume equality with your male coworkers regardless of their age or status. It puts you in a better position to go toe-to-toe with them when needed.

- Lighten up. You've got to have a sense of humor about being the only woman in the group. Develop some one-liners that you can deliver at just the right moment. If someone makes a joke about your being the only woman in the group, respond with something like "If you think it's strange for you—try being in these heels!"

- Wow them with your professionalism. Consistently lead with your expertise and ability. Do this, and over time gender will no longer be an issue. There's no arguing with talent.

ACTION ITEM

Mistake 30

Telling the Whole Truth and Nothing but the Truth (So Help You God)

*W*hy is it that women, more so than men, feel the need to blurt out the truth about themselves, even if it's self-disparaging or damaging to them? A study was once done in which men and women were asked to describe themselves. The men, regardless of appearance, described themselves in factual and positive (or at least neutral) terms. "I'm six feet tall, brown hair, 195 pounds, and have a mustache," said one portly, aging man. Right. And I'm Julia Roberts. Women were more likely to use more pejorative phrases, such as "My hair is graying, I could stand to lose a few pounds, I'm not *too* bad-looking…"

The same holds true when a woman is asked to debrief a particular project where something has gone askew. She'll blame herself and identify all the things she could have done differently. What do men do? Again, they're objective and Teflon-like in their descriptions. One man, when accused of designing an ill-conceived methodology, said, "The problem wasn't the methodology, it was that the methodology didn't reflect realistic measures of the process." And *who* designed the methodology to begin with?

Anne Mulcahy, former chairperson and CEO of Xerox, found out the hard way that telling the unadulterated truth can get you into trouble. At an investors conference early in her tenure, she told the world that the company had "an unsustainable business model." The next day, Xerox stock lost 26 percent of its value. Mulcahy originally thought that since it was no secret the company was losing money, it naturally followed that there was a problem with the business model.

"Looking back," said Mulcahy later, "I should have said, 'The company recognizes changes have to take place in the business model.'" She advises people to continue being straightforward, but also to make sure "you don't provide sound bites that can be used out of context...."

It seems Mulcahy hadn't yet learned the art of putting a "positive spin" on a situation. Telling the truth doesn't require you to cast yourself in a negative light. It requires an honest, objective description of facts without blame or self-flagellation.

COACHING TIPS

- Listen carefully to the question you're asked and answer it simply and objectively. The question "Why wasn't the project done on time?" isn't an indication that the person expects you to point the finger at yourself. More than likely, there are good reasons why the project wasn't completed on time, and *those reasons* are what you should offer in response. An appropriately honest answer would be, "There are two primary reasons. First, we didn't have the staff required to meet the unrealistic deadline; and second, the information required to complete the data wasn't made available to us until two days before the deadline."

- Even when you legitimately bear responsibility for a blunder, don't make it worse by embellishing it. Avoid the tendency to agree or explain, and, whatever you do, don't allow yourself to feel bad about it. We *all* make mistakes. Replace apologetic, explanatory, or defensive responses with more neutral ones. Practice saying, "I understand what you're saying, and I'll keep that in mind in the future." You are neither agreeing nor disagreeing—simply acknowledging.

- Counter or pair every negative with a positive. This is what positive spin is all about.

Change This:

- "I have to admit, I could have done a better job of making sure we remained under budget."
- "I wish I had done a little more inquiry before making the final decision about that candidate."
- "I don't think I'd be the right person for the job—I don't possess all the qualifications listed in the job description."

To This:

- "Although we didn't come in under budget, we did complete the project ahead of schedule."
- "Although the employee proved to be a bad match for the job, we learned a good lesson in what we really want."
- "It's true that I don't have *all* the qualifications listed, but what makes me a viable candidate is my depth of hands-on experience."

ACTION ITEM

Mistake 31

TMI (Too Much Information)

This mistake has taken on entirely new proportions since the first edition of this book was written more than a decade ago. Back then, there was no Twitter, Facebook, Myspace, LinkedIn, or the numerous other sites available for staying connected and sharing information. Now, people announce their every move and most intimate thoughts electronically. And it should come as no surprise, given women's propensity toward affiliation, that according to a study conducted by the research giant Nielsen:

- Women are 8 percent *more* likely than the average adult to build or update a blog / men are 9 percent *less* likely to do so.
- Women are 6 percent *more* likely to have created at least one social networking profile / men are 7 percent *less* likely to do so.
- A total of 68 percent of women use the Internet to stay in touch with friends and family / only 54 percent of men use it in the same fashion.

So what does this mean for you? It means you are a lot more likely than the guy in the cubicle next to you to be sharing too much information electronically! No one except your spouse, child, or *maybe* your mother really needs to know where you are at any given moment. I don't need to receive your e-mails with your opinions about an upcoming election, gay marriage, war, peace, or anything else. If I want your opinion, I'll ask for it. For heaven's sake, why in the world would you give your employer, or a prospective employer, ammunition to make a judgment about you?

And that's just electronically. How about face-to-face? The woman who shared this thought with me was a manager who noticed that the women in her department were much more likely than men to reveal complicated personal situations that could later be used against them. The example she gave was of a woman in her department who was experiencing performance problems on the job. At a one-on-one meeting, the employee broke down crying and told a long, involved story about how her mother was dying, her sisters wouldn't assume any responsibility, the burden fell on her to make all the health-care decisions, her husband was out of a job...

Relevant? Yes, but more than her boss needed to know. It gave the boss the impression she couldn't handle stress well. When a project came up that the boss knew would be stressful, she didn't want to take the risk of giving it to this employee. Sharing personal information isn't in and of itself a mistake—it's sharing *too much* of it that can come back to bite you.

COACHING TIPS

- Be selective about the personal information you share, how you share it, where you share it, and with whom you choose to share it. Remember, once in the ethers, always in the ethers.

- Less is more when it comes to divulging personal information. A little goes a long way.

- If you're a manager or supervisor, be even more careful. The rule of thumb I recommend is "Be the best friend you can be to your employees, but don't think for a minute they're your best friends." Your peers, the ones you may choose to confide in, are other managers and people at your level.

- Whether you're a manager or not, don't entirely withhold personal information. I've seen women do this, and it backfires. It makes you look secretive or dishonest. Sharing appropriate amounts of personal information enables others to see the human side of you and, in turn, builds relationships.

- When a personal situation is impacting your ability to perform your job, be honest, but be brief. It's enough to say, "I'm going through a rough time right now, but my job is important to me. I'll work on paying closer attention to the details."

ACTION ITEM

Mistake 32

Being Overly Concerned with Offending Others

*A*n interesting phenomenon I've observed is that when a man is controversial or offers a different viewpoint, neither men nor women respond as if they've been offended. They may be angry or hurt, but the man is rarely accused of acting inappropriately. Because women are more likely to encounter resistance by being told they're out of line, they tend to agree (even when they don't really agree) and fail to confront tough issues.

This is just another one of those ploys people use against us— and we unwittingly buy into it. If someone acts offended by a legitimate request or concern of yours, the implied message is that you've acted inappropriately or done something wrong. As a result, they know you're more likely to back down. When you back down often enough, you've trained others to feign offense as a defensive posture. It becomes a self-defeating catch-22.

Karl Marx used the term *mystification* to refer to the process whereby those with power and affluence denied the fact that there was a problem between the social classes, then denied they were denying. Here's how it sounds at work:

> **Employee:** It's been two years since I've had a raise, and I'd like to talk to you about why I think I deserve one.
>
> **HR manager:** Are you accusing me of overlooking your well-being?
>
> **Employee:** No, I'm not accusing you of anything, I just want to talk about getting a raise.

HR manager: Well, you obviously think there's a problem.

Employee: In fact, I do think there's a problem with not getting a raise in two years, but I'm not blaming you.

HR manager: We have a system in place that ensures our staff is fairly treated.

Employee: But if I haven't gotten a raise, then the system isn't working. I don't think you see that from your perspective.

HR manager: Now you're saying I don't see the problem.

Get the picture? This is a convoluted and circuitous method that never quite solves the problem and causes women to back down or not even try to bring up sensitive topics for fear of offending someone.

COACHING TIPS

• Use the DESCript method (see Mistake 91) to prepare for difficult conversations.

• Read *Crucial Conversations: Tools for Talking When Stakes Are High*, by Kenny Patterson, Joseph Grenny, Ron McMillan, and Al Switzler. If you're one of those people who avoid confrontations because you're afraid of hurting someone's feelings, you'll find terrific guidance in this book for how to say what must be said and in a way that won't damage the relationship.

• When expressing a controversial or different viewpoint, use the technique of contrasting what you do want and what you don't want: "I don't want to make it appear that I haven't heard what you said, because I have. I do want to express a different way to look at the situation."

• Let the other person know when what you're about to say is difficult for you by beginning your sentence with "This is a bit difficult for me to say, but I do want to let you know how I see the situation." This cues most people to be more patient with you.

• If you know you've expressed yourself inoffensively, and the other person is still offended, don't acquiesce. Instead, respond with a simple acknowledgment of his or her feelings—"I can see you feel offended by this"—and revert to listening. Avoid the inclination to backpedal and negate your true sentiments.

ACTION ITEM

Mistake 33

Denying the Importance of Money

$\mathcal{I}$know all the statistics about gender disparity in pay and benefits. You probably do too. I don't want to downplay the significance of these factors—they're real and they're relevant. But unless you're an equal-pay activist, you have no control over those factors. The real question then becomes, *What are you going to do about it?*

A year after *Nice Girls Don't Get the Corner Office* was released, the second book in the series, *Nice Girls Don't Get Rich*, was published. In that book I talked about the many mistakes women make with money because of their complex relationship with it. I spoke with women and asked what kept them from being rich. Almost to a woman, they responded they didn't have the need to be *rich*; they only wanted to be *comfortable*. For crying out loud! I've been comfortable, and I've been rich, and believe me, I'd rather be rich—and you should too. You can think of rich as *having all the money you need to live your life the way that you want, free from concerns about money.*

Money is power, and power is something women misinterpret and avoid. Ask a woman if she's powerful, and she'll give you five reasons why she's not. This translates into feeling uncomfortable with the subject of money and thinking she actually deserves less than she's due. Or worse yet, she doesn't give money a second thought except in terms of needing enough to pay the bills.

What you focus on is what you get. If you're not earning a fair salary or not being given the raises you deserve, it's time to focus on money. It won't mean you're any less committed to your work—only that you're equally committed to your well-being and that of your family.

COACHING TIPS

- If you think you're underpaid, do research into the pay ranges typical for your job or industry. You can do this online, through a professional association, or by asking trusted friends at other companies what their ranges are (don't ask what they earn). Because salaries differ from city to city and field to field, I can't give you a website that is comprehensive, but from your browser type in "salary surveys" and you'll be given a host of choices.

- If it turns out that you *are* underpaid, use logic and facts to make a case for why you should get a raise. Include ways in which you've helped the company to make money, save money, or improve efficiencies. And whenever possible, use numbers. For example, "Since I took over this role, we've increased sales by 23 percent and reduced customer complaints by 39 percent." Ask a friend to help you practice delivering the message.

- Subscribe to (and make a point of reading) a magazine that focuses on money and career issues. Several to consider are *Fortune*, *Money*, and *Smart Money*.

- Overcome the notion that talking about money is crass or impolite.

- Join, or start, a women's investment club.

ACTION ITEM

Mistake 34

Flirting

*H*ow many thousands of women have met the person of their dreams at work, fallen in love, and gotten married? It happens all the time and it's not such a bad thing, but it is a potentially danger- ous one. Just ask Monica Lewinsky or Paula Broadwell. As I told a reporter who asked me if an attractive woman should use her looks to her advantage to get the job she wants, "Sex sells, but not in the long term." It's more likely than not to backfire.

I once coached a woman whom everyone assumed was having an affair with the department manager. Whether she was could never be determined, but that wasn't the point. Her behavior toward him led others to believe she was having an affair with him—and percep- tion is reality. Her flirting, which caused others to be suspicious of their relationship, took the form of laughing a little too loud at his bad jokes, offering to run errands for him, siding with him in meet- ings when others expressed a different viewpoint, and inviting him to lunch at least once a week (when most others—both men and women—worked through their lunch hours).

What's a little harmless flirting? you ask. We know people find partners at work all the time. The harm is that it's the women who flirt—not the men—who most often become the butt of office jokes and who are more likely to suffer the consequences. In the case above, people excluded her from the grapevine (an important source of information), and from other discussions to which she should have been privy, for fear she would share the information with the boss. It reduced their trust in her and diminished her ability to perform effectively.

Another woman learned from her 360-degree feedback report that her peers thought she flirted too much. The feedback floored her because she had no inkling how others could perceive that. Then one day I happened to see her at lunch with her boss and understood perfectly. As he chatted away confidently, she smiled and listened with her head slightly tilted. I could see how it might be perceived as flirting, but what it really came down to was that the woman came from a traditional Irish family where she'd learned to acquiesce to men. Her way of showing respect to men, whether in one-on-one situations or in meetings, was to "dumb down" her actions and words.

COACHING TIPS

- Don't overtly flirt with coworkers. Knowing glances, whispered conversations, and laughing at stupid jokes don't belong in the workplace.
- If you *are* dating or having an intimate relationship with a coworker, be discreet. Conduct your personal business outside work and work-related activities.
- Don't be so naive as to think you can keep these things secret for long. There's nothing wrong with dating a coworker—just be up front about it.
- When you become personally involved with the boss (or—if you are the boss—with an employee who directly reports to you), you're playing with fire. Seriously consider the personal and professional risks and don't hesitate to get outside counseling if needed.

ACTION ITEM

Mistake 35

Acquiescing to Bullies

*I*t's not often I run into bullies. Most people in corporations know how to express themselves tactfully and diplomatically, seeking to solve problems, not create new ones. Such was not the case in a recent meeting with a vice president, however, who was clearly angry that he had been inadvertently double-billed for a particular service. None of the usual techniques for defusing difficult situations worked. I listened, paraphrased, reflected his feelings...and none of it made a difference. Finally, I said, "I'm not accustomed to being personally attacked." A third person in the meeting tried to intervene by saying, "I think you're getting defensive, Lois." To which I calmly replied, "When I'm personally attacked, I get defensive." After the meeting, the person who intervened said he thought I could have handled it differently. My response was "The guy is a bully and I wanted him to know I wouldn't be intimidated."

When we're bullied, we do one of two things: counterattack or acquiesce. Neither serves to shift the dynamic. By simply letting someone know how you feel, you stand a better chance of eliminating the offensive behavior—something that will never happen if you acquiesce. Even if the behavior doesn't change, you've put the person on notice that you won't tolerate it, and, as such, you've maintained your self-respect. By the way, the dynamic did change after my remark to this bully, and we were ultimately able to find a solution that met his needs.

COACHING TIPS

• Use the techniques I mentioned—listening, paraphrasing, reflecting feelings—as a place to begin defusing a bully. More often than not, they work.

• Don't roll over and play dead when someone tries to intimidate you. It's a tactic some people regularly use to make their point or get their way. Ask yourself what you're feeling in that moment and express it as an *I* message. Rather than "You're not listening to me," say, "I feel I'm not being heard." It's less accusatory, and no one can argue with your feelings.

• Turn the discussion to problem solving by acknowledging what you've heard and asking what the person would like to do: "I understand that you're frustrated with the fact that the shipment has not yet gone out. Let's talk about what we can do to get it to you as soon as possible."

• Avoid the inclination to apologize. If apologies are appropriate, you can always do so later. Apologizing to a bully only fuels the fire and reinforces the notion that you are a victim.

ACTION ITEM

Mistake 36

Decorating Your Office Like Your Living Room

*O*ffices are often an extension of personal homes. In many cases, women spend more time there than they do in their own living rooms. Nevertheless, this doesn't mean that your office should look like your living room. More so than men, women love the aesthetics involved with decor and frequently want to create a warm and comfortable setting, not only for themselves but for those who enter their work space as well.

I've been in the offices of women who've replaced overhead lighting with table and floor lamps (creating a more ambient environment) and scattered overstuffed couches, throw pillows, and personal memorabilia throughout their space. Depending on the message you want to convey, this can work for or against you. I don't recommend it for most women. It's more appropriate for people responsible for counseling employees than it is for those in other positions.

At the other extreme is someone like Christine, a physician at a metropolitan hospital, who had *nothing* on her walls. At our first coaching session I was struck by how austere and cold her work space was. As we worked together and I received feedback from her staff, I realized that this was simply a reflection of her personality. One of my coaching tips to her was to warm up her office with family pictures and artwork that would humanize her space.

A little later we'll be talking about personal branding. Your office also represents your brand. Think of it as a marketing tool. Ask yourself how others might describe your office. Would they say it's cluttered? Stark? Warm? Chances are, whatever they would say about your office is what people will be saying about you. Yes, your office or work space can be a reflection of who you are and what's important to you. But unless you're an interior decorator by profession, play it safe. Use your office space to emphasize your organization, good taste, and professionalism.

COACHING TIPS

• The decor of your office should be consistent with the kind of firm in which you work. In a more conservative culture you should select artwork, colors, and furniture that are tasteful and understated. More creative fields can tolerate a bolder approach.

• Given that your office or work space makes a statement about you, do pay attention to decor. In most offices you're assigned furniture, but how you accessorize it is up to you. Choose accessories that reflect your personality without overly emphasizing the feminine side of you.

• If you lean toward minimalism, then minimally have family pictures or other photographs displayed where people can see them. They serve to humanize you and act as conversation starters. One single woman I know has a framed picture of her dog on her desk.

• Look at your office with fresh eyes. If someone very special were coming to visit you at work, what would you change? Why? What adjectives would you attach to your work space if you didn't know who worked there? Are those the adjectives you want to be used about you?

• Keep your visible work space neat and clean. It conveys the impression of being organized and on top of things.

ACTION ITEM

Mistake 37

Feeding Others

*U*nless you're Betty Crocker, there shouldn't be home-baked cookies, M&Ms, jelly beans, or other food on your desk. Hillary Rodham Clinton may have been lambasted for her comment about not staying home and baking cookies while her husband was running for president, but her point was well taken. We don't ascribe a sense of impact or import to people who feed others. It may seem like a small or inconsequential thing, but the fact is, you rarely see food on men's desks. Similarly, men don't bring in leftovers from dinner the night before to share with coworkers.

The act of feeding is equated with nourishing, and nourishing is *definitely* a stereotypically female attribute. Additionally, food on the desk is often an invitation to stop and chat a moment (people can't just "eat and run"). Combined, the aspects of feeding and encouraging conversation emphasize stereotypically feminine qualities, often in the very women who don't need to emphasize them quite so much!

There are, of course, exceptions to every rule, and this is one of them. Lise Dewey, formerly manager of training and development at Universal Entertainment, told me she often coaches her own employees (especially men) who are perceived by others to be a bit *too* brusque, domineering, or downright abrasive (emphasis on the word *too*) to put a candy dish on their desks. The reason is obvious—she wants them to "warm up" their image and balance their more aggressive behaviors. In this regard, the food is used as a strategy to create balance in a personality that might not be perceived as warm.

Similarly, Lise has a huge candy bowl on her own desk—in part because *she* wants to eat it (although you could never tell by looking at her), and in part because she is in a role where people often come to her office to discuss personal and confidential matters. The candy is designed to make people feel comfortable with her. Again, she's using it strategically.

If you don't want to be perceived as stereotypical, think twice before putting food on your desk or in other ways feeding people at work. This is especially true if you're a woman who makes many of the other mistakes contained in this book. As with many of the tips in this book, it isn't the food alone that's lethal—it's the combination of mistakes that diminishes your credibility.

COACHING TIPS

- Unless feeding people is a conscious strategy, just say no to feeding people at work.
- If you're worried about them going to waste, take the leftovers from a weekend party to a homeless shelter rather than the office.
- Don't volunteer to organize the company potluck lunch. There are much better things you want to be known for being good at.

ACTION ITEM

Mistake 38

Minimizing Your Emotional Intelligence

The intelligence quotient, or IQ, that you're born with doesn't change much over the course of your lifetime. And new research shows that it isn't even the most important factor contributing to success. As I mentioned earlier, your emotional quotient, or EQ, plays a far greater role in determining how successful you will be in a variety of arenas. For example, Nobel Prize–winning psychologist Daniel Kahneman found that people would rather do business with someone they like and trust than with someone they don't, *even if the likable person is offering a lower quality product or service at a higher price.* A study of hiring practices by L'Oreal showed that salespeople who were hired based on their emotional intelligence earned $90,000 more annually than those hired through traditional methods.

In the past, we called these the "soft skills"—most likely because women exhibited them to a greater degree than men. As I frequently chided my male clients who disparagingly used this term to refer to the work we were doing together, "If they're so soft, what makes them so hard for you?" The good news for women is that we surpass men on four of five measures of emotional intelligence: self-awareness, self-regulations, empathy, and social skills. (Men and women are equal on the fifth measure, motivation.) Yet, despite the fact that we possess these critical skills, we often don't value them, nor do we consciously use them to our advantage. Instead, we focus on working harder and longer—neither of which will ensure success absent high EQ.

Earlier I cited research that shows having more women in leadership roles correlates to greater financial returns for a company or firm. Why do you think that is? Robin Cohen and Linda Kornfeld, managing partners at the law firm Dickstein Shapiro, claim that it's because women exhibit the following behaviors to a greater degree than men:

- working to form connections with others in order to develop relationships;
- focusing on team building and working collaboratively toward a common goal, rather than individual success;
- developing and motivating others through positive reinforcement; and
- talking through business approaches and incorporating the ideas of others before making final decisions.

In short, using your EQ not only helps to further your career, it adds to your company's bottom line as well.

COACHING TIPS

- Read *Emotional Intelligence 2.0*, by Travis Bradberry and Jean Greaves. This book contains the opportunity to assess your EQ and provides insights into how you can develop and use yours to your fullest advantage.

- Put words to the emotions that are often present but rarely expressed in meetings. For example, when tension is running high, say something like "It's clear we all have strong feelings about this subject. How about if we take a breather and come back to the table to discuss it further?" Doing so will cause you to be seen as someone who can read a room—an invaluable asset to any group.

- Begin meetings with casual conversation that expresses an interest in the other person. Although most people will welcome the opportunity to talk about themselves or matters that are important to them, some won't, in which case you can shift to the business at hand sooner rather than later.

- At social events, use your EQ to make introductions between people with common interests or backgrounds. Others will appreciate your efforts to make them feel comfortable and welcome in a group.

- Don't hesitate to comment on someone's unspoken mood. If it looks like a coworker seems a little down, an overture such as "Is everything okay? You don't seem like yourself," will let them know you see them as a human being, not just a human doing. If they don't want to discuss it, they won't, but they will remember that you showed concern.

ACTION ITEM ☐

Mistake 39

Being a Doormat

$\mathcal{A}$rtist Pablo Picasso once said, "There are only two types of women—goddesses and doormats." And since you're reading this book, I have a hunch you don't quite see yourself as a goddess—yet. What's the difference? Let's take a look.

Doormats	Goddesses
Do whatever is asked of them.	Get others to do what they ask.
Tolerate mental and physical abuse.	Banish abusers from their presence.
Believe it is their responsibility to care for others.	Believe it is the responsibility of others to care for them.
Are disrespected.	Are worshipped.
Never ask for anything for themselves.	Feel entitled to get what they want.
Can't say no.	Won't take no for an answer.
Give others permission to walk on them.	Walk away from people who walk on them.

Would you rather be the pigeon or the statue? Being a doormat might make you feel superior in a Mother Teresa sort of way in the short term, but it won't get you where you want to be in the long term.

COACHING TIPS

- Learn to manage expectations by clearly stating what you are willing to do and what you're not willing to do. Without ever having to say "no," you can let others know the boundaries of your flexibility. For example, if you're asked to deliver a report in an unreasonably short period of time, you can say, "I am happy to do the report. In the amount of time you've given me, however, it won't be thorough, so if you want a better end product, my recommendation is to extend the deadline by two days."

- Trust your feelings. If you feel as if you're being abused or taken advantage of, you probably are. In such instances, let the other person know how you're feeling and what you would like to change. Although you can't control the actions of others, you can remove yourself from unhealthy situations.

- Don't wait to be given what you want—ask for it. Too often women expect others to be mind readers and are disappointed when people prove they're not particularly adept at that particular skill. If you don't ask, you don't usually get.

ACTION ITEM

Mistake 40

Offering a Limp Handshake

*W*omen may not have the exclusive rights on this one, but we are more likely to hold back when offering a hand in greeting. For fear of appearing too masculine, we let the pendulum swing the other way. A handshake is how you make your first impression upon initially meeting someone. It says something about you before you ever open your mouth. Although you don't want to develop a bone-crushing grasp, you do want to be certain your handshake conveys the message *I'm someone to be taken seriously.* One good pump and a concise greeting (such as "I'm delighted to finally meet you"), combined with solid eye contact, will do the trick.

COACHING TIPS

• Practice your handshake with both male and female friends or colleagues. Get their feedback about whether yours is too limp or too strong. You may have a different handshake for men than for women. Continue practicing until you find a place where both men and women tell you your handshake conveys the message you want it to.

• Here's a tip a colleague's father taught him when he was a young boy: Keep extending your hand until you hook thumbs (try it and you'll see how it works). Don't stop with just grabbing the fingers. (And by the way—how many fathers taught their daughters how to shake hands?)

• When meeting someone for the first time, if he or she doesn't offer a hand first, offer yours. It's a sign of confidence.

• Depending on the situation, you may want to convey a sense of sincerity or warmth. This may be the case when meeting someone in person for the first time after speaking by phone for some extended period. To do this, loosen the grip just a bit and briefly place your left hand on top of the person's right hand as it shakes yours. Again, practice this until it comes naturally.

• While I'm on the subject of greetings, the question often comes up as to whether it's appropriate to greet an associate with a hug. This one is tricky. My advice is to never hug someone unless he or she does so first. Not only is it a matter of invading another person's space, but it also softens the greeting.

ACTION ITEM

Mistake 41

Being Financially Insecure

*V*irginia Woolf said every woman must have a room of her own. There are other women who will tell you a bank account of your own is even more important. Whether you're dependent on a husband, a domestic partner, or an employer, financial dependence translates into a loss of career choices and power. Having no money of your own, having your financial affairs in disarray, or not adequately preparing for your financial future equates to having no freedom.

But why is this a potentially career-busting mistake? Because if you don't have financial security, you wind up acting in ways and making decisions counter to your best career interests. Women are more likely to remain in dead-end jobs and be forced to work beyond the normal point of retirement because they can't afford to leave. Women are less likely to make tough but necessary decisions because they're afraid to rock the boat and lose their jobs. And women are often less able to understand the financial implications of business decisions because they don't pay close enough attention to their own financial affairs—the place where they *should* be learning about financial matters and extrapolating the lessons to business.

Women are also often forced to reenter the workforce ill prepared for success because they were dependent on someone who decided to discontinue financial support. I fully understand that being a homemaker teaches a woman many skills that are directly applicable to a job, but try telling this to the hiring source. As a result, late entries to the workforce are at a career disadvantage and wind up in low-paying entry-level positions.

In another scenario, Carrie worked her entire life for one employer, and worked hard. She was single with no children, and, although she owned her own home and created somewhat of a nest egg, by the age of sixty-two she still hadn't accumulated enough to retire. When the company was sold, the old managers who knew her and respected her work were all given golden parachutes to leave. Because she wasn't high enough up in the company, she was not one of the people offered this benefit.

As new managers took their place, she discovered the skills she had honed over the years weren't the same as those the new owners wanted in staff earning as much as she did. It wasn't so much that they could hire a younger person more cheaply; it was more a matter of hiring someone who more closely met their expectations. At her age and salary, Carrie didn't have many choices. She was forced to remain in a company where she was no longer respected and do menial tasks for which she was overqualified because she hadn't planned properly for her financial future. As personal finance columnist Liz Weston, my friend and fellow author, says, you need to have F.U. money—a "forget about you" stash of cash.

COACHING TIPS

• Read *The 10 Commandments of Money: Survive and Thrive in the New Economy*, by Liz Weston. Liz writes in a way that enables you to totally understand key concepts related to money and provides great tips for how to gain financial literacy.

• Have a financial goal. Every woman I know has a number in mind for what she wants the scale to read when she steps on it. Now you need a number in mind for how you'll know when you've become rich.

• Select a good financial planner, and with his or her help develop a solid personal financial plan.

• If you don't already have one, go out today and open an IRA or other retirement account for yourself. Deposit into it the maximum allowed yearly. If you're over forty, create a budget that allows you to contribute even more. It doesn't matter if you start it with fifty dollars or five hundred, do it. Hopefully, you're going to grow to be an old woman and you want to be a rich old woman, not a poor one.

• When you go to the store to purchase only a few items, pay with a twenty-dollar bill and put the change in a jar at home. When the jar is full, transfer the coins and dollar bills to your savings account.

ACTION ITEM

Mistake 42

Helping

$\mathscr{K}$risten is a new manager. She prides herself on not asking anyone on her team to do anything she herself wouldn't. At a recent off-site where her team was working in small groups and she was shuttling among them to offer assistance, one group asked her to bring them coffee. Thinking this wasn't a big thing, she brought it. Then they asked her to make some copies of their work product, which she did. The final request was for fresh Magic Markers.

At first blush it doesn't seem like anything was wrong, but closer scrutiny reveals the reason why certain members of Kristen's team often missed deadlines and ignored her requests for information. In her desire to help her team, they had begun to view her as a functionary. While she was getting coffee, fetching Magic Markers, and making copies, several of the men on the team were providing the real leadership the group needed.

A study conducted in the early 1980s interviewed 135 women to determine, among other things, how women gain knowledge. The researchers found that many of the people with whom they spoke said helping others, through either providing assistance, listening, or teaching, actually gave them more insight into themselves and greater self-confidence. Why? Because women are taught early in their lives that others know more than they do, so knowledge and self-confidence must be attained *externally*. Helping others is one way capable women gain external validation for their self-worth. This certainly accounts for why so many women go into helping fields.

Although I'm a staunch believer in the servant leadership philosophy espoused by Robert Greenleaf, many women take this to the extreme and encounter the same problems as Kristen when they're promoted to the management ranks or asked to lead a project team. They fail to transition from doer to leader. If you're busy doing, you don't have time to provide the vision, guidance, technical support, and oversight required of a leader.

COACHING TIPS

- Read the *Harvard Business Review* article "What Leaders Really Do," by John Kotter. The article helps you to take a look at higher-order behaviors expected at the more senior levels of any organization. Even if you aren't there yet, reading this will help you to get there.

- Differentiate *helping* and *being used*. If you're truly helping, you're providing the resources and support needed to allow others to get the job done efficiently and effectively. If you're working harder than everyone else on your team or task force, you're being used.

- Rather than offering to do the work of another, offer to teach him or her how to do it. Even though it may take longer in the short term, it will pay dividends in the long term.

- Ask yourself if you're helping because you think you'll be liked for it or because it's something you really want to do.

ACTION ITEM

Chapter 4

How You Think

*C*hanging how you *think* about how you work is essential to changing self-defeating behavior. Most of us have notions about what will get us recognized and what won't. These are called *superstitious behaviors* because we come to believe that if we don't do them, something catastrophic will happen. *I'll be rewarded only if I work harder than everyone else*, and *My boss will fire me if I tell her what I really think* are examples of superstitious thinking. These thoughts are often built around parental messages about work that may have been true for our parents but are no longer valid for us. Similarly, they're often reflective of behaviors that may have been functional early in our careers, but they're usually not as helpful later. What we do as entry-level workers to get respect and attention is more related to the task at hand than it is to exhibiting behaviors related to leadership capability, relationship skills, and the like. It's thus difficult to relinquish these beliefs because they've worked—up until now.

One of the most difficult aspects of coaching is getting people to try new behaviors. It's a little like letting go of old worn-out tennis shoes. They're comfortable. You've broken them in. You know exactly how they're going to feel when you wear them. They looked great three years ago, but you can't wear them in public anymore. This next section focuses on some of those beliefs you may have formed early in your work life that need to be retired before you do.

Mistake 43

Thinking Like an Employee

*M*any years ago I read an article, the gist of which was that jobs were created during the industrial revolution in response to the need for narrowly defined manufacturing functions. For example, in the automobile industry, one person put the wheels on the car, another person installed the steering wheel, another painted it, and so on. So each job was narrow in scope. The advent of robotics and a deeper understanding of workplace productivity changed all that. Even in Detroit those "jobs" have gone the way of the Model-T, with more car companies using teams of people endowed with broad responsibilities to assemble the vehicles.

The impact for you is that you can't just come to work and do your job. That's thinking like an employee. As one who has been an employee and who has also been an employer, I can tell you we do think differently. Add to that the myriad tasks required of women in their daily routines and the belief that we have to do things right (rather than do the right thing), and you have a nice girl with little time to think broadly about her *role*, as opposed to about her *job*. Trust me, your boss does not want you to be an employee. Your boss wants you to be a partner in the process of working toward goal attainment. The following chart may be helpful in illuminating the differences.

An Employee	A Partner in the Process
Does her job.	Thinks about ways to make the company money, save the company money, or improve efficiencies.
Doesn't question authority.	Diplomatically questions directives or assignments that don't seem logical or efficient.
Collects a paycheck.	Gains valuable transferrable skills through experience, training, and seizing new opportunities.
Performs the duties described in her job description.	Expands the boundaries of her job description by doing things that aren't asked of her but that need to be done.
Thinks day-to-day.	Thinks long-term.
Waits for assignments.	Seeks opportunities, gathers data, presents proposals, and makes it happen.

The problem for many women is that they are so overwhelmed with what they *have* to do, they can't carve out time for thinking more broadly and strategically. In the next mistake I address what you need to relinquish so that you can become the partner your boss wants and your company needs, but for now consider the following coaching tips to help you start that shift.

COACHING TIPS

• Ask the boss for assignments that will make his or her workload easier and at the same time provide you with opportunities to expand your skill set. Be up front about it when asking—it's not considered toadying if there's a quid pro quo.

• Consider how each of your primary duties interacts with the other functions in your department or throughout the company. Picture yourself as part of a complex network of functions, each interdependent on the other. Assume responsibility not only for your own success, but for the success of the company as a whole.

• Read trade magazines and professional journals that give you insight into trends in your field and make proposals for how to implement selected best practices. While you're at it, share articles or books about best practices and new trends with both the boss and your coworkers.

• Continually ask yourself, *What are we not doing currently that if we started doing would fundamentally change how we did business?* Then find ways to introduce changes that will enhance your company's bottom line.

ACTION ITEM

Mistake 44

Believing in the Myth of Work-Life Balance

*I*f climbing the corporate ladder is important to you, there is no such thing as work-life balance. It's not possible for men, and, given their additional family responsibilities, it's even less possible for women. We actually don't even hear the term *balance* referred to any longer. The new language around it is work-life integration, because the focus is on how to integrate the two aspects of your life as a working woman. Anne-Marie Slaughter, writing for *Atlantic* magazine, caused quite a stir with her article "Why Women Still Can't Have It All." In the article, she made the case for what I've been saying for years—yes, *women can have it all, but they can't have it all at the same time.*

As women, we're put in the untenable situation of having to make difficult choices involving our careers and our families. As one woman put it, "When I'm at work I feel as if I should be at home with my family, and when I'm home with my family I feel as if I should be working." You would think with women making up about half the workforce and data reflecting the myriad benefits of having women in leadership roles, by now American corporations would have figured out a way to enable women to have more balance in their lives. Sadly, that's not the case. Yet there are some things we do to *ourselves* that exacerbate an already difficult situation. Ask yourself how many of the following behaviors at home and at work impede your ability to have more balance in your life:

- Strive for perfection
- Rarely ask for help

- Have unreasonable expectations for how much you can accomplish in a day
- Feel guilty about never quite being who everyone else wants/needs you to be
- Don't negotiate
- Believe you have to work twice as hard to be considered half as good
- Allow others to dictate how your time will be spent
- Engage in excessive multitasking

Even if you own up to only two or three of these behaviors, that's enough to suggest that you're literally and figuratively working overtime. It's time for you to get more realistic about how to craft a life that's not only productive but meaningful, fulfilling, and rewarding.

COACHING TIPS

- Read Anne-Marie Slaughter's article "Why Women Still Can't Have It All" in the July/August 2012 edition of the *Atlantic* magazine. Not only is it a classic piece, it will help you to understand why you've been feeling (and rightly so) as if you're going out of your mind trying to keep all the balls in the air at the same time.

- Send guilt on a trip. It serves absolutely no purpose in your life. When you start feeling guilty, ask yourself what you can realistically change to make the situation better and act on it. If the answer is that nothing can be done differently, then move on.

- Focus on quality, not quantity. Staying at work additional hours doesn't make you more effective at your job or perceived as more valuable to the company (if overtime isn't a company expectation). In fact, it could make you seem overwhelmed and inefficient. Similarly, the amount of time you spend with your family isn't as important as the quality of that time. You can be at home physically and absent mentally. Strive to be fully present wherever you are and compartmentalize the various aspects of your life. Personally, I have a visualization exercise that I do when I'm feeling torn between two places. I picture myself putting my concerns or worries in a box and then placing that box on a high shelf in my closet. I tell myself that I can retrieve the box at a later time and deal with the issues then, but for now I must be fully present in the moment.

- Resist multitasking. As mentioned in Mistake 21, all research points to the fact that over time, multitasking makes us less effective and actually has long-term deleterious effects on the brain.

ACTION ITEM

Mistake 45

Making Miracles

*T*hink logically about this. When you look around at the people who get promoted and recognized, are they the people who make miracles? Women take pride in the fact that they can do more with less, meet or beat impossible deadlines, and get juice out of a turnip. They actually believe others will recognize and appreciate their efforts. What they don't realize is that every time they make a miracle, they've set the bar higher in terms of what people expect from them. Not only that, but while they're busy jumping through hoops, their male colleagues are doing things that give them more visibility and, ultimately, more rewards.

Take Anita, for example. She transferred from the advertising business into a Big Five consulting firm. Without a doubt she was an expert in her field—everyone said so. And as her boss said: "She inherited a mess." By coming in early, staying late, and working week-ends, she started to get a handle on the problem and made inroads into correcting it. No matter what was asked of her, Anita delivered.

Whereas the first year she could do no wrong, the next year she could do no right. People came to expect her to achieve the same results—and more—every day. To do this, Anita had to continue spending ridiculous amounts of time at the office. She had set the standard so high the first year that she couldn't possibly surpass it the second year—or even keep up the pace—although that's what everyone expected. This is not to say she shouldn't have given it her all the first year, or that she should in any way sacrifice excellence. It simply means that you must be realistic about establishing work habits and not thinking you have to be superwoman to be effective.

During my keynote addresses, if there are men in the room, I will randomly choose one and ask, "When your boss asks you to make a miracle, what do you do?" Inevitably I receive one of three answers: "I laugh"; "I negotiate"; "I delegate it to a woman." Women, on the other hand, almost always answer, "I do it." Remember, miracle workers get canonized; they don't get recognized.

COACHING TIPS

• Manage expectations. Always be willing to go the extra mile, but provide choices that focus on what's reasonable and realistic. For example, if you're asked to put together the company holiday party on a budget of $500 for 250 people, you can manage expectations by saying something like "I'm happy to work within that budget. Given that it amounts to $2 per person, I can make the party alcohol-free and ask everyone to bring a dish; or, if you'd like to increase the budget to $1,000, I can bring in deli trays and we can have soft drinks. What would you prefer?" This puts the onus of responsibility on the person making the request, rather than making you the scapegoat for a lousy event or making you feel as if you have to make a miracle— which even at the holidays is an unreasonable expectation.

• Set realistic daily or weekly goals. Women think there are thirty-four hours in every day. Remember Parkinson's Law: "Work expands to fill the time available." If you come to work in the morning with the notion that you can work until 9 p.m. if you have to, then you will. If you come in with the idea you're going to leave at 6 p.m., you'll probably be out not long after.

• If you're understaffed, *ask* for help or negotiate reasonable deadlines. You can always say, "I'd love to get this to you by five o'clock as requested, but we don't have the staff to achieve that kind of turnaround. Tomorrow at five is more realistic." From there you may have to negotiate, but you're less likely to work until midnight.

ACTION ITEM

Mistake 46

Taking Full Responsibility

*T*his is a variation on the miracle theme. Just because you're assigned a project doesn't mean you're the only one who *can* do it or *should* do it. It only means you're the one responsible for making it *happen*. You get no brownie points for doing a project alone. You get brownie points for getting it done. In fact, you may be looked upon more favorably if you're able to delegate parts of the project or influence others to help you. It shows that you know how to manage a project. Haven't you ever noticed that when a man is given a project, the first thing he does is begin delegating?

I once coached a woman who'd been given responsibility for developing a plan for corporate philanthropy. The company had never before funded grants to the nonprofit community. The thought of doing this was daunting to her. She had no idea where to start. As we discussed it, she began to realize she didn't have to do it all today— nor did she have to do it all herself. Engaging various stakeholders in the company and in the community would actually be better because she would get their buy-in from the start and could take advantage of their ideas, energy, and resources. She left the meeting feeling as if a burden had been lifted off her shoulders.

COACHING TIPS

- When assigned a project or task, avoid the tendency to start *doing*. Take time to think it through, plan it, identify resources, and so forth. Break it down into small parts with benchmarks that enable you to measure and report progress on an ongoing basis, rather than when the project is completed. It also makes everything on your plate more easily digested.

- Continually build relationships throughout your company and your professional community. When you need a relationship, it's too late to build it. I'll speak more to this a little later in this section.

- Don't reinvent the wheel. What I've come to realize is that there's not too much new under the sun. If *I* have to do something, it means other people must have done it before. Find these people and ask them to share their expertise.

- Learn to delegate. Even if you don't have staff reporting directly to you, call on the relationships you've built to help with providing assistance.

ACTION ITEM

Mistake 47

Obediently Following Instructions

This isn't true of all women, but some of us, when given an assignment, become like dogs with a bone. We're so anxious to get the job done quickly or get the pat on the head we crave, we can't see what's on the periphery that would help us work smarter. We tend to look at the details, not the big picture. People who get ahead know how to balance the tactical with the strategic.

There are two women in my office who are really good at this. They were hired to manage the many new projects and clients that come through the door. Because I tend to see the big picture but not the details, I had in the past always assumed I needed to surround myself with detail-oriented staff and hired accordingly. Kim and Jessica have shown me the error of my ways and have spoiled me for all time.

When given an assignment, rather than jumping in to immediately start it, both women begin by first thinking about it, then asking lots of good questions. This saves an incredible amount of time—not to mention money and frustration on their part—because we no longer get halfway down the road only to realize my original idea for the project was less than well thought through. They add value to the company by not obediently following my instructions but rather by thinking and planning—which is what *you* want to be known for.

COACHING TIPS

- Spend time brainstorming with colleagues before beginning complex or large assignments. Choose people who don't necessarily think the way you do to ensure you're getting a 360-degree view of the project landscape.

- Rather than responding to the details of an assignment, before beginning consider how it could be done faster, cheaper, or more effectively. Then go back to the person who gave you the assignment and discuss changes that you propose for making it more efficient while at the same time providing better outcomes.

- Take a stress management class to overcome the need to treat every assignment with the utmost urgency. Here you will learn techniques to manage anxiety that may accompany high-stakes projects.

ACTION ITEM

Mistake 48

Viewing Men in Authority as Father Figures

*C*arolyn was an upwardly mobile career woman who was smart and assertive—that is, with everyone except those men who were senior to her. When they asked her a question, she became tongue-tied and childlike. She came to coaching because she knew she wasn't projecting the image she wanted to with these men. She acted like a little girl, and, in turn, she was treated like one. Early on I realized that giving her tips for being more assertive or speaking articulately wouldn't work. She already knew how to do that. The problem was, she couldn't do it with certain people.

During one of our early meetings I asked her to tell me about her father. As it turns out, he was a former colonel in the army and ran his family as he might a platoon. She described him as authoritative, critical, and impossible to please. When I inquired into how she survived childhood, she said she'd learned to be a good girl, obey all the rules, study hard, and not do anything that might displease him. When she entered the workforce, she responded to men senior to her as if they were her father and she, the dutiful daughter.

Conversely, Suzanne's father was nurturing, loving, and compassionate. He encouraged her to pursue her dreams and emotionally supported her in the process. She came to coaching because she couldn't understand why she never pleased the boss. Surely she must be doing something wrong, she thought. I knew her boss and, although I didn't tell Suzanne this, he was widely known as a critical, egotistical know-it-all. There wasn't anything she—or anyone else— could do that would please him. What Suzanne didn't understand was that not all men are like her father, and she couldn't expect them to treat her as he did.

What Suzanne and Carolyn had in common was inappropriately viewing the boss as a father figure. Expecting the best from him, or expecting the worst from him, doesn't allow you to build an independent, objective relationship with your boss or other senior executive.

COACHING TIPS

- If you find yourself responding to the boss or other male authority figures in a way that is unlike you in other situations, ask yourself these three questions:

    1. *Whom does he remind me of?*
    2. *How do I act when I'm around him?*
    3. *Why do I give up so much power to him?*

- The answers will help you see why and how you see the boss as your father.

    o Use self-talk to differentiate male authority figures from your father. When you're in a meeting with the boss, tell yourself he's not your father and you are his equal. Do it as often as needed to believe it and act accordingly.
    o Lower your antenna for feelings and focus on the message a male authority figure gives you, not the manner in which it is delivered. This will enable you to hear it objectively and respond appropriately.

ACTION ITEM

Mistake 49

Limiting Your Possibilities

In her classic book *Women's Reality*, Anne Wilson Schaef observes that in our culture, those with less power live their lives in a zone circumscribed by people with more power. White men, being on top of the hierarchy, decide what's appropriate behavior for everyone else, including women. In many ways, *Nice Girls Don't Get the Corner Office* is about how women live according to the rules established by men. Men define the rules for the playing field, heavily influence behaviors that are acceptable for women and people of color inside and outside the workplace (it certainly isn't the other way around); and we live in a society where laws are passed by legislators and Supreme Court justices who are predominantly men.

Schaef points out that without even realizing it, living our lives this way narrowly circumscribes the choices we make. Like air pollution, if you live in it and breathe it long enough, you come to believe that's just how the air is supposed to be. It's not until you see the beautiful blue skies of some unspoiled territory that you realize things can be different. For women, the air is polluted all the time, so we don't often have the opportunity to see how things can be different. We come to believe that our possibilities are limited, when in fact they're limited only because we allow them to be.

Not too long ago a woman was referred to me because she wanted to explore a career opportunity for which she was qualified but uncertain about tossing her hat in the ring for. For many years she had worked at a nonprofit organization as the second in command. She had seen directors (all male) come and go and never really thought of herself as a contender for the top job. The board of directors was made up exclusively of conservative men, and they had never considered her for the job when the top position became available. This made her believe she would never be considered a viable candidate.

After our first meeting, it was clear to both of us that she had the talent and the experience to do the job; she just didn't have the confidence. She'd grown up in a household where an older brother was the anointed superstar of the family, and she was given the message that she was good, but not nearly as talented as he was. It was pretty clear why, up until now, she was satisfied in positions where she played second fiddle.

At our second meeting I wanted to know why now, after all these years, she wanted the top spot. She said she'd been looking around at women colleagues who had begun their careers in pretty much the same position she had—and they were all now executive directors and presidents of their nonprofit institutions. Part of the shift in thinking was out of embarrassment, and part was because she was bored and ready for a new challenge.

By our third meeting the woman had put together a plan for how she was going to express her interest in the job and show why she was the best-qualified candidate. Within two months (this was a very slow-moving board!) she was the lead contender for the job, and within three months she was sitting in the director's corner office.

Women are given so many subtle and not-so-subtle messages about "where we belong" that we all too often remain inside an artificially narrowed box. One of the most powerful women in entertainment history is Sherry Lansing, the former CEO of Paramount Pictures. Recognizing that the chance to run her own studio would never be handed to her, Lansing started her own production company. When her company produced such blockbuster films as *Fatal Attraction* and *The Accused*, the studio heads took note. Within a short period of time, she was invited back to play with the big boys and given the top spot at Paramount. Having had the opportunity to speak with her, I can tell you she did it all without lowering herself to some of the typical entertainment dirty tricks but rather by exhibiting a huge

EQ and LQ. The lesson here is: *If you live your life within the boundaries circumscribed by others, you'll never know the full scope of your potential—nor will anyone else.*

COACHING TIPS

• Consciously expand your world of possibilities by enumerating your choices at every fork in the road. If you can't see them, brainstorm with a friend.

• Listen for limiting self-talk such as:

I could never do what Kathy did. I'm not that brave.
They'll never approve of this idea no matter how many facts I present.
I may as well not even apply for that job. I'm not the best qualified.
I'm not smart enough to get a PhD.
I'll never have enough money to retire early.

• Avoid the tendency to disregard unconventional choices. Before making a decision about a direction, sleep on all your choices. One that you may initially discount could be the right one for you.

• Read biographies of successful women and learn how they broadened their possibilities.

• Ignore naysayers. People told Mary Kay Ash she couldn't possibly start a successful cosmetics company—and look what she did! One of her favorite sayings that you would do well to remember was "Aerodynamically the bumblebee shouldn't be able to fly, but the bumblebee doesn't know that so it goes on flying anyway."

ACTION ITEM

Mistake 50

Ignoring the Quid Pro Quo

*P*eople don't like to talk about it, but inherent to every relationship there's a quid pro quo—something that's exchanged in return for something else. The quid pro quo can be obvious, such as *I give you a salary and in return I expect you to do a good job*, or more subtly, *I give you a recommendation and in turn expect you'll help me get my expense check processed faster*. It's an unspoken system of bartering that goes on in relationships. Women aren't very good at capitalizing on the quid pro quo. Instead, they give away favors and expect little or nothing in return.

An important part of building relationships at work is identifying the quid pro quo. What do you have that others want or need, and what do others have that you want or need? Every time you give people something they need, a (figurative) chip is deposited into your account. The trick is to always have more chips in your account than you need. The only way you can do this is by interacting with others with generosity of spirit.

A former client of mine called not too long ago to let me know that she was now at a new company. She said it would mean a lot to her if I would come and speak with the company's women's group. When I asked what her budget was, she said there was none. She was hoping I would do it as a favor to her. Given that this is how I earn my living, speaking to groups, it was a big favor to ask, but I did it at no charge. The woman is well-connected, and I thought one day I might need her help with something.

About eighteen months later, I needed a location to hold a non-profit event and I knew the woman's company had several spaces large enough. So I called her and asked if she might be able to help me out. I never mentioned the favor I did for her, although I had no doubt she remembered it. After some hemming and hawing, she said she didn't think she could arrange it and I politely told her not to worry about it. When I finally found a location for the event, I sent her an invitation, fully expecting she would reciprocate the favor I did for her by buying a ticket for the fund-raiser (even if she couldn't attend). But this didn't happen either. So two years later, when she made a career move to another company and once again called on me to do her a favor, I chose not to. The quid pro quo had been broken. With a limited amount of time, I choose to spend mine helping either people who can't help themselves or those who support me and my goals.

It really isn't as manipulative or mercenary as it sounds. We do it all day long without realizing it. Say, for example, that I finish up a report for you because you have to leave early for a doctor's appointment. I collect a chip. Several weeks later I need some information that I know you've collected through your research. I cash that chip in when you give me the information. Sometimes the quid pro quo is verbalized ("Remember when I loaned you my laptop last month? Well, I've got a favor to ask..."), but more often it's not.

COACHING TIPS

- When you go out of your way for people, be sure to let them know. A subtle way to do this is by saying something like "Can I finish this report before I leave? Well, I was planning on meeting a friend after work, but why don't I call him and let him know I'll be late." You've just collected a chip.

- Don't make things look so easy. Try saying something similar to "I'm happy to report that I convinced the IT department to repair your laptop ahead of several other requests. I knew you would need it before you left on your trip." There's another chip in your account.

- Don't underestimate the barter value of things such as verbally supporting someone in a meeting, public praise, a listening ear, or grapevine information. They're all valuable workplace commodities.

- Cash in your chips sparingly, but don't be afraid to use them. If you're applying for a job and someone you've collected many chips from has information about the hiring source, ask for it. When you need someone to help out in a pinch, ask someone you've extended the same courtesy to in the past. Keep in mind that the exchange of chips isn't always one-to-one, it isn't always immediately following the point of collection, and it doesn't have to be made obvious.

ACTION ITEM

Mistake 51

Skipping Meetings

*L*ose the notion that meetings are supposed to be valuable, interesting, or worth your time. That's really naive. It's the unusual meeting leader who knows how to achieve all three of those achievable, but rarely recognized, goals. Also lose the inclination to stay at your desk and work because you believe *that's* really important. Wrong again. I realize that most meetings are an incredible waste of time if you think the content is what they're all about. It's not.

They're called *meet*ings, not *work*ings, for a reason. Meetings provide the ideal opportunity to see and be seen, meet and greet, or play show-and-tell. It's part of the branding and marketing you'll read about in chapter 5—something most women need to do *much* more of.

COACHING TIPS

- Don't skip meetings. (How's that for direct and to the point?)
- Use meetings as an opportunity to showcase a particular skill or piece of knowledge (provided it's not note taking or coffee making). If you're good at facilitating, then offer to lead the meeting (it's much better than sitting there bored). Or if you want to build a relationship, support what someone else says (but only if you really agree with it).
- Ask to be invited to meetings where you'll have the chance to meet senior management or make a presentation about something for which you need support.
- Choose a role to play in meetings. The book *Mining Group Gold*, by Thomas Kayser, provides suggestions for what you can do to be perceived as an invaluable member of your team. From helping to clarify what others have said to asking the questions no one else wants to ask, there are numerous roles you can play that will keep you engaged and get you noticed.

ACTION ITEM

Mistake 52

Putting Work Ahead of Your Personal Life

*D*on't make work your life. The CEO of one Fortune 100 company (a man, of course) told me, "If my staff can't get the job done and have a life outside of work, they're doing something wrong." When all is said and done, do you really want written on your tombstone: "She always put the needs of the company ahead of her own"? You owe the company an honest day's work for an honest day's pay. You owe the company a reasonable amount of overtime (with or without pay, but always without complaint). You don't owe the company your soul.

My experience with women who give up what's important to them to meet the needs of the job is that either they don't have anything to go home to or they don't want to deal with what they do have to go home to. Like any other "ism," workaholism is usually in the service of avoidance. Having activities and people outside work that are important to you helps you remain positive and productive. It's a fallacy that you have to give up your life to have a successful career. All work and no play makes Jill a very dull girl.

COACHING TIPS

• Think twice before canceling plans because you're asked to or because you're swamped. Weigh the rewards against the risks involved with doing so. There are legitimately times when you have to cancel, but if these are the rule instead of the exception, something's wrong with the picture.

• Never cancel plans with your children because of a workplace request unless your job is on the line. Even then think twice. You obviously can't risk losing a job you need for financial reasons, but you might want to ask yourself if you wouldn't be better off at a company that embraces family values.

• Develop outside hobbies and interests. If you don't have one, *create* a reason for leaving work.

• What *do* you want written on your tombstone? Now go do it.

ACTION ITEM

Mistake 53

Letting People Waste Your Time

I just *know* we must have "Go ahead—waste my day" written on our foreheads. Why else would people think they could spend so much time talking to us about nothing? I cannot understand why anyone—man, woman, or child—would come into my office and say, "Would you mind if I ask you a question? Bob is busy at the moment." Like *I'm not?* Your time is one of the most precious commodities you have. Once it's gone, you'll never retrieve it.

So we're supposed to be nurturing and kind and blah, blah, blah, blah, blah. Well, I'm here to tell you, being nurturing and kind is not mutually exclusive of being protective of your time. There's a time and a place for everything, and when you've got a tight deadline, a five-thirty hairdresser appointment, and your in-laws are coming for dinner—it's *definitely* not the time.

Christine Reiter, president of the Pasadena-based consulting firm Time Strategies, works with clients to maximize the use of their time. When I asked her how women differ from men in terms of time wasters, she told me, "The urge to please everyone and not be able to say no is the biggest time waster for women. We don't like conflict and confrontation. As a result, we have difficulty setting boundaries and making our positions clear."

Don't leave this page thinking my suggestion is that you *never* make time for others. Doing that would only irreparably damage relationships and prevent you from collecting chips that you can later barter. But do think about how you allow others to take advantage of your time, especially when you just don't have it to give.

COACHING TIPS

- Differentiate the times when people *need* to talk from those when they *want* to talk.
- Repeat after me: "You know, I would love to talk more, but I'm on a tight schedule today. How about if we continue this conversation tomorrow?"
- Use tricks of time management, like keeping a pile of papers on the extra chairs in your office; not putting your pencil down when someone walks in; answering your phone, voice mail, and e-mail only during specified periods of the day; and putting a "Please Do Not Disturb" sign on your door when you've got a tight deadline.
- A few more tips from Reiter:

  1. Clearly set boundaries about how much time you have—or don't have—to share, and know the world will not fall apart because of it.
  2. When people ignore the boundary (as they inevitably do with women), enforce it by saying something like "As I said before, I'd love to spend more time with you, but today's schedule won't allow me to."
  3. If others keep you waiting more than twenty or thirty minutes for a scheduled appointment, leave. This includes business lunches, doctor's appointments, and casual encounters with friends.

ACTION ITEM

Mistake 54

Reluctance to Negotiate

$\mathcal{A}$uthors Carol Frohlinger and Deborah Kolb have worked with thousands of women to help them be more confident and competent at negotiation. What may surprise you (because there's so much misinformation out there) is that women achieve negotiation outcomes as good as or better than men do—unless they are negotiating for themselves. It doesn't matter whether they are negotiating for a raise, a promotion, or credit for the work they've done, the fact that they themselves are the beneficiaries is the root of the trouble.

Carol and I have had several opportunities to discuss why this is the case and what women can and should do about it. Let's start with the fact that beginning with our time on the playground as children, we are socialized to behave in accordance with stereotypical gendered roles. And, as you know by now, nice girls let others take the lead, don't talk about money, and don't toot their own horns. Carrying those messages into adulthood, nice girls are reluctant to advocate on their own behalf—it just doesn't seem like the right thing to do. Instead, they work hard, hoping that someone will notice and give them the rewards they deserve. Clearly, this is a fallacy. "Failing to proactively negotiate at work costs nice girls not only money but affects career opportunities and job success as well," says Frohlinger. "Women have to raise their hands to let people know they're interested when a bigger job becomes available. They have to request the resources required to get the job done. They have to reach agreement on project parameters and deadlines. And, yes, they certainly have to advocate when it comes to compensation."

While writing *Nice Girls Don't Get Rich*, I had the pleasure of interviewing Dr. Lisa Barron, an assistant professor in organizational behavior at the Graduate School of Management at the University of California, Irvine. Linda published an article, "Ask and You Shall Receive? Gender Differences in Negotiators' Beliefs About Requests for a Higher Salary," based on a study she conducted with male and female MBA students. The scenario involved all students' being offered a job with a salary of $61,000 and a bonus of $5,000. They were also told that other students from their program were offered similar jobs at another company with a salary of $67,000 and a bonus of $10,000.

The students in the study were given information that would allow them to negotiate not only their salaries, but also tuition reimbursement and vacation. In the end, both men and women negotiated for more money, but men wound up receiving significantly more—because they *asked* for more. Lisa found three primary themes that emerged with the amounts men and women asked for:

1. **Entitlement.** The men felt they were entitled to even more than what their colleagues had been offered at the other company, whereas the women felt it would be "fair" to get equal to what their colleagues received. In other words, men had more of a sense of entitlement and women more of a desire to ask for what they thought was "fair."

2. **Worth.** The men equated their salaries more with what they thought they were worth. If a colleague was receiving $67,000 annually, they believed they should get more because they were worth more. Women were uncomfortable with the notion of worth, didn't think of themselves as worth more, or couldn't measure their worth.

3. **Proving oneself.** The women in the study were hesitant to ask for more money before they could prove they deserved it, whereas the men used past experiences as a rationale for getting more money.

4. **Consequences.** Both men and women considered the consequences of asking for more money but men weren't concerned

that damage done in the present could hurt them down the road. The women were more worried that the recruiter would think poorly of them or think they were greedy or not nice.

The tricky part is that it is not enough for women to just ask, they must recognize that stereotyped expectations about whether and how they should negotiate are alive and well. To ignore them is at their peril; women are expected to be too "nice" to negotiate. The best way for women to bargain without blowing themselves up is to make every effort to appear selfless, linking what they want to what's good for their companies.

Then there's the issue that many women equate negotiation with confrontation. It doesn't have to be that way. In fact, the "win-win" negotiation described by Roger Fisher and William Ury in their classic book, *Getting to Yes: Negotiating Agreement Without Giving In*, is not only a more comfortable approach for most women, it is the only approach that makes sense when the negotiations are taking place with colleagues and clients. Why? Because everything we do before, during, and after the negotiations should enhance the relationship. Furthermore, because this brand of negotiation demands an understanding of the other party's needs, women, generally considered skilled listeners, are well poised to be excellent at it.

And there's still more good news. Negotiating is a learnable skill; you can improve the outcomes you get (and reduce the stress in getting them) if you are willing to invest in yourself. After every important negotiation, think about the things that worked (and why they worked), and also consider what you will do next time to be even more successful.

COACHING TIPS

Carol Frohlinger provides these tips for how you can better negotiate more effectively for what you want:

- **Deliver excellence always.** You have leverage when negotiating if your work consistently exceeds expectations. Because you clearly provide value to your company, the powers that be will want to do everything they can to keep you satisfied. After all, it's disruptive when productive people leave the company.

- **Do your homework.** Benchmark as much information as you can about what others in your industry (and even better, in your company or department) have received. Use the Internet as one way to gather data, but don't rely on online sleuthing exclusively; draw on your networks as well to find what you need to know. Having this data will enable you to establish reasonable objectives for your negotiation.

- **Be clear about what you want.** If you don't know what you want, you can't get what you want. At the same time, think creatively about ways your needs can be met. For example, in order to secure more resources, you may be willing to accept a larger project scope or a shorter deadline.

- **Have a "Plan B."** Consider the alternatives you have if you are unable to reach agreement with the other person or persons. How good or bad are the alternatives? This is the negotiation concept described in *Getting to Yes* as BATNA (Best Alternative to a Negotiated Agreement). The better your alternatives, the more leverage you have in the negotiation. Also consider the other party's BATNA; they may have as much to lose as you do if you are unable to reach an agreement.

- **Anticipate pushback.** Anticipate the pushback you are likely to get and plan how you'll respond. But keep in mind, it's one thing to know what you are going to say, but it's another to actually get the words out of your mouth effectively. That's why, if it's an important negotiation, you should go one step further and enlist a friend to practice with you. Provide your friend with enough information about the situation and the person with whom you are negotiating so that she or he can play the role convincingly.

ACTION ITEM

Mistake 55

Prematurely Abandoning Your Career Goals

$\mathcal{S}$uccess breeds success. Eleanor Roosevelt said, "You gain courage and confidence from doing the things you think you cannot do." The problem encountered by many women is that they often allow others to sidetrack them from their early dreams and career goals. Mary Catherine Bateson, daughter of anthropologists Margaret Mead and Gregory Bateson, wrote a wonderfully insightful book titled *Composing a Life*. Her observation is that women's lives, unlike men's, are not linear but rather constantly shifting. "Our lives not only take new directions," she writes, "they are subject to repeated redirection, partly because of the extension of our years of health and productivity." It's this redirection that gets in our way of making plans and pursuing them through to completion. As a result, when we're interested in returning to them, we may find the workforce is no longer interested in us.

When I worked at ARCO, I saw numerous well-educated, bright women who were considered only for entry-level positions because they had abandoned their early career goals. They erroneously thought they would be able to pick up their careers where they left off. I once interviewed a woman for a position within corporate communications who had many starts and stops in her career. She had earned a college degree in English, intending to go into the newspaper business as a writer or editor. For the past twelve years she'd held various administrative positions for short periods of time (eight to eighteen months) as she moved around the country with her husband's job changes. She was a lovely woman who was clearly bright but, when asked, admitted she was not up to speed with state-of-the-art office technology and equipment. Combined with a spotty work history, she wasn't someone I could in good conscience further to the next stage of candidacy.

If she had at least kept up-to-date with technology, I would have considered her along with other candidates. If she had achieved any of her personal goals—regardless of how minor they may have appeared—I would have assessed her as more likely to perseveringly pursue the goals of the communications department. Instead, like many other women in her situation, her best chance of eventually getting the position she wanted would be to begin with an entry-level secretarial position and work her way up.

Even if circumstances prevent you from achieving your goal of being editor in chief of a major metropolitan newspaper, remain involved with your interests and up-to-date with your field of interest. You may have what it takes to be successful, but if you lose yourself in someone else's priorities or societal expectations, you will be judged not by your potential but rather by your history.

COACHING TIPS

- Rather than completely abandon your career goals when life throws you a curve, come up with a strategic life plan that allows you to keep abreast of developments in your field. Talk to friends and family and ask for their support in helping you to remain on your path.

- Consider the importance of a college degree not only to your success but to your self-confidence as well. Even if you don't need it for work, do you want it for you? If so, start downloading the application.

- When others attempt to derail you from your path, look at it as normal—but don't give in to it. When any "system" changes, whether it's a political system, an ecological system, or a family system, the system tends to want to maintain its equilibrium by going back to the status quo. So guess what? People are used to the status quo being to put your needs on a back burner—and if they had their druthers, they'd keep it that way.

- If you decide to be a stay-at-home mom for a while, remain involved with your field through participation in professional associations or community college courses.

- Volunteer to do work in your field of interest that will allow you access to the technology and equipment you will need when you return to work.

ACTION ITEM

Mistake 56

Ignoring the Importance of Network Relationships

*O*nce upon a time, in a decade very far away, people would do their jobs, collect their paychecks, go home, and know that as long as they did their jobs well, they could sleep easily at night. They would be taken care of. Only in a fairy tale would this scenario be true today. There was a time when IBM was notorious for its full-employment policy. Even during difficult financial times, you wouldn't be laid off. Your hours might be cut or you might be transferred to the boondocks, but IBM founder Tom Watson prided himself on the full-employment policy. Not anymore.

Many women still believe in that fairy tale. They go to work, do a good job, try not to make any waves, and think this is enough to protect them from career derailment. As Judge Judy would say: "*Wrong.*" You are in the center of a complex network of people.

Your job includes building a relationship with everyone on that wheel. You don't have to do it on the golf course or over beers after work, but you do have to do it if you want to ensure long-term success.

Rather than share with you a story about a woman whose career was negatively impacted by her failure to maintain network relationships, let me tell you one about a woman whose career was saved by those relationships. Alexis is an executive with responsibility for the North American sales group of an international toy company. After quite a few years of working for the company, her boss left and was replaced with someone from outside the firm. Alexis and the new boss didn't see eye-to-eye on many issues, and dissatisfaction on both ends inevitably arose.

NETWORK RELATIONSHIPS

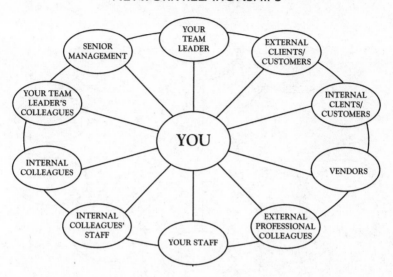

The new boss was ready to fire her and asked human resources to help him do so. He admitted she did a fine job, was a hard worker, and always met her sales goals, but they disagreed on some significant changes he wanted to make in the business. To bolster his case, he suggested they conduct a survey of people in her network, asking for feedback about her performance. He assumed that if *he* didn't get along with her, then others must not as well.

Well, was he surprised by the results. It turned out that Alexis was a superb networker. She built strong relationships not only with customers of the company, but also with vendors, coworkers, and people reporting to her. To a person they praised her for her work ethic, integrity, and attention to customer needs. From reading their comments, you would believe they'd named their first, second, and third children after her. It was pretty clear that if the new boss fired her, he would lose goodwill throughout the company's community of employees and customers. Instead, as a result of her network relationships, he was forced to find a way to work more effectively with her.

NETWORK RELATIONSHIPS

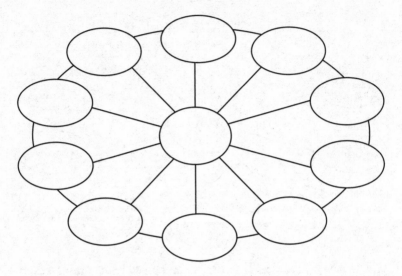

Alexis's story demonstrates the power of network relationships. Most of us aren't in situations this dramatic, but we all do need to call on relationships every now and then to help us out professionally. And remember: *When you need that relationship, it's already too late to build it.*

COACHING TIPS

- Go back to the blank network diagram on page 162, and in the circle for each category write the names of actual people who impact your work and career.

- Develop a plan for how you're going to build (or maintain) a relationship with each of them. Remember to take into consideration the quid pro quo inherent to each of these relationships: what you have to offer and what you need in exchange.

- Join and actively participate in a professional association.

- Tell yourself, *Spending time building relationships is not a waste of time*. And it's not. The more relationships you have in place, the more access you have to information and resources.

- Create a database that includes the names of all the people you meet and the information they share with you.

ACTION ITEM

Mistake 57

Refusing Perks

*T*oni was promoted to a senior management position in her firm. The company, like many others, had a policy about which levels of employees were entitled to which offices. You know the story—those on the bottom of the food chain get an inside cubicle, next up get a cubicle with a window, next up a double-sized cubicle, and so on up to a corner office, with a door, mahogany furniture, and a predetermined color of carpet. (When I worked in corporate America, I used to say, "I want to be promoted to a door.") Toni was entitled to an office, with a window (and a door) and faux mahogany furniture. When she was informed it was time to move from her double-sized cubicle with a window, she refused. She didn't see the need to go to the trouble and expense to move. Mistake!

Nancy experienced a similar situation. Due to a promotion, she was entitled to a new office, furniture, PC, and so on. In her case, Nancy expected to move into her new space and was waiting for the green light to do so—but the green light never came. One day she went to her boss and asked what was up. He informed her that he'd recently hired someone for whom he would need the office she'd expected. You guessed it: The new hire was a man. Rather than make waves, Nancy stayed in her cubicle, grateful for even being promoted. Even bigger mistake!

COACHING TIPS

• You don't take a perk because you want it or think you deserve it. You take it because it manages the impressions others have of you—and those you have of yourself.

• When a perk you've earned is—shall we say—"overlooked," bring it to management's attention. It could legitimately be an oversight. Then again, they could just be hoping you'll act like most women and never bring it up.

• When you're not given perks commensurate with your position, and you know it's not an oversight, ask why not. At a minimum, make someone look you in the eye and tell you why you're not getting what everyone else in your position gets.

• If you feel strongly about the slight and are willing to accept the consequences, bring the matter to senior management for a final decision. Without being whiny or pointing fingers, explain the situation, what you would like to have happen, and in what time frame. The worst you will hear is no, in which case you let it go unless it's the hill you're willing to die on.

• When you get a promotion, be sure to ask what it includes. Often information either doesn't flow automatically or is delayed.

ACTION ITEM

Mistake 58

Making Up Negative Stories

*M*y mother was a master at making up negative stories when things went wrong. If someone was a bit cool to her, she would think out loud, "Maybe the gift I gave him wasn't nice enough." If I didn't get a particular job, it was "Maybe you didn't wear the right dress." If my father didn't get a promotion, he heard, "Maybe you insulted the boss." As a result, whenever things didn't go quite as I had planned, I assumed I'd done something wrong—and I know I'm not alone. Many women suffer from this same phenomenon, and for the same reason!

At work, making up negative stories will serve to continually put you in a position of having to second-guess yourself or, worse yet, being hesitant to take risks for fear of something coming back to haunt you. It can also be immobilizing.

Let me give you an example. A former client called to discuss a promotional opportunity being offered to her. She would be moving from an individual contributor to manager of her department. Since she had been with her firm for a relatively short period of time, it was quite a compliment to be offered this position. Within hours of being offered the job, however, she had made up so many negative stories about what could go wrong that she became hesitant to accept the assignment for fear of failing at it.

It wasn't that she was wrong in her diagnosis about the potential pitfalls; it was that she couldn't overcome this negative thinking long enough to find the many ways there were to obviate them. Had she not been capable of handling the challenges inherent to the position, she never would have been offered it in the first place. She did wind up accepting the position, and (to no one's surprise except perhaps her own) she's doing beautifully.

COACHING TIPS

• To begin, replace negative stories with more neutral ones. Consider alternative scenarios that could explain what has happened that have nothing to do with *your* doing something wrong.

• Focus on solutions to problems, not the problems themselves. Wallowing in a sea of negativity will cause you to miss the obvious solutions.

ACTION ITEM

Mistake 59

Striving for Perfection

*H*aving been made to believe we're totally flawed, imperfect beings, women overcompensate by striving for perfection. Intellectually we know it's impossible, but emotionally we go there every time we feel insecure or less than competent. What a waste of time and energy! We would be much better off using the time we spend perfecting already good work products or relationships on new and creative endeavors. Elsewhere in this book I talk about how we allow *others* to waste our time. Well, this is one way in which we waste our *own* time.

Julia is the perfect example. Before she came for coaching, she would drive herself crazy checking and rechecking—then checking one more time—everything that left her office. Her compulsion around perfection caused her marriage to fail, created physical problems for her, and made the people who worked with her absolutely nuts. No one wanted to have her on their team because she was known for being so nitpicky. Her career was severely limited by her inability to let go of the small stuff. She unintentionally conveyed the message to others that nothing was good enough for her. She made them feel as if *they* weren't good enough. Who wants to work with or for someone like that?

This is an area where guys really get it. They know when good enough is good enough and move on to the next thing. Where do you think they find the time to network, go to lunch with colleagues, and attend professional association meetings? They do it by realizing it's more efficient to go back and correct a mistake (if there is one) than to keep reviewing a project to possibly catch one.

COACHING TIPS

- Consciously reduce the amount of time you work on any given day or spend on any one piece of work. If you know you have only one hour to proof a report, then you'll do it in an hour. If you leave the schedule open-ended, perfection-seeking behavior will result in your putting in more hours at work than necessary.

- Ask for feedback. Before putting in extra time on what might already be a completed product, ask a colleague what he or she thinks. It may be that it's perfectly fine as is.

- If your behavior borders on obsessive or compulsive, consider seeking professional help for the purpose of assessing whether medication could be helpful in soothing the anxiety often associated with being perfectionistic.

- Strive for 80 percent perfection. The difference between 80 percent and 100 percent won't be noticed by most people but will buy you more time to shift to other important tasks.

- Read *The Gifts of Imperfection: Let Go of Who You Think You're Supposed to Be and Embrace Who You Are* or *I Thought It Was Just Me (But It Isn't): Making the Journey from "What Will People Think?" to "I Am Enough,"* both by Brené Brown. You may have seen Brown on the TED talk that encourages us to embrace our vulnerability as a means of living life more fully. Both books carry this theme in an inspirational way.

- Ask yourself often, *Is this a valuable use of my time?* If the answer is yes, ask yourself, *Why?* If your answer is tied to your self-image and what people will think of you, you may be guilty of striving for perfection.

- Relinquish the need to be seen as perfect and settle for being viewed as human. After all, you are a human *being*, not a human *doing*.

ACTION ITEM

Mistake 60

Nixing the Idea of an Entrepreneurial Venture

*W*hen I told my mother I was going to quit my job to start my own business, she replied, "It makes my stomach turn to think of you as unemployed." Now mind you, I have two brothers, both of whom have their own businesses—but they're not thought of as unemployed. Yet her comment illuminates why many women, dissatisfied with the opportunities presented in corporate America, are reluctant to venture out on their own. If we're not thought of as capable enough to run our own businesses, or not encouraged to do so, we're less likely to believe we can do so successfully.

In my case, I had more courage than brains. I had no idea how difficult it would be, but my mantra was "Failure is not an option." Almost thirty years later, I'm still self-employed and proud of it.

Going back for a moment to one of the women leaders I most admire, Mary Kay Ash, you can see the entrepreneurial spirit at work. When she started her business, the naysayers said she could not possibly start a cosmetics company. No one dreamed she would successfully compete with more established competitors like Revlon, Estée Lauder, and CoverGirl. She was a single mom who knew little about cosmetics and even less about running a business. But she had a vision: *to create work for women that would allow them to become financially independent and still allow them to lead lives where God could come first, family could come second, and work could come third.*

The vision paid off. She started the company in 1963 with her life savings of $5,000. By 2003, Mary Kay Cosmetics was one of the largest direct sellers of skin-care and color cosmetics in the world, employed more than one million independent beauty consultants worldwide, and realized annual revenues of nearly $1.8 billion. Each woman working for the company sees herself as an entrepreneur walking in the footsteps of Mary Kay. Interviewing several of them for my book *See Jane Lead: 99 Ways for Women to Take Charge at Work* was an inspirational experience. Not only did they believe their lives were changed by becoming independent beauty consultants, but they continue to live and espouse the values of the company founder.

The fact is, women have been starting businesses at a higher rate than men for more than two decades. According to the National Federation of Independent Business, women will create over half of the 9.72 million jobs expected in small businesses by 2018. If you're among the women disillusioned by corporate politics, the inability to live your life on your terms, and the lack of respect paid to women who opt for motherhood and a career, then you might consider how you can start a business that would allow you to be the boss in your very own private corner office.

COACHING TIPS

• For inspiration, read a few biographies of women who started their own enterprises. Consider starting with *On Her Own Ground: The Life and Times of Madam C. J. Walker,* by A'Lelia Bundles. Madam C. J. Walker was the "first black female millionaire" after developing and marketing African American hair-care products. She also opened up some great career opportunities for African American women.

• Read *Think Like an Entrepreneur: Transforming Your Career and Taking Charge of Your Life,* by Deborah A Bailey. The tips she provides will help you to compete successfully *anywhere.*

• Conduct some informational interviews with local entrepreneurs. Ask them how they got started, what their biggest challenges were, and what recommendations they would give to you about starting a business. Most women are more than happy to help other women get started.

• Find and join (or start) a Ladies Who Launch chapter. This group of entrepreneurial women are all about encouraging and supporting female-owned businesses.

ACTION ITEM

Chapter 5

How You Brand and Market Yourself

When you think about well-known name brands, which ones come to mind? If you're like most people, names like Kleenex, Coke, and Google immediately pop up. Not only are the names familiar, but they've also become synonymous with the product. When we go to a restaurant and ask for a Coke, we may or may not be served a drink made by Coca-Cola. We don't just do a search on the Internet, we Google it, regardless of the actual search engine being used. "Hand me a Kleenex" doesn't necessarily mean Kleenex brand. Brand names get a good reputation as a result of two things: consistent quality and marketing. One without the other doesn't equate to staying power or success in the marketplace.

Dr. Bruce Heller, president of the Heller Group in Encino, California, coaches professionals about the importance of thinking of themselves as brands to be marketed. "You have to look at the workplace as a marketplace," Heller says. "In this market, your product is you." You create a brand for yourself by first identifying what distinguishes you from other people in the workplace and then marketing those distinctions as a brand.

One of Dr. Heller's favorite phrases—"outta sight, outta mind, outta business"—is particularly important for women to remember. As young girls we often learn that we are to be seen but not heard. Carrying that forward to adulthood translates into doing our work in a quiet and unassuming way. I often hear women say they don't care if they're given credit; they're just happy to make a contribution to the bottom line. The result is that we are overlooked for promotions and assignments we've actually earned and deserve. The coaching tips in the next section are designed to help you define your brand, acknowledge the value of your brand, and develop a plan for marketing your brand.

Mistake 61

Failing to Define Your Brand

*N*ot too long ago I interviewed a woman with a doctorate in organization development for a vacancy on our coaching team. Her résumé was impressive. She seemed to have the kind of experience and education I sought, but I wasn't sure of her specialty area. Because we're known as a firm with subject-matter experts who can provide executives with unique expertise in their areas for development, one of the first questions I posed to this woman was "Tell me about what you're best known for." For the next thirty-five minutes she told me all about what she had done, what her interests were, and the many ways in which she could add value. The problem was, she didn't answer my question. Despite another twenty minutes of probing and asking the question in several different ways, I never learned what made her unique among all organizational psychologists.

Peter Montoya, whom I consider to be the guru of personal branding, wrote, "A personal brand is a promise of performance that creates expectations in its audience. Done well, it clearly communicates the values, personality, and abilities of the person behind it." That's what was missing from my interview with the woman who wanted to be on our coaching team—but wasn't selected because of her inability to clearly define her brand for me.

In another scenario, I was doing a radio show on women and money when a call came in from a woman asking how she could better market her day-care business. I asked her to "tell me what makes your day-care business different from all the others in your community." There was dead silence before she replied, "I guess I can't." As I told her, until you can clearly articulate what differentiates your brand from the others, you can't successfully market it.

COACHING TIPS

• Make a list of the three to five things that bring you the most satisfaction at work. We tend to be good at what we like, so focusing first on these will help to point you in the right direction. You might come up with responses such as *help others, listen, problem-solve, negotiate, write technical reports, manage projects, collect data, identify obstacles, implement solutions*, and more.

• Next, translate these behaviors into three key strengths you bring to your workplace. For example, "My ability to listen effectively enables me to gather data from reluctant sources. Tied in with that is my skill at writing, which allows me to report that data in an objective way. Third, once the data is collected and reported, I've exhibited the ability to identify and implement solutions to problems." Practice saying these words out loud so that when the time is right you can recite them fluently and confidently.

• Consider how these behaviors distinguish you from others. For example, the ability to gather and report data may be unique in a department or company known mainly for producing a product. Or having skill in building relationships may be unique and valuable in an organization where intellectual capital is the product.

• Finish this sentence: "There goes a woman who _____ _____." Now engage in the behaviors required to make that statement a reality.

ACTION ITEM ☐

Mistake 62

An Elevator Speech That Doesn't Go to the Top

$\mathcal{D}$ebra worked for a large entertainment company as an executive in charge of minority recruitment. The company took a table at a fund-raising event, and when she arrived no seats were left at the table. Not one to be shy, she looked around and spotted a table where there were empty seats. After asking if she could join their table, she sat down and was naturally asked where she worked and what she did. Debra said something like this:

> I'm the director of Minority Recruitment at one of the country's largest entertainment companies. I'm so fortu-nate to be able to enhance the company's bottom line by developing programs that attract and retain minority talent. Just this past year alone we increased the number of minority hires by 22 percent over the previous year and reduced minority attrition by 8 percent. It's been so rewarding to get people at all levels involved in the effort and see such great results!

For the remainder of the evening she chatted with the folks at the table and gave her business card to several people who asked for it. The next morning there was a message on her voicemail from some-one at the table who said he was so impressed with her enthusiasm and passion for what she did that he wanted to talk to her about a job opening he had coming up. After an interview he made her an offer she couldn't refuse, and the rest is history.

Contrast this to an exercise I do in leadership classes for women where I ask participants to introduce themselves. Inevitably, the first woman to go gives her name, what she does, and how long she's worked for her company. It's rare for anyone to give his or her job title and even rarer for them to expand on the impact they make on the company and its bottom line.

When you're asked to introduce yourself, what do you say? Are you like Debra, or more like the hundreds of nice girls I've encountered who provide lukewarm self-introductions? Does what you say make a memorable impression or get lost in the dozens of introductions we each hear during the course of a regular week?

Marketing your brand starts with your elevator speech. It must be factual, but should also emphasize your unique skills and how you make a difference. Many women tell me that to do so makes it seem as if they're bragging. Did Debra sound as if she was bragging or simply relating with gusto how much she loved what she did? It's not bragging if you speak the truth, use your title, and comment on a few things of which you're proud.

COACHING TIPS

- Prepare an introduction that takes about the same time as an elevator ride and that lets others know who you are, what you love doing, and how you impact your company's bottom line. This works equally well if you're an administrative assistant or vice president because it's all about branding yourself as someone others would want to "buy." If you don't believe you make a difference, why should anyone else?

- Practice your introduction until it rolls off your tongue without hesitation. This will take a little while, particularly if you're not used to extolling your own virtues. Ask friends if they'll give you feedback as to what they would think about you if they didn't know you and heard you say it. Go back and make adjustments as needed and as your situation changes.

- Pitch it with passion. It's not only what you say that makes a difference, but how you say it. Endow your introduction with energy and enthusiasm.

ACTION ITEM

Mistake 63

Minimizing Your Work or Position

*T*his goes beyond a lukewarm elevator speech. Way beyond. I can't tell you how many times I've heard women respond to the question "What do you do?" with a self-deprecating answer. "Oh, I just manage a legal office." "I'm only an administrative assistant." "I kind of run the information technology group." These comments don't sound like brands I would be interested in learning more about. Instead, they reveal a feeling of embarrassment or lack of pride in what the person does. Every job in every organization is critical to its operation. You may not be the president of Nestlé, but you wouldn't have your job if it wasn't necessary to run the business. Identifying why your business needs you is crucial to accurately marketing your brand.

Perhaps what bothers me most about this phenomenon is that, in many cases, women have diminished their brands because they are buying into what others have said about them or their roles. If at a party you overhear your spouse say that you don't have a career, when in fact you do temp work to augment the household income; or if your father loudly and proudly talks to anyone who will listen about your brother the lawyer, it might be hard to talk about a more modest career without feeling like a second-class citizen.

There's a joke that underscores this point. The first woman is elected president of the United States, and she asks her mother what she's going to wear to the inauguration. The mother indicates she's not going to go because she has nothing to wear. After much cajoling, the woman gets her mother to attend the event. Just before she's about to be sworn in, she hears the chief justice of the United States lean over and whisper to her mother, "You must be very proud of your daughter." To this the mother replies, "Yes, but her brother is a *doctor*."

As Scottish essayist Thomas Carlyle said, "All work, even cotton spinning, is noble; work alone is noble." Regardless of what you do, be proud of it and describe it in a way that allows others to see that pride and, in turn, builds your personal brand.

COACHING TIPS

- Don't allow others to place a value on the work you do. Only *you* can do that.
- Remove minimizing words from the description of your work.
- Whether you sweep floors or run a sweepstakes for a living, do it and describe it with pride.

ACTION ITEM

Mistake 64

Undervaluing Your Consultative Skills

If you've ever helped a coworker to solve a sticky problem, you're a consultant. If you've influenced your boss to take a different tact than one that was originally intended, you're a consultant. And if you've offered advice that prevented a major catastrophe from happening to a friend who was about to fall off a career cliff, then you're also a consultant. Women frequently overlook the ways in which building relationships contributes to being a "trusted advisor"—an invaluable skill, but one we often chalk up to being just a good listener. I borrow this phrase from a wonderful book with the same title, *The Trusted Advisor*, by David Maister. In the book, Maister illuminates the ways in which trust and confidence are built over time through listening and understanding. Although the book's primary audience is consultants, it's equally helpful to anyone who wants their brand to include the perception of strong consultative skills.

Because listening and helping others is part of the genetic makeup for so many of us, we don't place enough credence in the fact that this is a valuable and marketable commodity that can be traded on. Whereas nice girls routinely engage in consultative behaviors but don't emphasize them, smart women make them a hallmark of their brands.

COACHING TIPS

• Gain a deeper understanding of the consultative process inherent to the roles most of us play in our organizations by reading David Maister's *The Trusted Advisor*.

• Consider yourself an "internal consultant." Regardless of your position, your experience and expertise, combined with strong relationships, provide you with an entrée to this function. When branding and marketing yourself, don't forget to use the phrase to describe what you do.

• Don't feel as if you've failed as a consultant if all your suggestions aren't accepted or implemented. By nature consultants try to influence, but leave the final decision up to their "clients." Always leave the door open for continuing discussion.

ACTION ITEM

Mistake 65

Using Only Your Nickname or First Name

*W*hen was the last time you heard a male executive called by the diminutive of his name? Billy Gates. Donny Trump. Andy Cuomo. I don't think so. The diminutive of anything diminishes its importance. All nicknames and diminutives are used as a fond way of referring to children. As adults, it serves the same purpose—but most men drop it by the time they're teenagers. Michelle Obama may have been able to call the president Barry, but you wouldn't catch many others getting away with it.

I've also been amazed to watch as a woman introduces herself using her formal name, only to have the person immediately shorten it. A client of mine named Teresa tells me that within moments of introducing herself, she's called Terri. "I never heard anyone change Jim to Jimmy," she says.

Similarly, whenever I hear a woman answer the phone with only her first name, or leave a voice-mail message that says, "This is Sarah. Please leave your message....," it makes me wonder why she dropped her last name. One woman in a workshop told me she does this because using a hyphenated last name makes it seem too long and dropping it entirely is one way to shorten it. Why does she need to shorten it? Are we talking about the difference between two seconds and three seconds? It's your name!

Shortening a name is common among administrative staff—and entirely unnecessary. You will rarely hear a man answer the phone using only his first name. It's a small but significant difference. Using only your first name relegates you, once again, to a childlike status. Ask a child his or her name and most often you get only the first name. The combination of your first and last names moves you to adulthood.

COACHING TIPS

• Even if you've gone by Kathy, Debbie, Maggie, or Sandy your entire life, begin introducing yourself using your formal name. Over time, people will take your cue. Change your business cards, desk nameplate, or formal letterhead to read Kathleen, Debra, Margaret, or Sandra. You'll be much more likely to be taken seriously if you don't use your childhood nickname for professional purposes.

• Always use your first and last names on your voice-mail message, in your e-mail address, when introducing yourself, and when answering the phone.

• If people change your name to the diminutive, correct them by simply repeating the name you prefer them to use.

ACTION ITEM

Mistake 66

Waiting to Be Noticed

*D*uring a recent downsizing in her corporation, Jacqueline desperately wanted to stay on in either her current position or another one in the company. She knew that behind closed doors, decisions were being made about who would stay and who would go. While she waited nervously to be told her fate, I suggested she had nothing to lose by going to her boss and human resources representative to make a case for staying. It was as if I'd suggested she race nude across the executive floor. Not only couldn't she fathom coming up with something to say that could possibly make a difference, she couldn't picture herself going in and saying it.

Corporate downsizings and the trend toward flat organizations have created the need to be noticed in a positive way—before workforce reductions take place. When it comes to maintaining your job during layoffs, it can be as simple as making a case for why your unique brand will be valuable in the newly formed organization.

As for flatter organizations, the dearth of opportunities to move up makes assignments and projects that can offer you visibility or specialized training all the more valuable. Recipients of these assignments are often those who subtly (and at times not so subtly) call attention to the ways in which their strengths play to the requirements of the work. Waiting to be noticed will not get you where you want to be. You've got to know your brand and sell it when the opportunity arises. Women, especially those who are not particularly good at "selling" themselves, are often overlooked—not because of lack of capability, but because of modesty or the mistaken belief that their accomplishments will eventually be noticed.

COACHING TIPS

• If there's a vacancy or assignment you want, ask to be considered for it.

• When you're ready to make a career move, talk about it out loud. Let people know you're ready for the next challenge. The more people you talk to about it, the more likely you are to hear about opportunities when they arise.

• Continually showcase your achievements in subtle ways. One suggestion is to prepare a weekly or biweekly status sheet listing your accomplishments or those of your department. Another is to share your achievements in the form of "best practices." For example, at a staff meeting you could share with your colleagues how you solved a particular problem or overcame an obstacle that threatened a deadline.

• Develop a marketing plan. Envision your future and write down the specific steps you'll take to get there.

• Spend time engaged in learning, soliciting feedback or getting coaching, and doing something different than what you're already good at. These three things prepare you for unexpected challenges and opportunities.

• Ask someone in a position senior to yours to be an advocate for you by proposing your name.

ACTION ITEM ☐

Mistake 67

Refusing High-Profile Assignments

 $\mathscr{T}$ his entire book is the by-product of something a client told me when we were about to start a coaching session. As the director of operations at an East Coast branch of a manufacturing firm head-quartered in Los Angeles, Sandra was asked to sit on the executive committee of her company. She had long complained that she wasn't recognized for her achievements in turning around what had been a money-losing operation. The request to sit on the EC made a strong statement about not only her value to her own division, but also the contributions she could make throughout the firm. And what did Sandra do? She turned it down because in the past she had attended several of their meetings and saw them as "a waste of time."

The first words out of my mouth were "Honey, you gotta quit bein' a girl!" I couldn't help myself. Without considering the bigger pic-ture, she acted in a manner consistent with the values she'd learned in childhood—to work hard and not waste the company's time or money. And at that very moment all the mistakes I had seen women make throughout my career because of how they were socialized came flooding into my head. For years I had talked to men and women about the ways in which parental messages impact their careers, but I had neglected the fact that boys and girls get different messages. On the way back to Los Angeles from my meeting with Sandra, I outlined all of a book I called "Quit Bein' a Girl," which was later changed to *Nice Girls Don't Get the Corner Office*.

The opportunity to showcase your capabilities through a high-profile assignment isn't limited to something as grand as being invited to sit on your company's executive committee. Being asked to facilitate an important meeting, to make a critical client presentation, or to make a presentation to your senior management are all examples of high-profile assignments you can't afford to pass up.

I understand that we're all oversubscribed, that meetings can go on for what seems like an eternity, and that making client presentations can be a lot of work and a little risky. So what? Use these opportunities to profile your unique capabilities and build relationships with others who are viewed as movers and shakers. Remember, 90 percent of success comes from just showing up!

COACHING TIPS

- When you're asked to sit at the table, graciously accept the invitation. If you don't have the time, make the time. It's an investment in your future.
- When offered a position or assignment that's new to you, take it. If others have enough confidence in you that you can do the job, you should, too.
- Request potentially risky but high-profile projects. No guts, no glory.
- Volunteer to give presentations to senior management. The benefits typically outweigh the risks, and you can't get comfortable doing it unless you do it. Exposure to senior management is critical for recognition.
- Keep in mind that in the workplace, senior executives are your customers. Therefore, you need to be in situations where you can identify their needs and serve them.

ACTION ITEM

Mistake 68

Not Sitting at the Table

In the last mistake, I talked about *figuratively* not sitting at the table. Now I want to focus on *literally* not sitting at the table. My dear friend Diane, who manages a branch office for a large financial institution, was over for dinner one night, and I asked how her annual off-site with senior management went. My ears perked up when she mentioned that her division vice president invited her to sit at his table for dinner one night, but she left the seat open so that someone who has less regular exposure to him could have it. Before I could accuse her of being a nice girl, she added that a peer of hers (a man who has the same opportunities to interact with the VP throughout the year as she does) took the seat instead. Even Diane's husband's mouth dropped open hearing this.

As nice a thought as it is, leaving a seat open next to the most senior person in the room is a huge branding mistake. Not only does it deprive you of having the ear of the boss, it deprives you of being seen sitting next to the person in power. Whether it's a regular meeting or a special event, finding the chance to speak one-on-one with executives in your company is something you should be seeking out, not giving up.

Another way in which this happens that always surprises me is when a woman enters a conference room or other meeting room for what she knows will be a packed meeting. She looks around the room and sees chairs surrounding the table and others on the periphery of the room. Invariably, the nice girl will take a seat on the periphery to leave the seats at the table for "more important" people.

This is not Thanksgiving, and you are no longer six years old and relegated to the children's table. If you want your voice heard and to be seen as someone who belongs playing with the "big boys," then you have to *literally* sit at the table.

COACHING TIPS

- When you're invited to sit at the table, sit at the table!
- If there aren't enough chairs at the table to accommodate everyone, pull one up and squeeze it in.
- When given a choice of seats, sit next to the most powerful person in the room. Their power will cascade over to you.

ACTION ITEM

Mistake 69

Being Modest

*B*oth boys and girls are taught in childhood to be modest—but women take the lesson way too far. There's a time and a place for modesty. When you've moved a mountain, broken the sound barrier, or produced a miracle, it's neither the time nor the place. When people fail to notice your major accomplishments, it's your job to illuminate them. Making things look easy or seamless when in fact they required herculean efforts isn't a great marketing technique.

Helena provides a great example of being much too modest. As director of executive development, she and her team are responsible for performing management assessments, designing individualized development programs for each top member of management, and providing executive coaching. When her company merged with another firm, the size of her job nearly doubled, yet the size of her team remained the same. Nonetheless, she found creative ways to get the job done with the people available to her.

During her annual performance review, Helena's boss commended her for the extra effort she put in and gave her a generous bonus. Pleased that he'd recognized her good work, she modestly responded, "It really wasn't anything." She had gone into the meeting wanting to bring up the need for additional staff, but when he complimented her and gave her the bonus, she was completely thrown off kilter and failed to parlay his recognition into a marketing opportunity. As a result of her modesty, she had to come up with another strategy for requesting more head count, since getting the job done "really wasn't anything."

Another example of modesty is the degree to which we display degrees, framed letters of commendation, or photos of us taken with dignitaries. I was in one client's office when she had to step out to take a call. While she was gone, I looked around the office at the many items of personal memorabilia and photos she had on her credenza. Then I spotted a picture of her with Hillary Clinton at a conference on women's affairs—hidden behind all of the other items! When she came back in I pointed to the picture and asked why she didn't have that particular picture front and center given that it was so impressive. Her reply? You guessed it. She didn't want to make it seem as if she was too full of herself.

I'm pleased to report that this client, fifteen years later, is now vice president of a division of her company, and in every office I've subsequently visited the picture is prominently displayed. Is this why she's been so successful? Of course not. But moving from hiding her accomplishments to letting others know about them did make a difference in how she marketed her brand.

COACHING TIPS

• Completely, totally, and permanently erase the statement "Oh—it was nothing" from your vocabulary.

• When reporting accomplishments, give them the import they deserve. Helena should have said something like "It took everyone on the team working long hours and weekends, but I'm proud of what we did and glad you appreciate it."

• When given a compliment, look the person in the eye and respond with a simple "Thank you." Avoid downplaying your efforts.

• Forward notes of appreciation or acknowledgment about your work to your manager.

• Prominently display awards, plaques, or other items that speak to your achievements.

• Keep an "atta gal" file—a collection of accomplishments of which you are proud: thank-you notes, outstanding performance reviews, and the like. Review it at those moments when you begin to doubt yourself.

ACTION ITEM

Mistake 70

Inappropriate Use of Social Media

$\mathcal{I}$ was recently called by a prestigious institution as a reference for a woman who once worked for me. She was a phenomenal employee, and I was happy to give her a good reference. After asking me a few questions about this woman, whom I highly recommended, he asked, "Do I have to worry about her doing anything that could be embarrassing to our organization?" The question caught me by surprise. As it turns out, he had googled her and found her Myspace page from years ago when she was barely in her twenties. There he found pictures of her with a nose ring, drinking beer, participating in a wet T-shirt contest.

We've *all* done things we wouldn't want a prospective employer to know about. I'm only thankful we didn't have social networking sites early in my career! Even as it is now, I had to figure out how to keep friends and family members from posting what I consider to be less than professional pictures and comments on my Facebook page. I encourage you to do the same. There should be *nothing* on any social networking site that could possibly tarnish your reputation or cause someone to question your values, behavior, or your brand. Once it's posted, it's hard to put the toothpaste back in the tube.

Here are a few other mistakes to avoid, contributed by branding expert Ryan Rancatore (personalbranding101.com):

1. **Incomplete Profiles.** They mean one of two things:
   o Your background is so empty that you can't even complete a simple profile.
   o You are lazy.

2. **Multiple Names.** Facebook, Twitter, and LinkedIn are all micronetworks that form your overall network. Are you confusing your connections with different messaging, names, and images across all these sites? The most powerful corporate brands know that a consistent image is key to building a memorable, identifiable brand. You should strive for the same consistency.
3. **Not Interlinking Your Profiles.** Why is this important? The more touchpoints that exist to connect with your network, the better. Seeing you come up again and again across social networks creates a memorable brand.
4. **Being a Robot.** Never, ever send a LinkedIn request with the stock message that reads "I'd like to add you to my professional network on LinkedIn." Rancatore says when he receives a message with this request, he reads it as "I'd like to add you to my professional network, but I don't have the courtesy to take ten seconds to include your name or a personal message."
5. **Tunnel Vision.** Do your postings scream, "ME ME ME"? A solid rule of thumb is that 90 percent of what you share should be made up of personal insights and thoughts along with a heavy dose of helpful links, while 10 percent should directly benefit you.

COACHING TIPS

Here are some tips from Poonam Sagar, digital media consultant and coach at PT Infotech Solutions (infotech.co.id) in Indonesia, for how you can use social networking to your advantage:

- Be friendly. It's called social networking, not social narcissism (although some people do confuse the two). Your social media outlets represent your personal brand, and, as I mentioned earlier, people want to affiliate with brands that are likable and emotionally intelligent. If you use your outlets to express negative emotions or critical diatribes about other people or products, your brand will quickly lose its luster.
- Be helpful and generous. There's a currency associated with sharing valuable information. Post links to articles or blogs that you know are of interest to others in your network. Others will come to see you as a resource—something you definitely want associated with your brand.
- Consider creating your own website. New technology has made it inexpensive and even somewhat easy (depending on your level of technical expertise in these matters) to get a website up and running in a matter of hours. The one that was recommended to me due to its ease of use is weebly.com. Check it out, and if you need help, it might be worth it to barter your expertise for that of a techie friend who can provide you with assistance.
- Post compelling and quality content online. Whatever you decide to share about yourself online needs to be engaging and optimized for search engines. If you're writing brilliant blog posts, or sharing the world's wittiest status updates, it doesn't do any good if nobody can find it.
- Choose your connections wisely and manage your privacy settings on social media platforms. Send and accept connections requests only from people you know, want to know, or who add value to your network.

ACTION ITEM

Mistake 71

Ineffective Use of Social Media

$\mathcal{I}$t's one thing to use social media inappropriately (in ways that can be damaging to your brand); it's another to use it ineffectively (in ways that don't benefit your brand). I am not exactly what you'd call an early adopter—someone who jumps on the technology band wagon early—but even I know the power of social networking. It's why I have Facebook and LinkedIn pages. (I do, however, draw the line at tweeting.) A few colleagues and I even had a blog for a few years—until the blogosphere took over the Internet and it was clear people couldn't possibly absorb all the information available to them. The outlets I use serve the purpose of disseminating career information that complement my writing, speaking, and coaching. In short, keeping the Dr. Lois Frankel brand in the public eye as a resource for women's career issues.

I've already talked about the risks of not getting into the social media game. Now, ask yourself if you are using social media as effectively as possible to help you build or maintain your brand. As a woman, we already know you're doing more social networking than your male colleagues, but we also know that the nice girl in you is most likely not using it to your advantage. As a recovering nice girl, I myself am loath to ask for recommendations and introductions that could be valuable to me. What was that your mother always told you? *Do as I say, not as I do!*

Digital media consultant and coach Poonam Sagar gives us more insight into what you should be thinking about when it comes to your online brand, as well as tips to put into practice:

Who are you? What expertise do you have? What do you want to be known for accomplishing? How do you want to be known and recognized by colleagues, other professionals, and potential employers? The information you put in your social media profiles and what you post develops your online brand. Google yourself and reflect on the "person" that emerged from the search—are the results congruent with who you want to be online?

The three basics of effective online social networking are:

- **Familiarity:** What are you getting into? Don't sign up for a social networking platform or web application without understanding what you will use it for.
- **Consistency:** It's important to carry the same voice, image, and persona across multiple social networking platforms. Complete your profiles on the social platforms you wish to use with a crisp résumé and a professional photograph. Develop your personal tagline.
- **Participation:** Social networking is a gift economy. The more you participate productively with others, the higher your own profile will be.

COACHING TIPS

• Research online the social networking platforms to understand how they use your data, and the conventions that govern the way the community operates, before you create your accounts.

• Create a schedule that works for you for social media conversations. For example, fifteen minutes every alternate day. Remember that it doesn't have to take a lot of time.

• Control your personal information online with privacy settings. Post only information and pictures that you are happy for everyone to see. Remove tags from undesirable pictures that might have been posted online by friends. Connect only with people you want to communicate with online.

• Acknowledge and appreciate your connections. Share their posts, endorse or recommend them on LinkedIn and Twitter, and, finally, remember to thank them.

ACTION ITEM

Mistake 72

Staying in Your Safety Zone

I once asked a man why he'd applied for a particular position when he knew he did not meet the stated requirements. His reply was simple: "I'm smart. I'll learn them." Women tend to remain in positions too long for fear of getting in over their heads. Unless a woman is 100 percent confident that she meets all the expectations for the job, she won't consider throwing her hat in the ring. Men are more likely than women to seek stretch assignments—ones they've never done before but want to prove they can.

In the modern job market, we look at people who stay in a job too long in the same way we used to judge job-hoppers—as if there's something wrong with them. Staying in a job too long gives the impression of being complacent and, perhaps, not staying up on the latest technical developments in the field. Women even refuse assignments for which they are handpicked if they feel they're not qualified for the job. Big mistake. There's no surer way to be crossed off the list for future opportunities than by refusing an offer—and there's no greater burden than a good opportunity.

Ironically, even people who stay in their comfort zones aren't attracted or impressed by other people who do the same. Most folks consider those who are enthusiastic, take risks, and exhibit a can-do attitude as charismatic or people they would like to emulate.

COACHING TIPS

- Unless the responsibilities within a particular job change significantly, look for a new assignment about every three years—five years maximum.
- Don't let your fear of failure cause you to overlook jobs you could do with minimal training.
- Stay up on developments in your field by taking classes or reading books. If you haven't learned anything new lately, you're not growing.
- Volunteer for assignments that stretch your skill set or enable you to learn entirely new ones that will flesh out your portfolio. If you're willing to take the calculated risk of possibly failing, it's not selfish to learn on the job.
- Start looking for your next job the day you start a new one. You may not actually make a move for several years, but being open to the possibilities creates a proactive, preemptive focus in the job market.

ACTION ITEM

Mistake 73

Giving Away Your Ideas

*T*his story is all too common. Woman has idea. Woman expresses idea. Idea gets ignored. Man expresses same idea. Man gets promoted. Who's to blame? Woman. She let her idea be stolen instead of calling attention to the source. Why? Because she's unsure of herself to begin with and doesn't want to appear selfish, territorial, confrontational, or not a team player. Every time you give away an idea, you give away a little of your self-respect. Do this enough times, and your self-confidence begins to dwindle immeasurably.

Don't make the mistake of assuming your idea is overlooked because you're a woman. I've observed meetings at which women's ideas were ignored for the simplest of reasons: Perhaps they didn't speak loudly enough to be heard, or they whispered their concept to the man sitting next to them and he offered it as his own, or the timing was wrong. These are factors you can address fairly easily and unobtrusively.

It's not only about not giving your ideas away, it's also about finding ways to sell them. Your ideas have value in the marketplace called work. Each time you make a suggestion that's actually implemented, you've made a sale. Make enough of these sales, and you've collected more of those invisible chips that can later be subtly bartered for favors, plum assignments, or perks.

COACHING TIPS

- Get in the habit of asking a question *after* expressing an idea or making a proposal. Try something like "My recommendation is that we prioritize our solutions and select the top two for immediate implementation. Are there any objections to getting to work on this immediately?" This increases the likelihood of acknowledgment and discussion.

- When someone proposes the same thing you previously suggested (albeit in a slightly different way), bring the attention back to where the idea originated by saying, "Thank you for building on my original suggestion, Joe. Let me add a few things that I'm certain we'll agree on."

- Speak loudly enough to be heard.

- Take the risk of putting your ideas out directly and confidently.

- Whenever possible or appropriate, put your ideas in writing. It gives them a kind of credibility that just the spoken word lacks, and reminds people where the ideas came from. The written word is still one of the most powerful forms of communication, and some people respond much more favorably if they can "see" what you're saying.

- Whatever you do, don't lean over and whisper your idea to the person sitting next to you!

ACTION ITEM

Mistake 74

Working in Stereotypical Roles or Departments

$\mathscr{F}$or nearly three decades I've watched women in stereotypical roles—administrative assistants, personnel department staffers, clerks—go to school at night and earn college degrees in the hope of moving up the corporate ladder. I've also seen women with degrees enter the workforce in stereotypically female roles as a strategy to get a foot in the door in the hope of being noticed and promoted. Unfortunately, I haven't seen many who were successful in either scenario. Spending time in a "female ghetto" makes you more likely to be branded as unworthy of a senior assignment. Do I think this is right? Of course not.

Look around your company. Are there departments in your organization like this? Human resources and personnel often fall into this category. The fact that there are more women nurses than male and more women grammar school teachers than male has traditionally caused pay in these areas to be less than the work warrants.

Are you in one of these situations? If so, your status will not be viewed on a par with people working in departments where men and women are represented in essentially equal numbers. A good example of this is found in the banking industry. When tellers were predominantly men, the position was considered somewhat prestigious. As more and more women filled these roles, the pay scale for tellers declined and the position lost its glitter. Remaining too long in such a role or department will eventually limit your marketability.

COACHING TIPS

• Seek assignments in departments or fields where there are comparable numbers of men and women.

• When asked to take a stereotypical role, consider whether the long-term benefits outweigh the short-term ones.

• Never volunteer to make coffee or copies for a meeting. If asked, suggest the responsibility be rotated or assigned based on seniority.

• If moving out of a stereotypical role requires additional training or education, get it. It's worth the investment in your future.

• If you acquire the training needed to move out of a stereotypical role and it fails to yield results, consider the possibility that you've been "typed" and might need to seek a new organization.

ACTION ITEM

Mistake 75

Not Soliciting Enough Feedback (or Ignoring It)

*T*here's a word on the street about all of us. It's what people say about us behind our backs or when we leave a room. This is the stuff that succession planning meetings are made of. A bunch of executives sit around a room and give their impressions of you. Creating your personal brand allows you to influence those impressions. You cannot build your brand without getting feedback. Neither can you effectively market yourself without feedback. Feedback is a little like medicine. You resist taking it, but you know it will make you better.

Then there are the people who respond to feedback by either ignoring it (and hoping it will go away) or brushing it off with "That's just one person's opinion." *Perception is reality*. People do not know you by your intentions; they know you by your behavior. You can explain or justify your behavior, but that doesn't solve the problem of having a brand that doesn't meet customers' expectations. Sooner or later, people stop buying it. As we tell our clients: "When three people say you're drunk—lie down."

COACHING TIPS

- Ask your human resources department to conduct a 360-degree feedback assessment. This will allow you to see yourself as others see you and provide the opportunity to work on areas for improvement. If that's not possible, get in the habit of routinely asking people what you could do more of, less of, or to continue to be even more effective in your job.

- Make it easy for your boss to give you feedback by regularly asking for it. Here again, don't ask, "How am I doing?" but rather what you can do more of, less of, or continue to do.

- When given feedback, respond with a nondefensive inquiry: "Can you tell me more about how and when I do that?" Avoid responding with explanations for how and why you do something.

- When the feedback stings, ask for time to think about it. If you need clarification, get back to the person and ask for it when you can do so unemotionally.

- Most people are reluctant to give honest feedback, so when you get it, consider it a gift.

- If you ask for feedback, it implies that you're going to do something with it. Let people know what you're doing to address your development areas. It calls their attention to any changes you actually make.

ACTION ITEM

Mistake 76

Being Invisible

$\mathcal{D}$id you know that the capture of Osama bin Laden was made possible by a woman? Much has been made of the team of Navy SEALs who bravely carried out the mission, but it would not have happened at all had it not been for a dedicated CIA analyst. According to one of the SEALs, this woman "teed it up" for success. She obviously cannot reveal her name for security purposes, but what's most interesting to me is how many people don't even know she exists! Contrast that with the SEAL who went outside the bounds of propriety and actually wrote a book about the capture.

I facilitate a leadership program (for men and women) in which participants from the same company work in small groups to solve a real-world problem faced by their firm. Using a specified problem-solving model, they are asked to come up with a solution that includes problem identification, causes, and recommendations for overcoming it, as well as the preparation of a presentation for senior management. On the last day of the program, senior executives from the company are invited to listen to the presentations and comment on the viability of what is suggested. Many times the end product is so good that the proposed solutions are incorporated into the company's business plan.

Inevitably, the women in the program are the worker bees in this exercise. They keep the guys focused; they prepare the overheads or PowerPoint slides for the presentation; they ensure that everyone's opinion is heard and taken into consideration. When it comes to who will lead the presentation, it's entirely another story. In nearly twenty years of doing this particular exercise, I can't recall one time when a woman took the lead. Instead, they suggested that the most verbal man lead the presentation team.

Women are invisible enough without having to take extra steps to be doubly certain they aren't seen or noticed! These situations present the perfect opportunities to market your brand. Don't hand it over to a competitor—even if it is friendly competition.

COACHING TIPS

- Volunteer to chair regular department meetings.
- Submit a proposal to make a presentation in your area of expertise at a professional association meeting.
- Write articles for local newspapers, professional journals, or your company newsletter.
- When volunteers are asked to speak to senior management, seize the opportunity.
- In meetings, make certain you don't remain invisible. Voicing your ideas is a great way to market your brand. Make your motto "Early and often" when it comes to making your presence known.

ACTION ITEM

Mistake 77

Overlooking Opportunities to Re-Brand Yourself

*W*hat happens when you go back to school, get a degree or certificate, and everyone still sees and treats you as an administrative assistant? Or when you've gotten feedback that you're not coming across as you thought you were and you do a course correction, only to find no one notices? How about when you've been laid off from a job in a field that is going the way of the dinosaurs? Pamela Mitchell, founder of the Reinvention Institute in Miami, Florida, and author of *The 10 Laws of Career Reinvention*, would tell you it's time to reinvent yourself!

Here's a quick quiz from Pamela to help you determine if reinvention should be in your future:

1. On Sunday nights I feel:

    a) Excited—it's the final moment of the weekend, and I'm excited to get back to work tomorrow.

    b) Stressed—it's the final moment of the weekend, doggone it!

    c) Anxious—it's the final moment of the weekend, and I'm not looking forward to work tomorrow.

    d) Relaxed—it's the final moment of the weekend, and I enjoy it!

2. At work I feel:

    a) Energized—I have lots of great projects and/or a great team, and I enjoy going to work.

    b) Bored—I am doing the same thing I've been doing for a while.

c) *Jaded—I don't enjoy the people I work with, and I don't think things will change.*

d) *Challenged—I'm always learning something new, and I have fun at work.*

3. **My relationship with my boss is:**

   a) *Supportive—she or he goes to the mat to get the resources I need to do my job.*

   b) *Distant—I rarely get face time with her or him, and she or he doesn't come to me often for things.*

   c) *Antagonistic—I don't work well with her or him; there's a lot of conflict in our communication.*

   d) *Nurturing—she or he spends a lot of time helping me develop my skills and talents.*

4. **The senior team of my company views me as:**

   a) *Essential—I contribute a lot to the company's goals, and they know about it.*

   b) *Nonexistent—I'm not on their radar screen at all.*

   c) *A pain—there have been a few situations where I didn't agree with what was going on, and I made my feelings known.*

   d) *Competent—my boss tells them I do my job well.*

Now score your responses:

Mostly A's: You enjoy what you do, and you've got the momentum to prove it! It's not time yet to switch careers; instead, work on an annual reinvention plan as insurance for any unexpected changes.

Mostly B's: You don't feel passionate about your work, and that shows up in the office. It's time to lay out a reinvention strategy.

Mostly C's: You don't enjoy your job, and the people you work with know it. Time to get moving on a career change before you find yourself in a "forced" reinvention!

Mostly D's: You're still growing, learning, and taking pleasure in your job. Don't rest on your laurels; focus on using the opportunities in front of you to build your reinvention skill set.

Don't be a nice girl who suffers in silence or falls into the group of people Henry David Thoreau describes as those who lead "lives of quiet desperation and go to the grave with the song still in them." Follow these tips that Pamela shared on the Katie Couric show, *Katie*, for how you can start creating a "brand"-new you.

COACHING TIPS

• Begin with a mini-reinvention. Change your hair color, lose weight, or take on a new sport or hobby. These small steps will shift you toward thinking outside the box for the bigger changes you want to make.

• Grab a buddy. Reinvention is lonely work. Identify a friend or coworker who you know is struggling with some of the same things you are and schedule time each week to talk about what you both plan to do, what you have done, and your visions for your futures.

• Ban excuses. Excuses are simply manifestations of fear. Rather than talk about why you can't change, come up with not only reasons why you *can*, but why you *will*.

• Step outside your comfort zone. The life you want to live is just outside your comfort zone.

• Give yourself time. Most people want immediate results, but that's not realistic. Set goals and keep track of progress so that you can appropriately reward yourself for success along the way.

ACTION ITEM

Mistake 78

Ignoring Your Legacy

*W*hat is the forensic evidence that I existed? When they dust for fingerprints, what will they find?" This is how one executive described the desire to leave something of himself behind in the workplace where he had spent so many years devoted to his company. When I told a friend about this insightful comment, her response was "I don't think about leaving a legacy. I just want to do a good job." Ah, yes. Nice girls are selfless and self-sacrificing, when, in fact, if you are really doing a good job, then you are likely doing things that *will* leave a legacy.

Your legacy doesn't have to be a building with your name on it, a huge charitable foundation, or an endowed chair at your alma mater. Most of us leave much more modest legacies, but we don't think of them as part of our brands. Depending on where you are in your career at the moment, it might not be on your radar screen, but I encourage people at all levels to consider what they want their legacies to be so that they can engage in behaviors that will ultimately lead to the satisfaction of knowing their professional presence made a difference.

Studio City–based consultant and psychotherapist Susan Picascia and I developed the following chart to describe the various tasks inherent to each phase of our careers. These phases are not dictated by our ages, but rather the time we've each spent in the career of our choice. You'll note our chart is similar to Maslow's hierarchy of needs, but with a focus on career, because we believe that striving for professional fulfillment is part of everyone's developmental process. It's when that process is thwarted that we experience malaise or indifference to our work.

STAGES OF CAREER DEVELOPMENT

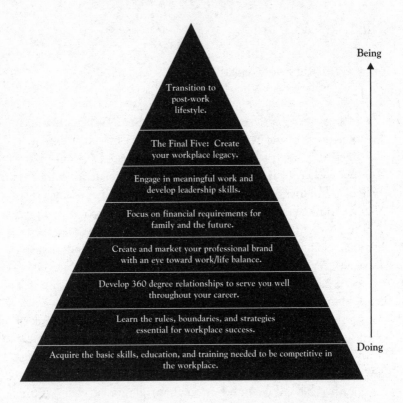

Being

Transition to post-work lifestyle.

The Final Five: Create your workplace legacy.

Engage in meaningful work and develop leadership skills.

Focus on financial requirements for family and the future.

Create and market your professional brand with an eye toward work/life balance.

Develop 360 degree relationships to serve you well throughout your career.

Learn the rules, boundaries, and strategies essential for workplace success.

Acquire the basic skills, education, and training needed to be competitive in the workplace.

Doing

On the chart you'll see many of the things we've already covered in this book, including personal branding and creating your legacy. These two things go hand in hand. I've seen too many women who've made remarkable contributions to their organizations underplay their impact and fade into obscurity, whether due to ineffective branding, changing jobs, or retirement. Existentialist philosopher Jean-Paul Sartre said that the loudest statement we make about who we are is our choice of career. The brand you establish in that career will be one of your greatest legacies.

COACHING TIPS

- Be a mentor. This you can do at any age or career stage. If you're not a mentor to people inside your company, then mentor young women in the community. The website mentoringgroup.com has a wealth of information to assist you with developing a meaningful relationship with mentees.

- Take risks—speak the unspoken. If you've reached the stage of your career where your reputation is established, the fact that you're still employed tells you the company values your contributions, and you most likely can "get away with" saying things that people on the way up can't. It's the perfect time to take some risks and be the voice for concerns you've had for a while but have never had the courage to express.

- Create new systems or processes. You have expertise and a perspective that others may not. Consider bringing together technical experts from all age-groups to work on a task force that will add value to the company's bottom line by developing new systems or processes. Use your external network of experts to help—you not only benefit from their expertise, but you also have a legitimate reason to stay in touch. And if or when you leave the company, you never know when or how you might need members of your network.

ACTION ITEM

Chapter 6

How You Sound

There's a Chinese curse that afflicts many nice girls: "May you have a wonderful idea and not be able to convince anyone of it." The best ideas fall on deaf ears if they're not communicated in ways that instill confidence and credibility. Dr. Albert Mehrabian, professor emeritus of psychology at UCLA, developed what is known as the "7%–38%–55% rule": 7 percent of your credibility comes from what you say (the content of your messages); 38 percent comes from how you sound (tone of voice, loudness, etc.); and 55 percent comes from how you look (dress, posture, nonverbal messages, etc.).

These factors also contribute to what's known as *gravitas*—what some believe to be at the core of executive communication. In a research paper on executive presence, gravitas is described by Sylvia Ann Hewlett and coauthors as "elegant packaging that attracts impressed attention, allowing your hardcore skills, accumulated knowledge, depth of experience and raw talent to stand out and draw others to you."

This next section examines behaviors contributing to how you sound and gives you specific language to practice. Try saying some of the Coaching Tips out loud to get a feel for how they might sound. Avoid the inclination to discard a tip just because it feels uncomfortable or awkward—it may be the one you need most. Remember, combined with how you look (which I cover in the next section), how you sound comprises more than 90 percent of the perception of your credibility.

COMPONENTS OF CREDIBILITY

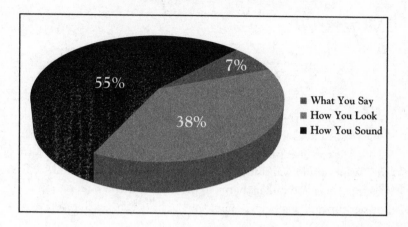

Mistake 79

Couching Statements as Questions

*T*his is one of the most common mistakes I hear women make: asking a question as a safe way of expressing an idea without being perceived as too direct or pushy. Such questions typically take the form of "What would you think if we..." or "Have you considered..." By asking a question rather than making a statement, we relinquish the ownership and outcomes of our ideas. Consider this exchange:

> **Ann:** Do you think we should budget more money for development this year so that we can meet unexpected but emerging needs?
>
> **Pete:** No. I think we should put more money into marketing. We first need to create buzz and then worry about filling the need.
>
> **Ann:** That's true, but we have to be prepared to fill the need upon demand, and that requires development funds.
>
> **Pete:** So why'd you ask me?

A senior woman I coached was having little success shaking the perception that she was intimidating. As a tall and imposing figure, and one who worked with military-like precision in the defense industry, it was easy to see how her direct reports might be afraid to stand up to or disagree with her. When I first met with her, we role-played a typical scenario where she wanted input from her team but wasn't getting it. She started by asking a question about what I thought of a particular process. When I answered, she responded with a "yes, but" question—"Yes, but don't you think..." This went on for several iterations, and I understood completely what was getting in her way.

The woman's questions weren't intended to engage discussion; they were intended (consciously or not) to get others to do what she wanted them to do. On the surface, it appeared she was interested in the opinions of others. But her staff knew that what they said wasn't going to make a difference, so they stopped telling her what they thought. I later learned that another coach had told her she should ask more questions to dispel the notion that she didn't care about what her staff thought. I'm sure that coach hadn't quite envisioned how the suggestion would be applied!

The result of posing your statements as questions is that others won't hear you as owning your ideas; rather, they'll see you as manipulative, or they'll assume there's room to pick apart your proposal or ignore it entirely. If you ask a question to camouflage a statement, it's a little like trying to teach a pig to sing—it frustrates you and annoys the pig. If you're worried about sounding too strident or pushy, consider adding language to the message that would make it more palatable—but at all costs avoid turning it into a question if it isn't truly a request for information.

COACHING TIPS

- Start making statements. Each time you find yourself couching an opinion in the form of a question, stop and turn it into a statement.

- Save your questions for those times when you legitimately need information or are interested in someone's opinion.

- Put ideas out in the affirmative: "I propose we prepare ourselves for emerging needs by putting the bulk of our budget moneys into development." Even if someone disagrees with you, your affirmative statement leaves you in a much stronger position to defend your proposal.

- Adding a tagline such as "I'm interested in your thoughts," or "You can hear I feel strongly about this, and at the same time I'd like to hear what others think," after a proposal or statement can make you more comfortable with being direct without making you appear uncertain.

ACTION ITEM

Mistake 80

Using Preambles

A preamble is a concoction of words and nonwords used before getting to the main point. It's like a closet filled with clutter. When there's too much clutter, you can't see what's in the closet. The same is true with words. The more words you use, the more diffused your message becomes and the less likely the listener will hear your unique message.

Women use preambles as a means of softening their messages for fear of being perceived as too direct or aggressive. What's your response to this preamble?

> You know, I was thinking about this problem we're having with productivity. In fact, I've been talking to other peo-ple about it, too. A lot of us share the same concerns over reduced productivity during the last three quarters, so I'm not alone in this. Come to think of it, it might be even more than just those three quarters. It's something we've known about for a long time but haven't measured. At any rate, we've all been trying to find a way to address it, and I think I may have come up with an idea. I'm not saying it's the best idea or the only idea—just that it's one idea. In fact, other people have ideas, too, but I'll leave it up to them to share those with you. Now, my idea involves…

And the point is…This person's motto must be "Why use fewer words when I can use more?" This same message could have been delivered powerfully and confidently using 75 percent fewer words:

"Productivity has been an issue we've struggled with for some time now, and I have a proposal for addressing it."

COACHING TIPS

• Give your bottom line first. Organize your thoughts before you open your mouth by asking yourself two simple questions: *What's my main topic?* and *What two or three points do I want the listener to consider?*

• Let your mantra be "Short sounds confident." If the message is an important one, practice before delivering it. Hone it using as few words as possible.

• Try combining affirmative declarations with short messages: "I propose we conduct a cross-functional analysis to determine the causes of and cures for reduced productivity during the last three to four quarters."

ACTION ITEM

Mistake 81

Explaining

*R*emember the old television show *I Love Lucy*? Since originally airing in 1951, there has never been a time when it was *not* on the air—it's been in syndication in dozens of languages for more than sixty years. In the show, whenever Ricky was exasperated with some stunt Lucy pulled, he sternly admonished her, "Lucy, you got some splainin' to do." With this, Lucy knew she was in trouble and a sheepish look would take over her face. By demanding that she explain herself, Ricky was relegating Lucy to the level of a child—and she responded in a childish way. Explanations coming from an adult woman make them seem unsure of themselves and, at times, somewhat childish.

The lengthy explanation is the counterpoint to the preamble. You finally make your point—then you undermine it with an even longer explanation that causes others to mentally check out. Preambles, combined with explanations, are lethal. Why do nice girls tend to pair these fatal flaws more than men? There are a few reasons. More words soften a message, and heaven forbid we sound too powerful. Another is that we fear we haven't been thorough or complete enough, so in an effort to be "perfect," we keep talking. A third reason is that our statements frequently are not acknowledged, so we continue talking in an effort to get feedback. And, finally, we overcompensate for our insecurity. We think the more we talk, the better case we make… when in fact the opposite is true.

Let's pick up the preamble from the previous mistake and pair it with this lengthy explanation:

I'm not saying it's the best idea or the only idea—just that it's one idea. In fact, other people have ideas, too, but I'll leave it up to them to share those with you. Now, my idea involves doing some kind of a climate survey. You know, the kind where we go out to the employees and ask them questions about their processes, job satisfaction, relationships with their supervisors, and so on. A lot of companies are doing this now. We can use either an outside consultant or our own staff. If it's all right with you, I would be willing to look into what the best way to accomplish this would be. Or, if you prefer, you can name a task force to investigate options. On the other hand, if you want I will investigate the options and get back to you.

As I said . . . lethal.

COACHING TIPS

- Shorten your explanations by 50 to 75 percent.
- Use the headline model to plan your verbal communications in advance, sort out your thoughts when responding to a question, and keep your messages succinct. The more you use this model, the more natural it will become.
- Here's what the entire message would sound like if you used all the coaching tips from the past three mistakes with the headline communication model (see next page):

I propose we conduct a cross-functional analysis to determine the causes of and cures for reduced productivity during the last three to four quarters. The results will give us three pieces of invaluable data: (1) where our greatest strengths lie; (2) what mistakes we're currently making;

and (3) where we should go from here. I'll be happy to take the lead on this. Do you have any thoughts?

• Resist the internal message that screams *INCOMPLETE*. Saying everything you know related to a topic isn't necessary. Depending on your level of expertise, it may be incomplete to you, but not to the other person. This is a case where less is more.

HEADLINE COMMUNICATION

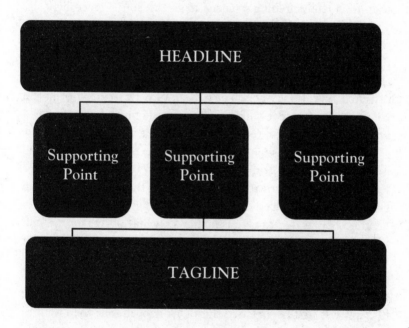

ACTION ITEM

Mistake 82

Asking Permission

*H*ave you ever noticed that men don't ask permission? They ask forgiveness. My hunch is that women ask permission more out of habit than from really needing someone to give them the green light. It's a variation on asking questions to play it safe—but potentially more self-defeating. In our society we expect children, not adults, to ask permission. Every time a woman asks permission to do or say something, she diminishes her stature and relegates herself to the position of a child. She also sets herself up to hear "No." By seeking permission before acting, we are less likely to be accused of making a mistake— but we're also less likely to be viewed as confident risk-takers.

Women ask permission for things as simple as taking a day off and as ridiculous as whether they can spend money on a particular service required by the department—despite the fact they have already been given signing authority. I'll never forget a woman who complained to me that she was denied permission for a one-day off-site for her staff while a male coworker took his team on a boondoggle to a local resort for three days. When I inquired as to how she went about making the plans, she admitted she thought she was being politically correct by asking the boss if it would be all right to have everyone gone for a day; his reply was that he preferred this didn't happen. She then went to her coworker and asked him how he'd gotten the boss's approval. He said, "It never occurred to me to ask."

Regardless of your position, you're entitled to take independent action within a given set of boundaries. Your job is to identify those boundaries, clarify them with your boss, and act within them. From administrative assistants to department managers, I observe many who won't make a move without first getting permission. Believe me, your boss wants you to take the ball and run with it. It's what you're paid for, and it makes his or her job infinitely easier.

COACHING TIPS

- Inform others of your intentions; don't ask for permission. By informing others you show respect for their need to know, but without your action being contingent upon their approval.
- Assume equality.
- Turn this: "Would it be all right with you if I work at home tomorrow? I'm expecting a delivery midday," into this: "I just wanted to let you know I'll be working at home tomorrow. I've got a delivery coming."
- You can assume that if people have a problem with what you're saying, they'll let you know. You can then negotiate from a position of greater strength.
- If using affirmative declarations is difficult for you, soften your message with a follow-up phrase. Rather than asking for permission, try something like this: "I plan to prepare a position paper to address each of the concerns of our client. When it's complete, I'd like to get your input before sharing it with the client."
- Similarly, don't fall into the trap of responding to statements posed as questions. You'll wind up in a spitting match.
- A legitimate question is one in which you are asking for information you don't have. By all means ask these types of questions, but avoid holding a group hostage with your questions. Be aware of the body language of others that suggests they're ready to move on. Ask additional questions off-line.

ACTION ITEM

Mistake 83

Apologizing

I was watching the British Open just after Tiger Woods had lost a tournament. The sportscaster interviewing him expressed sympathy for an obviously bad day in which he'd missed some easy shots and just hadn't played up to his normal standard. His response was "I didn't play poorly. The wind and the conditions were just against me today." It was a reminder of how even in the face of obvious errors and poor performance, men will deny or minimize the mistake rather than assume responsibility or apologize.

Women can take a lesson from this. Apologizing for unintentional, low-profile, nonegregious errors erodes our self-confidence and, in turn, the confidence others have in us. Whether it's inadvertently bumping into someone on the street or making a small mistake in the office, a woman is far more likely to apologize than a man. It's second nature to us and often done in place of confronting the real source of the mistake—the other person's poor communication. It's a conflict-reducing technique, but one that makes you look like you're at fault when in fact you're not.

Here's an example. A woman opened a coaching session by telling me that her boss had just finished berating her over the fact that she hadn't informed him of some meeting she'd attended that he wanted to attend as well. The fact was, she had forwarded to him an e-mail with the information about the meeting, but he'd either failed to read it or forgotten to mark it on his calendar. When asked how she handled the situation, I could tell she was proud of her response. Because we happened to have previously talked about the phenomenon of women apologizing, she knew she didn't want to do that. Instead, she very politely told him,

"I forwarded the e-mail to you the same day I received the information. If you're saying that in the future you would like me to check with you to be certain you receive information such as this, I'll be happy to."

This was a great response for a number of reasons. First, she didn't fall into the trap of apologizing. She reported that by not doing so she felt far more empowered and less like a child who was being scolded. Second, is there a boss anywhere who wants employees marching into his or her office to confirm receipt of a bunch of e-mails? By thinking on her feet, she came up with an alternative she knew he wasn't going to go for. Essentially, in a very diplomatic way, she put the onus on him to read his mail.

COACHING TIPS

• Start counting the number of times you apologize unnecessarily. Consciously reduce this number by saving your apologies for big-time mistakes (and there aren't many of those).

• When you do make a mistake worth apologizing for, do so only once, then move into a problem-solving mode.

• Turn the inclination to apologize into an objective assessment of what went wrong and ways to fix it.

• Combine the previous coaching tips with an unapologetic statement such as "Based on the information initially provided to me, I had no idea that was your expectation. Tell me more about what you had in mind, and I'll make the necessary revisions."

• Avoid using apologies that put you in a one-down position as a way of ensuring you're liked. Always begin from a place of equality—regardless of the level of the person with whom you are dealing. He or she might have a higher position than you, but that doesn't make the person any better than you.

ACTION ITEM

Mistake 84

Using Minimizing Words

*A*lthough women may not have cornered the market on the use of minimizing words, we certainly use them more than most men. Minimizing words are those that diminish the importance or size of an achievement. My cousin's teenage daughter recently demonstrated this, and the incident served as a reminder that this is something learned early in girlhood in response to the message "Don't brag or boast."

During a family event, her grandfather proudly announced that she had won several scholastic awards. When I expressed my congratulations and inquired as to which ones, she responded, "Oh, they're just Golden State awards." Now, I have no idea what these awards are, but I do know she had to do something above and beyond the norm to achieve them. By using the word *just*, she minimized the importance of the recognition.

The workplace equivalent is to downplay success or attribute it to something other than talent, hard work, or know-how. In response to congratulations or compliments, women will often say something like "It was really nothing," or "I guess I just got lucky." Say those phrases enough times, and you'll begin to believe them.

COACHING TIPS

• Practice saying, "Thank you for noticing," or "Thank you. I'm pleased with how it turned out." Say it again and again until it rolls off your tongue in response to a compliment.

• Objectively describe your achievements without using qualifiers. Avoid "It was only...," "I just...," or "I surprised myself..."

• If you want to be modest, try saying something like "Thank you. I am quite proud of what I achieved and must give some credit to those who helped me along the way."

• Read *Power Talk: Using Language to Build Authority and Influence*, by Sarah Myers McGinty. This book provides great insight into the importance of matching your communication to the situation as well as techniques for how you can ensure that your message is taken seriously.

ACTION ITEM

Mistake 85

Using Qualifiers

*A*nother way in which women calm their fears about being too direct, opinionated, or committed is to use qualifiers. They serve the purpose of softening, and weakening, your message. Qualifiers include comments such as:

> "It's kind of like..."
> "We sort of did..."
> "Perhaps we should..."
> "Maybe it would be better if..."
> "We could..."

Yikes! It's maddening. Equivocating comments prompt people to ask or think:

> "What *is* it like?"
> "What *did* you do?"
> "Should we or shouldn't we?"
> "Is it better or isn't it?"
> "Can we or can't we?"

COACHING TIPS

- Give your opinion in clear, certain terms. This doesn't mean dogmatically, just directly and without qualifiers.

- Here again, if you feel you need them, taglines can help you soften a strong opinion without invalidating it. For example, "I feel strongly that we should act now rather than wait for all the reasons mentioned. I'm curious to hear what others think."

- If you're really not sure, then preface your remarks with why you're not sure or what would make you more committed. "Given the facts we have so far, I'm not sure we should move so quickly. I would need more data before making a final decision," is still more clear than equivocating.

ACTION ITEM

Mistake 86

Not Answering the Question You're Asked

𝓗ave you ever felt like a deer caught in the headlights of an oncoming car when asked a question you didn't expect? You feel your heart start to pound. Your mind races trying to locate a few points that would make you sound halfway intelligent and informed. The seconds ticking by feel like hours. And what do you finally do? You start talking in an attempt to fill the silence and hope something will eventually come to you.

Consider this exchange between a senior vice president and one of her direct reports:

> **SVP:** Do you think we should tell our shareholders about the anticipated loss for the fourth quarter or wait until we're sure how much the loss will be?
>
> **DR:** Well, we could tell them now in preparation for the fourth-quarter financials. On the other hand, if we wait, we'll sound more credible in terms of actual numbers. If we tell them now, we'll have to deal with lots of questions we can't answer. If we wait, it may appear we're trying to hide something. There are pros and cons either way.

Guess what? The VP already knows there are pros and cons. She can probably articulate them just as well as you. What she wants is an answer. My Indonesian clients (who, regardless of gender, communicate in a stereotypically feminine way) call this *basa-basi*—"wishy-washy." Women often make the mistake of thinking they have the luxury of thinking out loud in response to tough questions. They believe putting all the options on the table is the most helpful and fair thing to do. The obvious problem is that it leaves the questioner without an answer. If you ask me, it's just another way women hedge their bets and play it safe. One colleague calls this "hiding in plain sight." If there ever is a time to make a declarative statement, it's in response to a direct question.

COACHING TIPS

- Directly answer the question you're asked. Just as in school, there are only four kinds of questions: true-false, fill in the blank, either-or, and essay. The question above was either-or: Should we share the information now or wait? The first words out of your mouth must be one or the other—or your own third alternative. In this case the sentence could begin with "Neither. I think we should let the results speak for themselves when the financials are announced."

- The inability to answer a question directly and succinctly can stem from the desire to have the perfect or "right" answer. I often hear people answer a yes-no question with "But I can't give you a yes or no answer." Oh yes you can. You do it by taking a risk and putting yourself on the line. It's better to err on the side of starting a debate than it is to sound wishy-washy.

- Go back to the headline communication model to organize your thoughts. Tom Henschel, president of Essential Communications, coaches clients to "chunk" answers mentally in terms of the bottom line and two or three pieces of supporting data. An appropriate response to the question above using this model would sound like this: "I suggest we share the information now. There are two primary reasons I advise this. First, I believe it's better to err on the side of full disclosure rather than be accused of withholding information. Second, we're pretty sure there's going to be a loss, but if we're wrong and there isn't, people will be relieved and we've lost nothing."

- When answering an essay question, use a numbered framework to order and express your thoughts: "I have three ideas...." or "There are two paths we can take...."

- Take an improvisation class. Part of being able to answer questions directly is knowing how to think on your feet. The techniques you learn in improvisation will be helpful to you in a number of ways.

ACTION ITEM ☐

Mistake 87

Talking Too Fast

*W*hen I was interviewed the first time on the *Today Show* by Ann Curry, I was thrilled. I don't know what got into me (probably high on the adrenaline rush I was experiencing), but after the interview I asked if I could give her a coaching tip. She hesitated, but then said sure. My tip for her was to speak more slowly because speaking so rapidly makes it seem like she's trying to take less time. Without being defensive, she replied that the control booth is always whispering in her ear, "Speed it up." As I told her, you don't hear Matt Lauer speeding it up—even though I'm sure they're telling him the same thing (or they're not because they know they can't get away with it with a man).

Was Ann replaced in the coanchor spot in 2012 because she spoke too fast? I don't think so. None of us really knows the answer to that question, but I can tell you she was a smart, gutsy woman with a lot of heart. Just before our interview started she looked me in the eye, gave me a fist bump, and said, "Let's do something good for women." My own opinion (and it's just that) is that Ann's departure was a case of being on the wrong playing field. The format and tenor of the *Today Show* changed over the years, and Ann is better suited to reports with more gravitas. The pieces she has done subsequently certainly showcase her talent in this arena.

But I digress! Many of us, having been given the message that we talk too much, are fearful of taking up too much floor time. We speed up our communications so that we can get our entire message out before being interrupted or given a sign that we've talked too much. We wind up sounding like the man in the old FedEx commercial who could talk at the speed of light. Much like physical space, taking the appropriate amount of time to verbally express ourselves is a sign of entitlement. That is: I'm entitled to be seen and heard.

Because so much of your credibility is dependent on how you sound, regardless of the actual content, it's important to convey confidence, accuracy, and depth of thought. Speaking too quickly does just the opposite. It can be interpreted by others as implying that you don't deserve the time you're taking from them or that your message isn't important enough for them to spend time on. Rushing through your message can be construed as not being thorough or thoughtful in your approach. These interpretations can, in turn, cause the listener to question the accuracy of what you are reporting.

COACHING TIPS

- Practice speaking at a moderate pace. Practicing a presentation to music is helpful—provided it's not a Sousa march.
- Join Toastmasters. These groups, which you can find in most cities, enable professionals to meet during the lunch hour and practice public speaking. Members give one another feedback at the end of each presentation. It's one of the best ways to gain comfort with not only talking, but public speaking, too. You'll find contact information in the appendix.
- Read *Smart Talk: The Public Speaker's Guide to Success in Every Situation* by Lisa B. Marshall. The book is filled with practical suggestions for how you can look and sound like a pro in front of an audience.
- Ask a friend or colleague to discreetly give you a sign when your speech speeds up.
- Tell yourself you're entitled to take all the time you need to convey your message (providing you do it in the way suggested in previous tips).

ACTION ITEM ☐

Mistake 88

The Inability to Speak the Language of Your Business

*E*very business and profession has a language and jargon all its own. We may joke about phrases such as "Let's make sure we're all on the same page," "She drank the Kool-Aid," and "Let's take this off-line," but when we fail to use the language, it conveys a lack of familiarity. Influence comes from knowing the business, and one of the best ways you can exercise your influence is to use language unique to your industry and profession. Women often assume if they know and are good at their piece of the business, that alone will make them influential. Wrong.

One woman we worked with wondered why she was continually overlooked for promotions. She received consistently good performance reviews and was frequently praised for her expertise and contributions to the department. In an attempt to identify high-potential employees, her company regularly administered management assessments to a certain level of staff. The assessment included a few tests and an interview with an organizational psychologist. The result: She was described in the report as being of above-average intelligence, a good problem solver, and potentially a good manager, but lacking in her ability to speak about parts of the business other than her own.

Do you know the ROI, bottom line, and performance indicators for your company? If not, it's time to find out.

COACHING TIPS

- Read the *Wall Street Journal*. It will provide you with not only information that could be helpful to you in your work, but also a common language of business.
- Ask someone in your finance department to explain the basics.
- Subscribe to industry magazines or newsletters.
- Take a class in accounting for nonfinancial professionals.
- Get involved with your own personal finances and budgeting.
- Attend professional association meetings.
- Research benchmarks and best practices in your field.

ACTION ITEM ☐

Mistake 89

Using Nonwords

*N*onwords are habitual sounds and phrases you use to fill up silence. When they infuse your speech, they make you sound unsure or hesitant. Nonwords can be *uh* or *er*, but can also be short interjections such as *Know what I mean?* or *See?*. Any repetitive sound used as a substitute for a brief pause becomes a nonword and detracts from your message.

If every sound you utter were transcribed, uh, well, you wouldn't, uh, want your speech to read as if you, uh, didn't know what you were talking about, know what I mean? Becoming conscious of these credibility busters can be the toughest part of changing the habit. Once you begin to track your nonwords, no matter how diligent you are, you're probably hearing only about a tenth of the ones you actually say.

COACHING TIPS

- Ask a trusted colleague for feedback about your use of nonwords.
- Set up a real-time feedback loop with friends or colleagues. For example, over a cup of coffee have them snap their fingers every time you use a nonword.
- Involve people outside work in your real-time feedback. The more feedback you get, the faster you'll break the habit.
- Videotape yourself making a presentation and review it for how you sound.
- Put a voice recorder on your desk and hit the Record button before you answer the phone or make a call. Listen to the recording later and count your nonwords.
- Become comfortable with silence—it can be a powerful tool in your communications.

ACTION ITEM

Mistake 90

Using Touchy-Feely Language

*Y*et another way women display their insecurity around being direct is to use the proverbial touchy-feely language. The best way I can describe this is to show you what it sounds like in comparison to non-touchy-feely language (I feel wishy-washy just writing it!).

Touchy-Feely	More Confidently Stated
"It feels like we should…"	"I believe it would be best to…"
"I might…"	"I intend to…"
"You could consider…"	"I would advise you to…"
"How would you feel if we…"	"What would you think if we…"
"One could argue that…"	"The opposition would say…"
"My thought is that we…"	"My proposal is that we…"

You get the picture. Both sides convey the same literal messages, but the ones on the right side are more assertive. They make a stronger statement about the speaker's commitment to what's being said and about her desire to become visible. You might think I'm just splitting hairs here, but our language strongly conveys meta-messages about us, our values, and our intentions.

COACHING TIPS

- Practice beginning your sentences with declarative *I* statements, such as "I think...," "I believe...," I propose...," "I intend...," "I would like...," or even "I feel..."
- Take more risks around stating your thoughts with conviction.
- Develop a more businesslike vocabulary by reading books and articles targeted to businesspeople.
- When writing letters or e-mails, go back and edit them with the intention of strengthening your written word.
- Don't entirely relinquish touchy-feely language—just be more discriminating in how you use it. It can serve a purpose when counseling or coaching coworkers.

ACTION ITEM

Mistake 91

The Sandwich

$\mathcal{I}$ don't know who came up with the idea for giving feedback using the sandwich technique, but it's manipulative and undermines your ability to be straightforward. The sandwich model suggests that when you're giving feedback, you should couch the negative between two pieces of positive feedback. Fageddaboudit. It doesn't work. It may be easier for you, but not for the recipient. I hesitate to give you an example of how it works because I don't want you to get the idea you should include it in your communication skills repertoire, but for the sake of clarity, here's what it would sound like:

> Greg, I'd like to talk to give you some feedback about your recent work on the Jackson project. I really like how you spent considerable time up front building a relationship with the client. They seemed to appreciate it. On the other hand, I would have liked you to put more time into doing the research necessary to create a robust proposal to them. Overall, I'd say you're doing a good job of managing the client's expectations.

Now, what is Greg going to walk away with? He's going to be asking himself if he's doing a good job or not. Even though the last message was a positive one, the middle, more critical message, is most likely what he's going to focus on. Separating positive and negative feedback is a much more effective way of delivering a clear message of expectations and reinforcing appropriate performance. Giving critical feedback is difficult no matter how skilled or practiced you are at it. It's one reason why I use the seven-to-one rule of feedback (described in the coaching tips below).

Women in particular often don't like being the bearers of bad news. In fact, most of us avoid it like a ten-pound box of chocolates. To be effective, feedback has to be specific, behavioral, and focus on positive results. A better way to approach Greg would have been as follows:

> Greg, I'd like to give you a little feedback about the Jackson proposal. It seemed to me that the research you presented wasn't thorough enough and left a number of questions unanswered for the client [specific]. In the future, I'd like you to conduct a more thorough review of what the competition is doing and contrast the benefits of using our process and people [behavioral]. This would enable the client to make an informed decision in a shorter period of time [positive results].

COACHING TIPS

- Giving critical feedback is much easier if you've followed the seven-to-one rule. Over time you must give seven pieces of positive feedback for every one piece of negative. This enables the recipient to hear your developmental message and not see you as overly critical.

- When you give positive feedback, make certain it's free from implied criticism. Like a left-handed compliment, it sounds something like this from your mother-in-law: "Dinner tonight was just delicious. It's sooooooooo much better than the last three meals you cooked for us."

- Keep in mind that ongoing feedback should be both positive and negative.

- Giving direct feedback can be made easier by using a model called the DESCript:

D = Describe why you're having the conversation.

Frank, I'd like to talk to you about something that happened last week when we were working together on the Acme project.

E = Explain in behavioral terms how you see the situation and Elicit from the other person his or her perceptions.

I felt the bulk of the work fell on my shoulders because you arrived late and left early four of the five days. I'm wondering how you see the situation.

S = Show that you've heard what's been said and Specify what you want to see happen.

I understand you had a family problem to deal with, and if I'd known that in advance, I could have made different arrangements or asked that someone else work with me. In the future it would be helpful if you would let me know when you're not able to devote 100 percent of your attention to a project we're working on together.

C = Tie the desired behavior to Consequences (positive or negative, depending on the severity of the problem or length of time it's been discussed).

Thanks for hearing me out. If we find ways to communicate better internally, we can provide increased value to our clients.

ACTION ITEM

Mistake 92

Speaking Softly

*W*hen I was about fourteen years old, I worked in a dry-cleaning store owned by a woman who was prone to migraine headaches. If you've ever been in a dry cleaner's midday during the week, you know there's a hum of machinery and pressing equipment. I was speaking quite loudly to someone working a few feet away, and the owner came over and whispered in my ear, "Don't you know that young ladies don't speak loudly?" For many years after that I was careful not to speak too loudly for fear of sounding unladylike. Three decades later I realized the woman most likely had a headache and just wished I would keep quiet. I wonder how many other young women have been given the same message—and for perhaps the same reason.

The volume of our voices is one more way in which we can manage others' impressions of us. Women tend to have softer voices to begin with. When we speak softly, the message conveyed is one of uncertainty or lack of confidence. Volume also impacts body language. The louder you speak, the more gestures you tend to naturally use. By combining appropriate volume and gestures, you immediately convey a sense of authority or subject-matter expertise.

COACHING TIPS

• When speaking before a group, pretend the person farthest away from you is a little hard of hearing, and speak loudly enough so that he or she can hear you.

• Take a voice, acting, or singing class to learn how to project your voice.

• If people tend to ask you to repeat things or to speak more loudly, consider this message something you must address.

• Videotape yourself making a presentation or even just discussing a subject in a meeting. If you find it difficult to hear what you're saying but everyone else can be heard just fine, this is another indicator that volume is something you want to work on.

• Listen to your own voice-mail greeting. Objectively assess how you would characterize the voice on the other end. Practice leaving a message that expresses self-confidence—this is frequently other people's first impression of you.

• Imagine your listeners as customers. Your voice should envelop them so they lean back comfortably in their chairs. If they have to lean forward, straining to hear you, you're not taking good care of those customers.

ACTION ITEM

Mistake 93

Speaking at a Higher-Than-Natural Pitch

*W*hy is it that a woman can be speaking with another woman in a natural pitch—but when a man comes into the room, she's suddenly a falsetto? This is not something you usually catch a man doing. When a woman's voice reverts to sounding high and thin, it becomes like a little girl's voice. What does a little girl's voice sound like? Coy, demure, sweet, and not at all authoritative. Which is probably the effect some women want their voices to have.

Again, people respond not only to the content of your message, but to the sound of it as well. Higher-pitched messages, which are stereotypically more feminine, tend to be discounted. Why do you think for so many years during early broadcasting that newscasters were all men? Walter Cronkite was someone we trusted even though we knew little about the man's character. To this day, male voices predominate in the national evening news. From Anderson Cooper to Charlie Rose and Scott Pelley, men are the so-called voices of authority.

Although I can't tell you why it happens, I do know that lower voices are accorded more attention and respect. As voices go up in pitch, credibility goes down. Perhaps it's simply ingrained in our culture that lower voices are typically male, and we tend to grant more authority in general to men. Even men who have higher-pitched voices face the same problems with credibility as do women. Ross Perot's somewhat diminutive physical stature, combined with a voice that was higher-pitched than normal for most men, didn't help him in the political arena.

Think about the voices of Meg Whitman, CEO of Hewlett-Packard, and Queen Elizabeth. Although the queen is largely seen as a titular head of state and Whitman heads one of the world's largest companies, their voices contribute to how seriously we consider what one has to say over the other.

COACHING TIPS

• When you wake up, make a noise. It can be any noise, like *Ummmmmmm* or *La la la la la*. You'll notice that this is your natural, unconstricted pitch—one you should try to maintain throughout the workday.

• Join a choral group and find your pitch. You won't be able to sing falsetto for long.

• Consciously breathe and relax your neck and shoulder muscles. Vocal pitch often rises because of tension and the restriction of the vocal cords.

• Imagine your neck and chest cavity to be large, spacious openings. Picture your voice rolling around inside you. Reframe any small, constricted images of your voice.

ACTION ITEM

Mistake 94

Trailing Voice Mails

$\mathcal{W}e$ used to joke that my mother-in-law didn't know how to say good-bye. Long after she and I had finished discussing the last item on either of our agendas, she just couldn't bring herself to close the conversation. The same holds true for many women when they leave voice-mail messages. Regardless of how succinct and articulate the initial part of the message is, it winds up something like this: "Okay, well, I guess that's everything. Uh, call me if you have any questions. That's it, I think. Okay. Bye." Trailing voice mails can undo the effectiveness of your initial (and most important) message. They can make you look indecisive.

I once worked with a client who told me that people left her rude, abrupt voice mails and she didn't know how to respond to them. I asked her to save a few for me to listen to during one of our meetings. I also asked her to save some of her own voice-mail messages by asking trusted colleagues to forward them back to her. Upon listening to both sets of messages, it was immediately evident that those she had problems with were from men. They weren't rude and abrupt; they were just succinct. Hers, on the other hand, used more words than necessary as she thought out loud and scrolled through her mental agenda. In comparison, they sounded softer—because they were softer. More words soften a message. Fewer words make it more memorable.

COACHING TIPS

• Most business voice-mail systems give you the opportunity to go back and listen to your message. To find out if you're guilty of leaving messages that trail off, go back and listen to a few before sending them.

• In advance of your call, create a mental checklist of what you want to cover so you'll know when you're finished and it's time to hang up (my mother-in-law could have really used this tip).

• If you find that this is a mistake you make, force yourself to end after you've made your point. Stop talking. Say good-bye. Hang up.

• Prepare a standard tagline for the end of messages (voice mail or otherwise). Saying something like "Call me if you have questions" and hanging up immediately will work.

ACTION ITEM

Mistake 95

Failing to Pause or Reflect Before Responding

I'm sure you've heard the term *pregnant pause*. It's a brief period of time that causes others to anticipate and pay attention to what you're about to say. In your desire to please others and not take up too much time, you may respond to questions too soon, not giving yourself enough time to reflect on your answer. A pregnant pause before speaking is a powerful tool to add to your communication skill set. Remember the old commercial: "When E. F. Hutton talks, people listen."

A pause before speaking does several things. It conveys a message of thoughtfulness about what you're about to say. It generates interest on the part of the listener. A pause and the ensuing silence give others the impression that you're self-confident. And they give you time to put your thoughts into a concise framework.

COACHING TIPS

• Practice counting to three before replying to a question—even when the answer is on the tip of your tongue.

• During the pause, ask yourself what the main point is that you want the listener to take away. Let that point be your lead sentence.

• Use the second hand of a clock or watch to time a three-second pause. In the middle of a conversation it may seem to you like an eternity, but, as you will see, it's only momentary.

ACTION ITEM

Mistake 96

Overrelying on One Communication Style

*M*ost of us have a preferred style of communication that involves focusing primarily on:

- Data
- Feelings
- Action
- Ideas

I use the word *primarily* because we typically use at least one of the other modes in many of our day-to-day communications. So think about this. If you're the kind of person who communicates your ideas using feelings (as many women prefer), and you're trying to influence someone who likes to communicate using facts (as many men prefer), then you're going to encounter a natural disconnect. When you say, "I feel this is the right thing to do," the other person is thinking, *I don't care what you feel; give me a logical reason why we should do this.* In situations like this, great ideas are often overlooked or even ridiculed because they weren't communicated in a way the other person could easily process.

The antidote to this dilemma is to vary your communication style based on the preferences of the person you're trying to influence. If you think this smacks of being phony, think again. Your message doesn't change, just the words you use to deliver it. Use your EQ here to observe individual preferences and apply the right style to each interaction.

COACHING TIPS

- Try using this chart to help you identify the right communication method to use with different people:

If the other person...	Then...
Has an office that looks like no one works there, is always extraordinarily well-groomed, and doesn't like small talk...	It's likely they will want you to communicate using data, facts, and figures. Do not try to schmooze with them; it will backfire. Come prepared with all the information needed to make or support your case so that a decision can be made logically and rationally.
Is someone who is always organizing the holiday parties or picnics, remembers everyone's names (and the names of their dogs), and who has a lot of personal memorabilia in the office...	It's likely they will respond best to communications using feelings, values, and precedents. Start your conversations with a little small talk, then shift to the business at hand. When trying to influence this person, show that you've checked with others and your proposal was well-received or explain how it will benefit the people impacted by it.
Usually has little time or patience for long conversations, has an office that looks like a bomb went off in it, and shows little concern for style or fashion...	Use an executive summary, communicating only in bullet points. Present your ideas in a way that suggests action can be quickly taken and results will be happening sooner rather than later. Be prepared to answer questions, but don't provide more information than is absolutely required to make your point.
Seems like a big-picture thinker, someone who sometimes lives in a world of ideas more than reality, can be creative, and has an office that sports toys, novelty items, or modern art...	Your best bet to effectively influence them is to present your ideas as state-of-the-art or cutting-edge in ways that will competitively position your company or department. Speak logically and factually, but with an emphasis on the future or how your proposal will distinguish the company from others in the field.

- Take the free communication styles inventory at keirsey.com. This will enable you to identify your own preferred style of communication and those of others. While there, check out the books available that go into more depth about communication style preferences.
- If it looks like you're not getting through to someone, try shifting your communication style. Sometimes that's all it takes to get their attention.

ACTION ITEM

Mistake 97

Ambivalence

*O*ne of the things that drive our male coworkers nuts (and probably male spouses, too) is the apparent ambivalence that women seem to have with making a decision and committing to a direction. I carefully selected the word *apparent* here because that's how men perceive the cognitive process employed by many women who lack the confidence and courage to jump into the pool with both feet. A professor in graduate school called this "the "Coney Island dip." We dip our toes into the water and see if we're prepared to go all the way.

Ambivalence, or the inability to make a choice due to conflicting internal messages, isn't the exclusive domain of women, but we exhibit our fair share of it. There are a number of factors that can cause ambivalence, among them:

- Lack of data
- The belief that others know more than we do
- Having been criticized in the past for decisions made
- A genuine desire to weigh all options
- Fear of making a wrong decision
- Not wanting to hurt someone's feelings

Regardless of what contributes to *your* appearing ambivalent, the result is that others perceive you as lacking the capability of making a commitment, having the courage to stand by your convictions, and possessing the resilience to turn around a decision that didn't pan out as planned.

COACHING TIPS

• Develop time frames within which to make decisions. When the boss asks you to take a lateral assignment in a different city and your immediate response is ambivalence, put a specific time frame on when you'll get back to him or her. Say something like "I'm honored you would recommend me for this position. It's a big decision and I'd like to think about it for a few days. I'll get back to you within forty-eight hours." A response like this does not appear ambivalent, but rather thoughtful.

• Be clear about why decision making is postponed and use data to support it. For example, "I'm not inclined to make a decision about this just yet. We've surveyed only one-third of our clients, and additional data is needed to be certain we're on the right path. A good decision will require input from at least 60 percent of the clients this action will impact."

• Avoid thinking out loud as a routine way of communicating. When you think out loud, you are cueing the listener that you're reflecting on a number of options or issues. It's okay to do this once in a while, but do it too often and you'll be labeled indecisive.

• Use a trusted friend as a sounding board, not your boss or management. If you're the kind of person who truly needs to thrash ideas around before making a commitment, then do it with a friend or family member.

• Keep in mind that most decisions are adjustable. For this reason, it's better to commit one way or the other than to appear wishy-washy.

ACTION ITEM

Mistake 98

Confusing Problem Solving with Complaining

I have one inviolable rule in my office: "No complaining without an accompanying solution or request for help with finding a solution." Unaccustomed to their right to present alternatives to problems without being accused of being pushy or overstepping their bounds, nice girls tepidly put a problem on the table then tiptoe around it. No one likes a complainer—even if there's legitimacy to the expressed concerns.

Men complain among themselves, but rarely to management. It's that stiff upper lip thing that probably precludes them from wanting to be seen as a crybaby. Instead, either they suck it up when something bothers them or they strategically try to figure out a way to solve the problem or find a way around it. Women, on the other hand, take things to heart and often wind up making mountains out of molehills, much to the consternation of their male colleagues.

COACHING TIPS

• Never ever, ever complain. Instead, follow Winston Churchill's wise maxim: "Never ever ever give up." If something bothers you, identify what would make the situation better and then do it or propose it (but don't ask permission to do it!).

• Don't be duped into being the mouthpiece for the complaints of others. Even if there's a critical mass behind a concern, it doesn't mean *you* should be the one to bring it up. Do that enough times and you'll be seen as a malcontent. The exception is when it's your legitimate responsibility to take action on concerns because of your position or your role.

• If you don't have a clue how to solve a problem, approach others with it in the spirit of true problem solving by brainstorming and applying creativity to sticky situations.

ACTION ITEM

Chapter 7

How You Look

When I coach, I typically begin with behaviors that are easily identifiable—and changeable. This gives people a quick success, because others can readily observe the efforts they put into replacing self-defeating behaviors with more functional ones. This section examines the things you may unconsciously or habitually do that contribute to perceptions of being less capable and competent than you really are. Don't be fooled by the apparent simplicity of some of these mistakes. Few women make only one of them, and combining several *significantly* contributes to the appearance of diminished competence.

Let's start by dispelling the biggest myth of career mobility: "The best and the brightest are rewarded with promotions and choice assignments." Wrong. Those who possess a competitive degree of competence *and* look and sound the part of a professional are the ones who move fluidly through their careers. Competence is only table stakes. It's what gets you in the door. You're expected to be competent, but competence alone won't move you forward.

Many women, especially young women, bristle at the idea of being judged based on how they look. We may have an idealistic view of what *should* constitute success or simply reject Madison Avenue's depiction of what a woman should look like. It certainly presents a challenge for all of us who are far from a size 2 and don't have flawless complexions, blue eyes, and blond hair. On top of that, it's so subjective. Beauty is, after all, in the eye of the beholder. Still, there are some things we can do to look the part of a professional without feeling as if we're being inauthentic, and that's what is focused on in this chapter. As my friend and communications coach Tom Henschel says, "If everyone else comes to work looking like Monday morning and you come in looking like Friday night, it's not going to work for you in the long run."

As cited earlier, research shows that about 55 percent of your credibility comes from how you look. How you sound accounts for an additional 38 percent. Only 7 *percent* of your credibility is based on what you say. If you don't look the part, you won't be recognized as a competent professional—no matter how smart or educated you are. Fortunately, it's also one of the easiest things you can address on your path toward forging the impression that you are a credible and competent professional.

Mistake 99

Obvious Body Ink and Piercings

A huge shout-out and thank-you to Christine Yelda and the women at Genentech in south San Francisco for introducing me to the term *tramp stamp*. For those of you who, like me before I was enlightened, have no idea what it means, it's a derogatory term for a tattoo on a woman's lower back that shows between her pants and top when she bends over or if she wears revealing clothing. The buzz on the Internet is not particularly flattering to the women who sport them. *Urban Dictionary* claims, "Fair or unfair, these tattoos have a socially constructed connotation associated with them. These women are labeled as tramps, whores, or other derogatory sexually promiscuous terms."

How about tattoos on other parts of your body? I'll forgo the lecture about why in the world you'd want to have one. I know they're trendy and one wild evening out with your friends can result in one, but I gotta say you can't have them showing in *most* workplaces. Exceptions might be highly creative or artistic arenas.

Despite the fact that one in five adults now have tattoos, a study conducted by career website Vault.com suggests that 85 percent of respondents think that a tattoo or body piercing negatively affects a candidate's ability to get a job. Bryan Caplan, an economics professor at George Mason University, went so far as to suggest there's an inverse correlation between tattoos and lifetime earnings.

I had an interesting experience with a woman I hired a number of years ago. During the interview she wore long sleeves. Only after hiring her did I learn that those fabric sleeves covered up tattoo sleeves (her forearms were totally covered in ink). Had I seen those tattoos during the interview, I would have never hired her because I think they show poor judgment for people who want to be considered serious professionals. Similarly, I don't like people who hide things during the interview—whether it's a tattoo, being fired from a last job, or a drug problem. The fact that you're *hiding* something speaks for itself. In this woman's case, she turned out to be a disaster despite my best efforts to overlook the ink when I walked into the office. Her poor judgment was evident in her decision-making skills and the manner in which she interacted with clients and coworkers. She didn't make it past the ninety-day probationary period.

The real question is, do you want tattoos or piercings to be what people are talking about? Do you really want them to define your brand?

COACHING TIPS

• Don't get a tattoo or an unusual body piercing if you've had even *one* drink, toke, or snort. You'll be likely to regret it. Similarly, don't be goaded into getting one by your sorority sisters, girlfriends, or someone you're dating who thinks they're hot.

• If you just have to get a tattoo or piercing, put it in a place *no one* at work will ever see. One woman who worked for me knew how I felt about visible tattoos in a consulting office. It took her months to get up the nerve to show me where she put one—on the nape of her neck, covered up by her long hair worn down during working hours! As long as I didn't see it...

• If you already have prominent tattoos or piercings, hide them during the workday. If it means you have to sweat all summer in long-sleeved blouses, so be it. It's the price you pay for being part of this trend.

ACTION ITEM

Mistake 100

Smiling Inappropriately

We reached the point in a Leadership Skills for Women workshop where we were discussing how to get people to take us more seriously. A petite Asian woman, an engineer from the Jet Propulsion Laboratory in Pasadena, California, raised her hand to question why her male colleagues ignored her input. When she finished, a ripple of laughter crossed the room. The reason was obvious to the rest of us: The entire time she spoke, she displayed a rather large (and inappropriate) smile.

Girls are socialized to smile more than boys. Parents smile more at girl babies than at boy babies. When men don't smile, they're taken seriously. When women don't smile, we're often asked, "What's wrong?" It's no wonder we aren't even aware when we smile at the wrong times.

COACHING TIPS

- Pay more attention to when you're smiling. I constantly coach women to "watch the smile."
- Consciously match your facial expression to your message. Aim for congruence between your body language and your message.
- Before delivering serious messages, rehearse in front of a mirror. This will give you a better idea of when you're smiling inappropriately.
- Don't quit smiling entirely—it contributes to your likability quotient, and likability is a critical factor in achieving success.
- Be discriminating about how and when you choose to smile. For example, a smile can be intentionally used to soften a less serious message or to convey empathy.

ACTION ITEM

Mistake 101

Taking Up Too Little Space

*T*he use of space is one way we make a statement about our confidence and sense of entitlement. The more space you take up, the more confident you appear. The next time you're on an airplane, take a look at the differences between how men and women sit. Whereas men sit down and spread out using both armrests, women tend to keep their elbows tucked in close to their sides, trying not to take up too much space. Another place to observe this is on elevators. Most people, men and women alike, are conscious of making room for others as they enter. As the elevator gets crowded, however, it's more likely you'll see a woman cower in a corner for fear of taking up too much space.

The same phenomenon often occurs when a woman steps in front of a room to make a presentation. She tends to stand in one place, moving only slightly within the space she occupies. When you combine taking up too little space with using too few gestures, the overwhelming impression conveyed is that of being demure, careful, unwilling to take risks, timid, or frightened, with little to contribute.

COACHING TIPS

• When giving a presentation, use the full amount of space available to you by slowly walking side to side, forward and back. Even if you're on a large stage, you should come out from behind the podium to take up about 75 percent of the space available.

• Choose a seat at a meeting that will give you freedom to move around. Don't sit where you'll be forced to keep your elbows glued to your sides. Keeping your elbows on the table and leaning in slightly conveys a message of being more alert to what's being said. The exception is if you have to pull a chair up to squeeze into the table, as I described earlier.

• When standing in front of a group, stand with your feet about as far apart as your shoulders are wide.

• When seated, use the coaching tips on gestures provided with the next mistake to appear more expansive and less constrained.

• Request a lavaliere or handheld microphone when one is needed. It will allow you to move about more freely than if you have to speak into a stationary microphone.

ACTION ITEM

Mistake 102

Using Gestures Inconsistent with Your Message

𝒯he use of gestures is an outgrowth of not taking up enough space. Like all other parts of your self-presentation, gestures should be integrated with your energy. If you're working to make your presence larger and to take up more space, working on your gesturing is an easy way to begin. The problem is, most women have never learned the art of gesturing. It's little wonder why. We've been taught to sit demurely with our hands folded in our laps. When we have used gestures, we've been given the message that we're too emotional. For fear of being called unladylike or emotional, we've let the pendulum swing the other way—no gestures.

Comedian Joan Rivers is an example of someone who takes up lots of space with her gestures because she wants to convey the message of being larger than life. Her hair, makeup, and gestures all contribute to this impression. Unless you do stand-up comedy, I wouldn't recommend that you emulate her.

Hillary Rodham Clinton, on the other hand, uses the prototypical gestures of a politician. She appears tense and almost too conscious of the use of gestures and often reverts to being an "ax gesturer." You know the move. It's when points are emphasized using repetitive karate-chop-like gestures. Predictable, consistent gestures distract from the message.

Gestures should complement, not detract from, your message. A woman who does this well is Christine Lagarde, head of the International Monetary Fund (IMF). Her communications, including her gestures, convey the message of authority while simultaneously maintaining her elegance and natural femininity. The next time you see her on television, turn off the sound and just watch her. You'll see that she nonverbally communicates a sense of confidence without the brashness of Rivers or the rehearsed look of Clinton.

COACHING TIPS

- Allow your gestures to flow naturally from your spoken message and your energy.
- Be aware of when you wring your hands because you're anxious—and stop.
- Match your gestures to the size of your audience. The larger the group, the larger the gesture.
- Emphasize your points by enumerating them with your fingers (one, two, three).
- Communication consultant Tom Henschel advises clients to use gestures that "break the silhouette." That is, when you stand with your hands at your sides or in front of you, your silhouette shows no gestures. When you work on taking up more space, your gestures should move outside the line of that silhouette. You can do this whether you're sitting at a conference table or standing in a doorway having a chat.
- Put energy into your gestures and enjoy taking up the space!

ACTION ITEM

Mistake 103

Being Over- or Underanimated

$\mathcal{A}$ communication colleague—Allen Weiner, president of Communication Development Associates in Woodland Hills, California—uses the term *carbonation* to refer to a person's degree of animation, which includes not only gestures, but also facial expressions, speed of talking, and other forms of body language. We've all listened to and watched people who are overcarbonated. They look and sound as if they're a can of soda that was shaken before being opened. Not only is this distracting, but it makes the person appear less confident than he or she may actually be. My contention is that women, more than men, are guilty of overcarbonation because we feel responsible for making everyone happy. As a result, women go out of bounds by putting more verbal and nonverbal energy into everything we do.

Conversely, if a woman has previously been given the message that she's too bubbly or emotional, she can fall into the trap of appearing undercarbonated, or flat and unanimated. In an effort to conceal her natural ebullience, she causes the pendulum to swing the other way. We ascribe characteristics such as low-energy, aloof, boring (or bored), or depressed to such people.

The friendship between actresses Carol Burnett and Julie Andrews often puts them on the same stage, where we observe Burnett's overcarbonation as a counterpoint to Andrews's undercarbonation. Especially early in Burnett's career, her exaggerated facial expressions and body movements contributed to her success as a popular comedian. In comparison, Andrews is less animated, more cautious, and ever the demure lady. Neither set of behaviors conveys the message most professional women want to project.

COACHING TIPS

• If you tend to be undercarbonated, speak more loudly. It's a natural way of increasing your animation.

• Because overcarbonation can result from anxiety, practice deep breathing and other relaxation techniques that will reduce overly animated behavior.

• Consciously strive to strike a balance between over- and under-carbonation. One way to do this is to observe yourself on a video-tape with the sound off. If you were standing outside the meeting, looking through a glass partition, how would you describe the woman you see?

ACTION ITEM

Mistake 104

Tilting Your Head

This is a small mistake with a big impact. The tilt of a head in conversation has the impact of softening a message. It's almost always used to either imply a question, signal that you're listening, or encourage the other person to respond. Women tilt their heads significantly more than men in conversation, and in this regard a head tilt can be a good thing. When trying to convey a direct message, however, it can be interpreted as uncertainty or a lack of commitment to what you're saying—even when you're dead sure of it. It's another one of those ways women have learned to communicate difficult messages in a socially acceptable but less assertive way.

The best place to observe this is on television where people are interviewed. On Sunday-morning programs such as *Face the Nation*, *This Week*, or *Meet the Press*, you don't see too many head tilts—by either the hosts or the guests. The topics are often of national and international importance, and therefore participants in these discussions typically want to convey a sense of seriousness.

But if you watch skilled interviewers such as Barbara Walters, Oprah Winfrey, or Katie Couric conduct interviews in which they really want a guest to open up, they effectively use tilting of their heads. They can ask the most personal questions and get away with it because, in part, the tilt of the head makes guests feel as if the host is really interested in what they're saying. Conversely, notice how these women lose the head tilt when they want to be taken seriously.

So the message here is not to stop tilting your head entirely. But do be aware of when you might do it at difficult moments as a means of softening a message that shouldn't be softened.

COACHING TIPS

• When conveying a serious message, avoid tilting your head. Look at the person straight on and in the eye.

• Use a head tilt to your advantage—such as when you're listening and want the other person to open up or when you want to convey that you understand how the other person may feel.

• A head tilt can also be used to bridge an uncomfortable silence—as if to say, "Take your time. I'm listening."

ACTION ITEM

Mistake 105

Wearing Inappropriate Makeup

*M*akeup is tricky. On the one hand, I don't want to perpetuate Madison Avenue's image of what a woman should look like. On the other, I know it's something people notice when it's too heavy or too light. I once asked the boss of a woman scientist for feedback about what she could do to overcome existing barriers to promotion. He thoughtfully explained how she could be more strategic, speak up more in meetings, and be a stronger advocate for her staff. After an uncomfortable silence, I suggested it seemed he had something to add. Somewhat sheepishly he said, "Maybe she could start wearing makeup." You can hear that comment as just another sexist remark— or as a valuable insight into what people expect as you climb the corporate ladder.

I was once shopping in Palm Springs, California, when I noticed a woman who was heavily made-up. Turning to a friend, I nodded and commented, "She looks like a caricature of Tammy Faye Bakker." As we approached the checkout line and I saw her husband at the time, Jim Bakker, join her, I realized it was Tammy Faye Bakker. In business you don't want to use the late Ms. Bakker or Lady Gaga as your makeup role model. Makeup is an accessory similar to a piece of jewelry or a scarf. People do notice it. Wearing too little can diminish your credibility as much as wearing too much.

COACHING TIPS

- Go to the makeup counter of a high-end department store and ask a salesperson (whom you consider to be appropriately made-up) for a free consultation.

- Ask a trusted colleague or friend who wears makeup that complements her features if she would be willing to give you feedback on yours.

- If you tend not to wear makeup, begin by using small amounts as recommended by a friend or consultant.

- Go to a Mary Kay or Avon consultant for helpful makeup hints.

- Stand with your back to a mirror and quickly turn around and look at your face. What's the first thing you notice? That may well be the place to use less—or more—makeup.

ACTION ITEM

Mistake 106

The Wrong Hairstyle

$\mathcal{H}$ air. Can't live with it. Can't live without it. Who hasn't struggled with a bad cut, not quite the right color, or just a bad hair day? Losing all of mine in 2006 during chemotherapy to treat breast cancer gave me an entirely new relationship with my hair—now I'm just glad that I have it!

The most common mistake I see women make is to wear their hair too long. One of the consultants in our office tells the story of when she received her doctorate in organization development and asked a physician in senior management at the hospital where she worked for feedback about how she could get a promotion she wanted. Looking at her beautiful, waist-length strawberry-blond hair, he replied, "Lose the Alice in Wonderland look."

I may not like how he gave her the feedback, but, as they say, feedback is a gift. In a predominantly male environment, long hair diminished her credibility by emphasizing her femininity. We'll never know if she got that promotion because she cut her hair—but even she agrees that cutting it made a difference in how people treated her.

COACHING TIPS

- Don't scrimp when it comes to finding a good hairdresser. A low-price leader may not be the best place to find a highly skilled professional.
- There's an inverse proportion of hair to age. Typically, your hair should get increasingly shorter as you get older and go higher on the

corporate ladder. Not only is shorter hair more professional, but longer hair tends to emphasize facial features of which we may be less proud as we age.

- If you don't want to cut your hair, wear it up to give it the appearance of being shorter.
- Hair, like makeup, is an accessory. Make certain it complements the rest of your appearance.
- If your hair is graying, consider a good colorist. Whereas gray or graying hair on men is viewed as distinguished, women aren't typically afforded the same compliment unless it's a pure white color and well-styled.
- Mary Mitchell, in an article titled "Dress for Success: 9 Tips for Professional-Looking Hair," offers these two tips:

1. Skip the Pat Benatar look. Heavily sprayed, scrunched, and gelled hair can be "the equivalent of wearing a skirt slit up to the thigh," says Jennie Brooks, stylist for Ovations Salon in Philadelphia. Instead, she suggests products that provide a softer, more polished look that won't distract from your professionalism. "It's possible to have an edge while still being professional. Think of an altogether polished look."

2. Match your style to the vibe of your workplace, no matter what level you're at. At the prestigious Hotel Bel-Air in L.A., all employees are required to look sophisticated and yet low-key (so they fit in but don't rival the star-studded guests). The director of human resources, Antoinette Lara, tells employees, "Think about how you'd wear your hair at a club on a Saturday night. Then do the opposite when you come to work."

ACTION ITEM

Mistake 107

Inappropriate Attire

*T*he workplace casual trend has made professional attire a bit more complicated. It used to be simple. Women wore dresses or suits to work. With workplace casual now the norm on days more than just Fridays, the margin for error increases. Interestingly, just recently the newly appointed CEO of a major food manufacturer made one of his first edicts to do away with workplace casual. When I inquired why he would want this to be his initial foray into his role, the employee I was speaking with said that he thought coming to work dressed casually on Friday makes you think you've already started the weekend and productivity goes down.

It's the same rationale I used nearly twenty years ago for why I didn't like workplace casual on *any* day of the week. Then a friend pointed out to me that at companies like Google and Apple, employees dress casually all of the time, and you can't say those companies aren't productive and showing huge returns to their investors. But I still say, follow the maxim "Dress for the job you want, not the job you have," and you won't go wrong. Short skirts, seductive clothing, stiletto heels, unshined shoes, and ill-fitting or wrinkled clothes won't get you where you want to be—at least not in the business world. Like it or not, people notice not only the style of clothes we wear, but also their quality. Even when your office subscribes to what one client of mine calls *casual intensity.*

Are there exceptions to the rule? Absolutely. There's a brokerage firm I work with that has a fairly strict and conservative unspoken dress code. When I coach women from this organization and the issue of dress comes up, as a way of arguing the point they inevitably bring up one woman who breaks every single rule of dress outlined above. I mean every rule. And to this I reply, "She's the exception, and not many of us get away with being exceptions." It just so happens the woman is superb at what she does, has been with the company for many years, and is known for being eccentric. Not only her dress but also her behavior is tolerated because of the value she adds. Most of us wouldn't get away with it—and shouldn't even try.

Can how you dress be a deal buster for hiring, promotions, and assignments that you want? Yes. It's the kind of thing that, when you get it right, you get no credit for, but when you get it wrong, people notice. Again, as my colleague Tom Henschel says, "If everyone else comes to work looking like Monday morning and you come to work looking like Friday night, there's a problem."

COACHING TIPS

- Look around at the successful women in senior positions in your organization. That's how *you* should dress.
- Nicole Balkenbusch, senior financial analyst at Procter and Gamble, offers this tip: If you wonder whether or not something is appropriate to wear to work, it most likely isn't—so don't.
- Even if your office subscribes to workplace casual, dress just a little better than most of the people around you.
- When you know you're going to be making a presentation to management or clients, dress to impress. You'll rarely go wrong.
- Go to the department that sells professional women's clothing in Nordstrom, Bloomingdale's, or other similar stores and ask for fashion advice.
- View clothes purchases as an investment in your future. Budget enough money to buy several really good outfits a year. When you feel good in clothes, you act more confidently.
- Have your color chart done. Wearing colors that complement your natural features has a bigger impact than you might think.

- Freelance writer Wendy Allen (@WendyCAllen on Twitter) offers this advice to young women looking to establish a great work wardrobe:

Invest in these items first, as they offer the most versatility and will help anyone look professional from the get-go.

- o Dress pants: Dress pants are likely to get the most wear out of anything in your work wardrobe, so it's essential to choose a style that suits you and get them tailored to fit. Wool blends will be the most durable, and every woman should own at least three pairs in neutrals like khaki, navy, brown, gray, or black to take her through the week.
- o Blazer: A dressy jacket is another wardrobe basic that every woman needs, as it can instantly make any outfit look more professional and serious. While brown and beige can work, most experts advise going with black, gray, or navy.
- o Pencil skirt: A black pencil or A-line skirt is an excellent wardrobe staple. You can pair it with everything from a sweater to a suit jacket to adjust the formality of the look. If black is too boring for you, colors like navy and gray can also be good choices.
- o White shirts: Crisp, white shirts are essential for completing your professional look. While the classic tailored look is best, you could also add a few shirts that incorporate ruffles or short sleeves to mix things up. Add two to four of these to your wardrobe, and ensure that the fit is perfect, as you don't want any gaping or buttons coming undone at the office.
- o Black heels: Work-appropriate shoes are one area where you should feel comfortable spending a little more, as comfort is key when you'll be wearing a pair of shoes all day, every day. Look for high-quality leather pumps in black, with a mid-height heel. Ideally, they should be closed-toe, as that look is both comfortable and professional. You can always branch out later.

o A suit: If your workplace is formal or conservative, then you'll need to invest in a suit or two to take you through the week. Suits can actually be a great investment, as you can wear each piece separately, too, so you can get a lot of mileage out of a single suit. To start out, choose a suit in a solid black, navy, or gray. Later, when you're ready to get an additional suit, you can branch out and play with color and pattern. Like with dress pants, fit really matters on suits, so make sure to invest in alterations if necessary.

o Dressy tops: A few dressy tops should also become a key part of your workweek wardrobe. Solid colors or prints can be paired with blazers and suits to build outfits that can easily transition from the workplace to a night out.

o Leather belt: When starting out your wardrobe, you'll need at least one black leather belt to pair with suits and dress pants. Later on, you can add belts that cinch around your natural waist and can be worn over shirts, cardigans, and dresses.

ACTION ITEM

Mistake 108

Sitting on Your Foot

I'm not sure I would have thought of this one myself. It comes from Dr. Doug Andrews, chair of the Department of Business Communication at the University of Southern California. He has the opportunity to observe students, both young and older than average, in his classes. He described it as "this thing women do when sitting where they tuck one foot up underneath them." Dr. Andrews is absolutely right when he says it's something that he never sees men do and that it conveys the impression of being a little girl rather than a professional woman. I was recently in an antiques store where I was drawn to a photograph from the early 1900s of a six- or seven-year-old girl posed for her portrait. She had one foot tucked under her, and it softened both her and the picture.

You can also observe this phenomenon on television talk shows. A guest comes out, sits in the chair next to the host, and tucks her foot up beneath her. Can you imagine former Secretary of State General Colin Powell, Microsoft CEO Steve Ballmer, or New York Mayor Michael Bloomberg doing this? It's almost always a woman guest who does it, and she does it out of discomfort or shyness. It may be cute, but it's not professional.

COACHING TIPS

- It's simple. If you want to be taken seriously, sit with both feet on the floor with knees together. In a more relaxed situation, cross your legs at the knee. Never sit with your foot tucked beneath you.
- Remember, being "grounded" requires "both feet on the ground."

ACTION ITEM

Mistake 109

Grooming in Public

*W*hen was the last time you saw a man pull out a mirror and check his hair after lunch? (Well, okay, John Edwards did do a little primping.) How about file his nails during a meeting? Even the thought of it is ridiculous. No matter how discreet you think you're being, grooming in public is noticed and mentally logged by those around you.

Another habit (often unconscious) that women often reveal is that of flipping long hair behind the ears. It may be when she looks down to read something or it may be used as a coy, flirtatious gesture. Take a moment to think about a group of people who "play with" their hair. If you came up with teenagers, you're right. Flipping your hair behind your ears makes you appear less mature than you really are. Public primping emphasizes your femininity and detracts from your credibility. Real women avoid PDG (public displays of grooming).

COACHING TIPS

• Never comb your hair or apply lipstick in public. If you can't resist, excuse yourself and go to the ladies' room.

• If you do go to the ladies' room to primp, keep it quick. Don't keep people waiting. Better yet, wait until you get back to the office.

• If you see your reflection in a mirror or glassy surface and notice something wrong, avoid the inclination to fix it there. Wait until you can do so in private.

• Avoid touching your hair unnecessarily. Think in terms of *Every time I touch my hair, I reduce my credibility by one year.*

ACTION ITEM ☐

Mistake 110

Sitting in Meetings with Your Hands Under the Table

*S*itting in meetings is not the same as sitting at the dinner table. You don't have to follow the rules learned in childhood for keeping your elbows off the table. Observe how men sit at meetings. When they're speaking, confident men almost always lean in with their elbows and hands resting on the table. When men begin listening to something that intrigues them, you can picture them sitting with their elbows on the table, chin resting on their clasped hands.

And what do we do? We often do as we were taught—sit coyly with our hands folded in our laps or under the table. The difference is striking. As uncomfortable as it may be at first, when it comes to being taken seriously, all research points to the need to "put it on the table."

COACHING TIPS

- In meetings, lean forward slightly, resting your forearms on the table with hands lightly clasped. Not only does this make you look more involved in the conversation, but it also puts you in a perfect position to gesture when needed.

- While we're on the subject of meetings, let me slip in two more tips. Whenever possible, select a seat next to the most powerful person in the room. For some unknown reason, that person's power permeates those around him or her. It also conveys the message that you're not afraid of power.

- Don't be afraid to sit at the head of a long or oval table. Again, this isn't the Thanksgiving dinner table. From the head of the table, you can see everyone in the room, and, just as important, everyone can see you.

ACTION ITEM

Mistake 111

Wearing Your Reading Glasses Around Your Neck

*T*his habit surely had to start with some librarian in the 1950s. Why is it that women, not men, buy those little chains to hang reading glasses around their necks? Are we more apt to lose our glasses than men, or are we just more willing to call attention to the fact that we're aging? In some department stores you'll even find these chains displayed as accessories. In the name of full disclosure, I must admit that since the first edition of *Corner Office* was released, I have taken to using one of these chains for my own reading glasses. *But*... I never use it in professional situations, but only when I'm shopping, on an airplane, or working at home so that I don't lose them.

At a workshop on developing presentation skills there was one woman, apparently in her mid-fifties, who held on to her reading glasses throughout her videotaped half-hour practice session. Not only did she hold on to them, but she also twirled them while listening to questions from the audience. Never once did she actually put them on—leading me to believe they were more a prop than a requirement.

At the risk of sounding ageist, I need to say once again that, unlike men, it's the rare woman who finds her credibility increasing with age. I'm on a one-way campaign to change this by attempting to be a role model for how to age with grace, so although I don't think it's something to hide or lie about, I also don't think it's necessary to emphasize it.

- If you're concerned about being able to read your notes during a presentation, type them in a font large enough to see without glasses. Using a PowerPoint presentation will also serve to keep you on target with your topic without having to put your glasses on and take them off.

- If you need a prop, use a marker or a pencil. There's nothing wrong with holding it; just take care not to tap, twirl, or click it, thereby creating a distraction from your message.

- A trick my ophthalmologist taught me is to wear a pair of plain glasses with the readers on the bottom. Even though I wear contact lenses to camouflage my severe nearsightedness, I wear the glasses over them so that I'm not continually putting on and taking off my readers.

- Since we're on the subject of glasses, keep in mind that they can be used as a prop to make you appear more mature if you have difficulty with being taken seriously because you look too young. Even if you don't require corrected vision, a pair with nonprescription glass can give you the appearance of being a bit more mature.

ACTION ITEM

Mistake 112

Accessorizing Too Much

$\mathcal{A}$ccessories can be your best friend—or your worst enemy. I once watched a videoconference in which former secretary of state Madeleine Albright was a keynote speaker. She wore a lovely tailored dress—totally appropriate for the event—but she had on her trademark huge pin. To me, this detracted from her message: Throughout the presentation, I found myself focusing more on trying to figure out what the pin was than on what she was saying.

I've learned to use accessories to manage the impression I often give that I'm very serious. In an effort to convey an impression of more levity, I accessorize with playful pins. One that frequently gets attention is of three women with wild hair and colorful dresses, arm in arm. It's my way of getting across the message that I may be serious, but I like to have fun as much as the next person. Of course if I'd been given feedback that I was too jocular, my tactic would be different.

Carefully chosen, accessories add style and personality to otherwise conservative corporate attire. They convey a message about you that may not be heard through your words and presence alone. But when inappropriate or overdone, they detract from your credibility. Accessories make a statement. Consider what you want yours to be.

COACHING TIPS

- Don't wear long, dangling earrings to work. Depending on your size and hair length, aim for posts—no larger than the size of a quarter.
- Add an inexpensive pearl necklace and earrings to your accessory kit. They never go out of style.
- Match accessories to not only your outfit, but also what you will be doing that day. A whimsical pin might be appropriate for a day in the office when you're meeting only with colleagues, but not necessarily for one when you're making a strategic planning presentation.
- Similarly, the bigger the group you're speaking to, the bolder the accessories can be. Just be certain not to make the same mistake as Secretary Albright.
- Do the same as was suggested in the section on makeup tips. Turn your back to the mirror and quickly swing around. Does anything stand out about your accessories? If so, consider changing it.

ACTION ITEM

Mistake 113

Poor Eye Contact

*T*here are a number of factors that contribute to the tendency to avoid another person's eyes. In some cultures it's a sign of respect to look away when speaking with someone who is older or has more authority or stature than you. There's research that suggests avoiding eye contact is a sign of deception. Children won't look at us when they know they've done something wrong or when they're being scolded.

When a woman avoids eye contact, it's usually a sure sign that she's uncomfortable or unsure of herself. If the eyes are the window to the soul, then you must use them to allow others to see your sincerity, self-confidence, and knowledge, and to see the other person's. A good place to observe this behavior is on television when someone like Ann Curry or even Ellen DeGeneres conducts an interview. Both of these women have learned the art of eye contact. Note how they look people directly in the eye, especially when asking difficult questions. Similarly, note that when they're embarrassed or someone has said something that catches them off guard, they look away. What also makes these women so good at what they do is that by looking the other person in the eye, they often get a sense of what he or she is thinking and base the next question on this. You don't have to be a television interviewer to use eye contact to your advantage.

COACHING TIPS

• When you go to the movies, observe how the more self-confident female characters use their eyes to convey a message. Make a mental note of the specific behaviors that contribute to this impression.

• If you have been given the feedback that you have a tendency to stare, get into the habit of looking slightly up or to the side when thinking about a response. This creates a break in the eye contact long enough to convey a comfortable pause.

• When greeting someone, be certain to look him or her in the eye. It puts you on an even footing with the person.

ACTION ITEM

Chapter 8

How You Respond

So far we've looked at the behaviors in which you actively engage that detract from or diminish your credibility. In this last section we'll examine how you respond to the ways others treat you. Often these responses are so automatic that we don't consider the ramifications they may have on us and our careers. Similarly, they can be formed by old experiences and interactions that are no longer relevant in the present.

For example, many women have been socialized to respond to inappropriate treatment in a polite, docile, or acquiescent way. One tragic example of this is a woman who told me what happened to her at a movie when she was about seven or eight years old. She and her older cousins routinely went to a Saturday matinee. One Saturday a man sat down next to her and began to molest her. She allowed this to continue for several minutes then told her cousins she wanted to change seats, but not why. When they moved, the man moved along with them and began doing it again. She became immobilized. She allowed it to happen until the movie was over.

In relating the story many years later, she wondered why she hadn't told him to stop or asked her cousins for help. Sadly, her response isn't unusual for women. We're not taught to defend ourselves or get angry when someone is disrespectful to us. In my book *Women, Anger, and Depression: Strategies for Self-Empowerment* (Health Communications), I contrast the messages little boys are given regarding anger to those given to little girls. Whereas boys are typically taught the art of self-defense, girls are taught to turn the other cheek. As a result, we're more likely to tolerate behavior we should never allow to happen. Unlearning those early childhood messages is a huge step on the path to living an empowered life.

Mistake 114

Airing Your Feelings in Online Public Forums

In 2009 Dawnmarie Souza, a paramedic in Connecticut, used Facebook to call her boss a "scumbag" and suggest in unflattering terms that he wasn't qualified to be a supervisor. The company had a policy that prohibited employees from using the Internet to say derogatory things about coworkers and the company, and she was promptly fired. Then the National Labor Relations Board (NLRB) found out about the termination and, believing that the policy was overly broad, filed a complaint against the company. The NLRB ultimately found that the policy violated the National Labor Relations Act, giving employees the right to "discuss the terms and conditions of their employment with others."

This is one that I definitely did not have to address a decade ago. Even if the laws are changing to protect your First Amendment right to free speech, it's just plain foolish to use social media to air your grievances—against *anyone*. It's a pitfall more for women than men because (1) we tend to be more emotional; (2) we use social media more; and (3) we want to show our support for others. Pamela Mitchell, Founder of the Reinvention Institute, whom I mentioned earlier, was telling me about a client of hers who has a bad habit of using her Facebook page to address every bone she has to pick with others. Whereas in the past people would pick up the phone and commiserate with a friend to get something off their chests, now they post their feelings on Facebook and get immediate reinforcement from their friends and colleagues.

As early as middle school, mean girls are using social media to write awful things about one another. It's the twenty-first-century version of the *slam book*—a notebook that was passed around in which students would make comments about kids they didn't like. This extends into adulthood with technology that has made it possible to say anything you want about someone else and in a matter of seconds have it distributed to hundreds of people in your network. The obvious problem is, it's also available for viewing by anyone with access to a computer.

COACHING TIPS

• Don't use social media as your personal pulpit for punishment. It will almost always come back to bite you.

• If you've got a gripe, go directly to the person. This is what grown-ups do. They don't talk behind people's backs or make anonymous comments. They give others the courtesy of being able to respond to their grievances. And if that fails, they move on.

• If you've got a legitimate beef with a company or institution with which you do business, use a recognized public forum such as tripadvisor.com, yelp.com, or angieslist.com to factually explain your concerns.

ACTION ITEM

Mistake 115

Putting a Stamp on with a Steamroller

*A*nother complaint men have about some women is that they never know if they're going to get Dr. Jekyll or Mr. Hyde. The inability to predict someone's reactions is one of the largest factors contributing to mistrust. We trust people who are consistent with us. They can be consistently nice to us or rude to us; it really doesn't matter. Either way, you come to trust how this person will treat you.

In many cases, inconsistent behavior is not the by-product of indecision, but rather the result of holding things in for too long. Nice girls can be like those old-fashioned radiators that operated on steam. If you let the steam build up for too long, the radiator would explode. When a nice girl finally has had enough and can't take it any longer, she blows up—and often at something that's inconsequential. There's a reason for the saying "It's the straw that broke the camel's back."

When this happens, we can be described as putting a stamp on with a steamroller. Far too much emotion for what the situation warrants. People then wonder about how rational we are, make assumptions about what time of the month it is, or question our mental stability. I recall once when I had a private practice of psychotherapy, I was working with a woman who was severely depressed. She held everything in, finding it too risky to say what she really wanted or needed at home and at work. Then one day her husband called in a panic and said, "You have to do something! She's gone crazy. She's breaking every dish in the house!" And that was her first step on the path to being more mentally healthy than she had ever been before in her life.

COACHING TIPS

• Take more risks around regularly saying what's really on your mind. When you hold too much in for too long, you're going to either be depressed or at some point (and usually not an opportune one) explode. Expressing yourself in the moment, or close to it, allows you to hold an adult conversation rather than throw a hissy fit.

• Give yourself permission to not react in the moment, but rather revisit an issue after you've had time to cool off. Women tell me all the time that they just can't think of what to say as a retort and as a result wind up feeling badly about an encounter they had with someone. You don't have to be quick on your feet, but you do owe it to yourself and those with whom you interact to circle back as soon as possible after an incident to discuss how you felt and what you'd like to see happen differently in the future.

• Trust your emotions. Many times we think we're making mountains out of molehills, so we overlook things that we actually have strong feelings about. Pretty soon all of those things we *thought* we had let go of become the straw that breaks the camel's back. Even if you don't address an issue directly with the person who caused you to have the feeling, you can talk to a friend about your reaction and use that as an opportunity to let off steam.

• For difficult conversations, practice using the DESCript method in Mistake 91. It really is a great tool to help you prepare what you want to say in a way that encourages dialogue and diminishes the likelihood of a blowup.

ACTION ITEM

Mistake 116

Holding a Grudge

*A*s the saying goes, "Hell hath no fury like a woman scorned." When I said this in a public forum I was accused of being sexist. Look, I didn't invent the saying; I'm just letting you know what people think when you can't move beyond a real or imagined slight.

A number of years ago I was brought in to do conflict resolution with two very talented women who could not stand to be in the same room with each other. This presented a dilemma for the boss (a male), who needed them to work collaboratively due to the fact that their roles in the company had some overlap. All he wanted them to do was play nicely together in the sandbox, and all each of them wanted was to be left alone by the other. Their behavior not only made his life miserable but also reflected negatively on him when his management would ask, "Can't you control your staff?"

I first met with each woman individually to get her perspective on the situation. As is usual in these cases, the story was like dual sides of the same coin, each with her own personal spin on what had transpired to result in a standoff. Then came what they thought would be the painful part, getting them in the same room to start the healing process. And here's how grudges can dissipate: *don't focus on the past; focus on what you need to move forward.* The only ground rule I have for conflict resolution sessions is that you can't rehash what happened in the past. It does absolutely no good. You've probably obsessed over the other person's transgressions for days, weeks, or months. Moving on requires you to identify what you want *and* need from the other person and what you have to offer them. The following coaching tips build on this premise.

COACHING TIPS

- Don't let slights fester. It's how they grow into seemingly unsolvable problems. Although an immediate, knee-jerk response to a slight is often counterproductive, sleeping on it and addressing it the next day should give you enough time to plan your communication.

- When addressing what you perceive to be a slight, start from a place that assumes the best of intentions rather than the worst. Most emotionally healthy people don't want to hurt your feelings. They do so in a moment of not thinking, haste, or frustration. Cut people a little slack until you learn their intentions.

- Prepare in advance for meetings that are designed to clear the air. Don't wing it. First, enter the discussion with a clear statement about your feelings concerning what transpired (not with a description of what happened). Something like "I was really embarrassed when you announced in front of the entire team that my department came in last for sales this quarter before you had the discussion with me." Next, let the other person know what you need from them in the future. This might sound like "What would be helpful for me to remain motivated and keep my team motivated as well is for you to give me a heads-up when those numbers come in so that I can discuss them with the sales folks." Finally, let the other person know what you have to give to them in return: "If you'll just do this, you have my word that I'll work vigorously to meet our sales quotas next quarter."

- Once you have this discussion, let it go by focusing on the future.

ACTION ITEM

Mistake 117

Internalizing Messages

*P*arents are guilty of giving children all kinds of messages that they carry with them for a lifetime. Not all of these are negative, but they do impact our self-esteem and how we see ourselves in the world. Whether it's "You're just like your father—you'll never amount to anything," or "You're such a sweet girl. You're going to grow up and get married and have lots of children," the message sets the stage for a self-fulfilling prophecy.

The messages are also not always verbal. Sometimes they're implicit expectations for how you should behave. Much of my coaching work begins with helping clients get in touch with those early-childhood messages and examine the impact they have on the present. Our greatest strengths are often learned in response to implicit and explicit parental expectations or demands. As a result, we tend to overrely on these and are reluctant to relinquish ones that are no longer effective.

Let me give you an example. Claudia was the oldest of seven children in her family. Both parents were alcoholic and depended on her to help raise the younger kids. As with many children who come from alcoholic homes, she was hypervigilant, very responsible, and quite protective of her siblings. No one told her she had to do this; she just did. These same behaviors served Claudia well early in her career. Her supervisors appreciated how she would show initiative, take new team members under her wing and show them the ropes, and always be on top of potential problems or barriers to achieving departmental goals.

Later in her career, however, these identical behaviors kept her from reaching her full potential. What was once viewed as being on top of problems was now described as being too critical. Whereas her willingness to take new people under her wing was once appreciated, now she was seen as intrusive and overly controlling. And one of her greatest strengths, initiative, was now interpreted as "grandstanding"—trying to get the best projects for herself.

Claudia had internalized the messages of childhood all too well—even though they were never actually verbalized. This will give you an idea of how well we must internalize verbal messages. Our work with Claudia was not to get her to stop doing all those things that served her well early in her career, but rather to provide her with a set of alternative behaviors from which she could choose when the situation called for it. For example, rather than always volunteering for difficult assignments, she needed to be more conscious of who else might benefit by learning from this project. And rather than being quick to point out mistakes, she might let some of the smaller ones go so that others could learn from them and not view her as quite so nitpicky.

COACHING TIPS

• Ask yourself which lesson learned in childhood contributes to your greatest strength and what complementary behaviors may be required to balance the strength.

• There's a tape that plays in our heads with childhood messages. When the messages on that tape hold you back from achieving your goals, use self-talk to tape over it. Consider therapy if the messages are so strong that you have difficulty taping over them.

• Post in a conspicuous place and frequently recite Eleanor Roosevelt's famous maxim: "No one can make you feel inferior without your consent."

ACTION ITEM

Mistake 118

Believing Others Know More Than You

*B*etty is an organization development consultant with her own practice. For many years prior to forming her consultancy, she was an organization development manager at the corporate headquarters of a nationally known fast-food chain. Between the two experiences, she can legitimately be called an expert in her field. One day she met with a prospective client who wanted to talk to her about doing a team-building session. As this aggressive, know-it-all executive laid out the problem, Betty began to think it wasn't team building he needed, but a conflict resolution intervention between two employees.

After the executive finished explaining what he wanted and why he wanted it, Betty suggested that team building might not be the appropriate path to take. She pointed out that when there is conflict between two employees and you do a team-building program, you may not get the results you want and needlessly include other team members in their dispute. The executive wouldn't listen. He had used consultants in the past for situations such as these, and he knew how they worked. He was certain the situation would be improved through the team building.

As with many consultants, Betty had to weigh the client's wishes against her best professional judgment. Does she walk away from the business opportunity to prove her point, or could she possibly help this group using the methodology demanded by the client? In the end she opted for the latter and facilitated a two-day off-site for the executive's department of twelve staff members. She thought that perhaps he was right—he made a convincing case for the off-site, and Betty was open to giving it a try.

The team building proved to be a total disaster. The majority of the time was spent trying to mediate the conflict between the two individuals whom the executive had mentioned in their first meeting. While at first Betty used the interaction between these two as a learning opportunity for everyone present (teaching listening and negotiation skills, for example), eventually the team tired of the tension in the room and began to mentally check out. In the end the conflict was never resolved, and the other team members felt that the experience was a waste of their time.

Betty learned the hard way that women often underestimate how much they know and put more stock in a stranger's opinion than in their own wisdom. From doctors to car salesmen, we think others know better. Betty acquiesced to the executive's assertion that he knew better than she—and the results were catastrophic. Her reputation within the company was damaged, and the executive wound up blaming her lack of expertise rather than recognizing that she was correct in her initial diagnosis and recommendation. In the long run she would have been better off saying no to the opportunity. Unlike men, we tend to admit it when we don't know something—but fail to trust ourselves when we do. Men can tell us something entirely wrong with more authority than any woman ever will. Worse yet, we believe it.

COACHING TIPS

• Before assuming someone knows more than you, ask a few probing questions to determine his or her expertise. "Why do you recommend that?" or "How do you know that?" will at least convey the message that you're not a pushover.

• Before asking someone else's opinion, be certain you really need it. As discussed earlier, asking a question to which you know the answer can diminish your stature.

• If something doesn't sound or feel quite right to you, it probably isn't. Buy time to think by insisting on a time-out to consider what's been suggested.

ACTION ITEM ☐

Mistake 119

Taking Notes, Getting Coffee, and Making Copies

*A*lthough it happens more covertly nowadays, at any minute during any given day there has to be a woman somewhere in the world tearing her hair out about this problem. How many times have I heard a man say, "Let's have _____ [fill in the blank with any woman's name] take notes. She has the best handwriting." Or, "Linda, would you mind making the coffee?"—as if it's really a question. Also, in certain female-dominated industries (which I will not name, but think *The Devil Wears Prada*), using employees to carry out your personal chores is common.

In workshops and seminars women frequently ask, "What should I do when I'm asked to make coffee for or take notes at a meeting?" The easy answer is, "Don't do it." What's harder is avoiding it. Each time we accept one of these tasks, we perpetuate the stereotype that a professional woman's role is to nurture, care for, and serve others at work. The inevitable result is that we feel either badly about ourselves or angry at the situation. Neither solves the problem. How can you respond to inappropriate requests? Well, it just so happens I have a few coaching tips.

COACHING TIPS

• Tell your boss about how you feel being given these tasks and suggest that the responsibilities be rotated. If he or she tells you it's no big deal, respond simply and nondefensively with "It's a big deal to me."

• When asked in front of a group if you'll make copies or take notes, practice saying in a neutral, unemotional way, "I think I'll pass, since I did it last time."

• Show that you're a good "meeting manager." Make a checklist of meeting tasks and suggest that the department administrative assistant be assigned them.

• Introduce your corporate culture to the custom of having the newest person on the team perform these tasks.

• When asked to do personal errands, let the boss know you're happy to do them when you have time, but otherwise you don't want to take away from being able to do a good job at what you were hired for. This may not be what he or she wants to hear, but consider your options. If you carry out the errands, you'll feel resentful; and if you don't, you may be fired. Pick your poison. If the errand requests persist, it's time to look for another job, ask for a transfer, or wait the boss out for a specified period of time.

ACTION ITEM

Mistake 120

Tolerating Inappropriate Behavior

*E*bonisha was transferred to a developmental assignment in the finance department at her company headquarters in December. She was given an office on the executive floor—but when she arrived, she realized it had no desktop computer. *Simple*, she thought. *I'll just call the IT group and get one.* When she called, she was told there were none currently available, but there should be one she could have in about a week. Two weeks passed and no computer. She called once again, and the IT manager apologized. His wife just had a baby and her request slipped between the cracks. The computer intended for her had been given to someone else (a man, of course). He'd see what he could do. By now it was Christmas and her office was closed for two weeks.

I met with Ebonisha in her office in mid-February—still no computer. She showed me a note she'd written to the IT manager:

> *I understand you've been quite busy and that you are short-staffed. However, I think two and a half months is a bit long to wait for a computer I need to perform my work. I would appreciate it if you would get the computer to me as soon as possible.*

What's wrong with the note? you ask. It's too understanding, too understated, and not specific. Here's my edited version:

> *It's been two and a half months since I first asked you for a PC, and, despite numerous promises, I still have not received*

it. Since this seriously impedes my ability to perform my job, I
will expect one in my office no later than Friday. If this is not
possible, or it does not arrive, I will assume it is due to matters
out of your control and will ask your boss and mine for assis-
tance. Please call later today to discuss further.

This **Describes** the problem. **Explains** why it's a problem. **Speci-fies** desired outcomes. Lays out **Consequences**. It contains all the elements of the **DESCript** method described under Mistake 91.

COACHING TIPS

- Take a self-defense class. Defending yourself physically will shift your thinking about defending yourself verbally.
- Use more *I* messages as opposed to *You* messages. The latter tend to be more confrontational and point the finger rather than solve the problem. Listen to the difference.

Turn this:
> *"You're always interrupting me!"*

Into this:
> *"I would appreciate it if you would let me complete my sentence."*

Or turn this:
> *"You can't do that to me!"*

Into this:
> *"I'm not happy with how I've been treated. I'd like to offer some alternatives."*

- Don't swallow your feelings—they'll only catch up with you in one way or another. Get in the habit of asking yourself how you *feel* when you're treated less than respectfully and express it in the form of an *I* message:

> *"I feel like a child when I'm spoken to in that way."*
> *"I feel disrespected when my ideas are ignored."*
> *"I feel that I'm being taken advantage of."*
> *"I feel that I'm entitled to a reason why my request is being denied."*

- Just because you don't react in the moment doesn't mean you don't have the right to go back and revisit an inappropriate encounter. When you're caught off guard, it can be difficult to come up with the right words. It's your prerogative to go back later and say, "I was thinking about something that happened yesterday, and I'd like to tell you how I felt about it."

ACTION ITEM

Mistake 121

Exhibiting Too Much Patience

It may be true that all good things come to those who wait, but women take the maxim to an extreme. When the term *impatient* is applied to a man, it means he's a go-getter, always on the go, or ready to move ahead. When the same term is applied to a woman, it means she expects too much, has a sense of entitlement, or doesn't understand how things work around here. Patience is not a woman's virtue.

In Kyoko's case, she was told to just be patient and she would get the promotion she had been promised. So she waited. And she waited. And she waited some more. After six months of waiting, her boss was transferred to another division. When she asked him about the promotion before he left, he told her the new person would handle it. Of course you know what happened. The new person came in and knew nothing about the promotion—nor did he care. Granting promotions wasn't exactly high on his list of priorities.

COACHING TIPS

• The squeaky wheel does get the grease—and it won't soil your skirt. One executive told me he has no problem if someone pushes him once, pushes him twice, but three times is too many. Until you've pushed at least once, you haven't advocated for yourself.

• Don't believe it when someone tells you you're impatient. It's only a way to get you to quit bugging him or her.

• When you're told to be more patient, ask the person to give you an idea of when you should revisit the matter. If he or she suggests a time too far in the future, press for a time frame that meets your needs. "That's much longer than I had anticipated or we had originally discussed. Why don't we say in two weeks rather than a month."

• If you're asked to wait longer than you think is needed, ask, "Why so long?" There may be a legitimate reason; if there isn't, you can explore other options you may have.

ACTION ITEM

Mistake 122

Accepting Dead-End Assignments

*T*here comes a time in everyone's career—man or woman—when an assignment is offered that has "dead end" written all over it. To take it or not to take it—that is the question. And the answer is: it depends. Don't be quick to accept an assignment just because you think you're supposed to or you don't want to appear ungrateful. You never know where it might lead. On the other hand, it may only lead to a dead end.

I once coached a young woman who was offered a transfer to a small, remote division of her company. Not only that, the division was losing money. Anxious to prove she was capable of turning around a struggling division, and wanting to make her mark so she could move on to bigger and better things, she took the job without a second thought. If she had only done a little more inquiring about the division and the person previously in the position, she would have found that he was leaving because there were rumors that the division was about to be sold. She'd been there only eight months when the deal was announced and she wound up working for a much smaller and less prestigious company. Don't think it didn't cross my mind that she was offered the transfer because she was (1) a woman; (2) young; and (3) naive.

COACHING TIPS

- Never accept any job assignment before first checking it out. Find out what the company has planned for the particular department or division, how it is perceived by others in the company, why the position is vacant, and to what future jobs the position typically leads.

- It's better to err on the side of turning down a dead-end job than to accept one in which others have failed or languished. You'll know this only if you do your homework in advance.

- Consider the following five factors a plus when deciding whether or not to take what appears to be a dead-end assignment:

    1. It has accessibility to senior management.
    2. There's potential for advancement within twelve to eighteen months.
    3. You have unique skills that would turn the dead end into a freeway.
    4. It allows you to significantly expand your network of contacts.
    5. You have nothing to lose.

- Consider the price of taking a lateral assignment. Although these can often be good opportunities to acquire new skills, they also delay upward mobility. If the economic situation is such that there aren't many upward opportunities or the organization is flattening, a lateral is a good move. Otherwise, ask around about how men in similar situations have been treated and ask that you be treated the same.

ACTION ITEM

Mistake 123

Putting the Needs of Others Before Your Own

*A*s women, we frequently find ourselves in positions where our needs come second to those around us. Whether it's taking care of a disabled parent, delaying your education until your husband completes his, or canceling your plans because a child has asked you to do something for her, the results are the same. Your needs don't get met. Of course, there are times when this can't be helped or it's the only right thing to do. But when it becomes the norm rather than the exception to the rule, it's time to take a look at what you do to perpetuate it.

In the workplace we see the phenomenon manifest itself when there are limited funds, perks, or opportunities. Wanting to play fair or be kind, a woman will put her requests on hold or lower her expectations. Pretty soon she feels as if she has no choice at all and doesn't see that she has created the problem.

COACHING TIPS

• Make sure you know what you need or want by routinely asking yourself what it is. Many times women are so accustomed to denying their own needs that they no longer know what they are.

• Between work and home, stop for twenty minutes and do something for yourself. It can be dropping by the library to read the newspaper, going to a park and listening to music, or calling a friend from your cell phone.

• Learn to negotiate. Whether you read a book or take a class, it's important to be familiar with the many techniques of negotiation. For example, did you know it's been proven that those who ask for more wind up getting more? Or that by dividing up your needs like a salami and asking for just one piece at a time, you are more likely to have all your requests approved?

• Avoid giving in just because it's easier or you don't want to make waves. This is another place where reading the book *Nice Girls Just Don't Get It*, by Carol Frohlinger and me, would be helpful. We provide tangible tools for getting the things you most want in life.

• As many times as it takes to believe it, tell yourself it's not selfish to have your needs met—even though it might inconvenience others.

• Make sure you have a life outside work that you want to go home to. Workaholism is often an excuse for not having a life.

ACTION ITEM

Mistake 124

Denying Your Power

*W*hen I had a private psychotherapy practice, I intentionally chose downtown Los Angeles for the location of my office. I wanted to serve the large community of businesswomen who spent the better part of their lives working in corporations around the city. My clients were well-educated and successful women. They also had something else in common: They could not see or acknowledge their own power.

As these women told me stories of how they were taken advantage of, ignored, or in other ways abused at work, I would often say something like "How is it that a powerful woman like yourself allows others to treat her that way?" To a person, the response was to deny she was powerful. "Powerful? I'm not powerful," was a typical reply. And this became the focus of my first book, *Women, Anger, and Depression: Strategies for Self-Empowerment.*

When I examined the phenomenon more closely, it became apparent that women denied their power because of the messages they received growing up. *Power* was associated with men and, as such, was a masculine term. Their perceptions of power had to do with who was in control—and they knew they weren't. Just looking at the top of most major corporations still proves this. As of this writing, only 4.5 percent of CEOs at the nation's one thousand largest companies are women. Wouldn't it be wonderful if a generation from now a woman finds this book and is not appalled, but rather amazed that statistic could possibly be true?

Juanita is an example of someone who, in denying her personal power, found herself depressed and falling short of her career aspirations. She was an attorney with one of Los Angeles's most prestigious law firms. She had been with the firm almost five years and didn't seem to be getting anywhere. Younger, less experienced male lawyers who joined the firm after her were given higher-profile client cases and, in some situations, more paralegal assistance. Needless to say, this contributed to feelings of depression and incompetence. Eventually, it became a catch-22 for Juanita—as she struggled with her depression, she was given even fewer "meaty" cases, which in turn exacerbated the depression.

As we explored why these other lawyers seemed to be surpassing her professionally, Juanita expressed resignation over the fact that it was simply an "old boys' club," and there was little she could do to change the situation. In other words, she felt powerless. When I suggested that she had more power in the situation than she was giving herself credit for (even if it was only to pick up and leave), she denied that she was in any way powerful.

It's not an insignificant fact that Juanita came from a family where she was the only girl among six children. Her father, a Mexican immigrant, presided over a traditional household where the boys were revered and Juanita was pretty much viewed as "just a girl." And so my work with Juanita was about helping her find and define her own brand of power. Without that, I knew the depression would continue, and she had no chance of either improving her work situation or finding a job where she would be better respected.

As is the case with so many women, Juanita had to reframe the definition of power so that it would apply to her as well as men. She knew her father and brothers were powerful—and she wasn't anything like them; ergo, she must not be powerful. As Juanita and I talked extensively about different kinds of power, she came to realize that for women power isn't defined as controlling others, but about having control of one's own life. Denying your unique brand of power erodes self-confidence and perpetuates a self-fulfilling prophecy. It was only after many months of taking baby steps in expressing her needs with both her family and her boss that Juanita's depression gradually lifted and she was able to see the connection between power and having responsibility for her life's direction.

COACHING TIPS

• Read my book *Women, Anger, and Depression: Strategies for Self-Empowerment.* It's designed to be a workbook to help you first identify childhood messages about power and anger and then find ways to express yourself in more empowered ways.

• Redefine power by considering the ways in which you have more control than you allow yourself to use. For example, you have the choice to say "enough" when you're being exploited or to say "no" to unreasonable requests. In many ways this book is about reclaiming your power.

• Use self-talk or posted affirmations to reprogram how you think about power. For example, write, "I am as powerful as I choose to be," or "Only I determine how powerful I am," and post it near your desk where only you can see it or in a portfolio you take to meetings.

• When someone suggests you're powerful, accept the compliment gracefully—even if you don't feel it at the moment. Over time the belief will become part of your self-messages.

ACTION ITEM

Mistake 125

Allowing Yourself to Be the Scapegoat

$\mathcal{E}$va is a human resources representative with a well-known toy manufacturer. She was providing counsel to an employee who was struggling with her relationship with a very difficult boss. One day Eva got a call from her own boss, the division's vice president of human resources, who told her that the woman's boss (also a vice president) wanted to fire the woman. Eva suggested she call the boss and schedule a meeting with him and the employee for the purpose of facilitating a dialogue. Wanting to preserve his own power in this scenario, the HR vice president said no; he'd arrange it. Eva, understanding the politics involved in such situations, agreed to let him broker the meeting.

When she heard nothing about the meeting, Eva called the HR vice president and left a message asking if the meeting had been arranged. She heard nothing back. She sent an e-mail. No reply. Based on feedback she was getting from others, it seemed things were improving, and Eva assumed the meeting wasn't necessary. Then she got a call from the woman's boss. He wanted to meet immediately. When Eva showed up for the meeting, the HR vice president was there, and the woman's boss was apoplectic over the fact that Eva hadn't made an appointment to come talk to him. The HR vice president, who'd insisted on scheduling the meeting himself, sat there silently. Eva could say nothing to assuage the man's anger as he ranted for the next forty minutes about her (Eva's) ineptitude.

Talk about sticky situations. If Eva told the man that the HR vice president had said he would schedule the meeting, she risked losing the support of her boss. If she didn't, she was the scapegoat. She decided it was better to be the scapegoat than to risk having two vice presidents angry with her.

COACHING TIPS

• Diplomatically let people know you don't like being scapegoated. What Eva should have done was speak with her boss after the meeting and let him know he'd failed to support her. Without pointing a finger or blaming, she could have said something like "I'm confused over what just happened in there. It was my understanding that you wanted to schedule the meeting. I left several messages for you and never heard back." At this point her boss would have only two choices. The high road would be to admit his mistake and apologize. Not likely to happen given the fact he'd sat silently in the meeting and let her take the heat. More realistically, he'd tell her it was her responsibility to follow up. Either way, just having the conversation would let him know she didn't appreciate being scapegoated, and would be the best shot at preventing it from happening again. Is this to say it wouldn't happen again? No—only that she'd put him on notice that she recognized what had just happened and was unwilling to silently shoulder the blame.

• Other language you can use to avoid being scapegoated:

  o "There's no need to point a finger or assign blame, but I want you to know I followed the instructions I was given. Why don't we focus on how to move forward?"

  o "I'm happy to redo the report if it's not what you want, but I would like to make clear it was prepared in accordance with our policy related to confidential information."

  o "What would be helpful to me in the future would be if we all would meet together to review the process. It seems different departments had different ideas about what the end product would look like."

ACTION ITEM

Mistake 126

Accepting the Fait Accompli

*Y*our office is redesigning its work spaces. There are two large offices with windows and three smaller interior ones available for staff of your department at your same level. When the floor plan comes out, you notice you've been put in one of the smaller offices while a male peer who has been with the company less time has been given one of the larger spaces with a window. When you speak with the space planning department about it, you're told, "Too late. The plan has already been submitted to office services, and they'll be setting up the phones and computers next week."

If you accept what they say, you've accepted the *fait accompli*—a French term meaning "an irreversible or predetermined decision." It's a technique people use when they don't want to change their plans. When it comes to dealing with women, they often bet on the fact you won't argue and will accept it as fact. It's also used as a negotiation strategy. An insurance company will send you a check to settle a claim before they've even spoken with you. They're betting you'll cash it rather than go to the trouble of contesting the amount.

Women are far more likely than men to go for the bait. Whether it's accepting a lower performance rating than you expected or a less convenient time to take vacation because you've been told "That's just how it is," you've taken less than you're entitled to without an argument. If you're like most women, you'll find a way to rationalize the decision and wind up believing it's what you really deserve. Instead, use the tips on the following page to enhance your negotiation skills.

COACHING TIPS

- If it's important to you, don't accept less than you deserve without a fight. There are times when it won't be worth winning the battle only to lose the war, but there will be other times when the principle matters.
- Always accompany your complaint with a proposed solution. Using the preceding scenario of the offices, an example would be, "Then it's not too late. The phones haven't been moved yet. I suggest the offices be assigned based on seniority or some other objective factor."
- Use the "broken record" to counter claims of fait accompli. Like a record with a scratch, you repeat your concerns, using different words, as many times as necessary to engage a dialogue. Here's how it works:

> **Space planning:** Too late. The plan has already been submitted to office services, and they'll be setting up the phones and computers next week.
>
> **You:** Then it's not too late. The phones haven't been moved yet. I suggest the offices be assigned based on seniority or some other objective factor.
>
> **Space planning:** I've already sent all the plans and change requests to office services.
>
> **You:** It may be inconvenient, but they haven't taken action yet. I'm sure adjustments could still be made based on a more equitable method of assigning space.
>
> **Space planning:** I really don't have time to redo the forms.
>
> **You:** I would be happy to help you once we agree on a fair way to assign space.
>
> **Space planning:** I don't have the authority to make the changes.
>
> **You:** Who does? I will speak with them or we can meet together.
>
> The broken record doesn't always yield the desired results, but it sure gives you a good shot at it—especially if you do it without anger or judgment.

ACTION ITEM

Mistake 127

Permitting Others' Mistakes to Inconvenience You

$\mathcal{T}$his story, a variation on the scapegoating and time-wasting themes, demonstrates how one woman handled being inconvenienced by her boss's mistake. Maria was an internal efficiency expert who went from division to division of a defense company, providing expert advice on streamlining processes. Before she went to one particular location, her boss told her that what the plant wanted was simply an outline for a training program. She developed the outline and met with the plant manager, who expressed disappointment over the brevity of what she had to offer. What he expected was a full curriculum with accompanying materials and for her to facilitate the training program. Maria appropriately told the manager it was her understanding that all he wanted was an outline, but she would double-check with her manager.

When she called her manager, he told her to just go ahead and give them what they wanted. She was dumbfounded. Maria, being an efficiency expert, had scheduled her work around other plant requests and didn't have the time to prepare a project of this magnitude. When her boss reiterated the need to give the plant manager what he'd asked for, she realized she was going to be working long nights and weekends for the next several weeks. His failure to ask the right questions of the plant manager caused her to be greatly inconvenienced.

Maria was savvy enough to know she had to do it, but she wanted to be sure this didn't happen again. Although she could have talked to the boss about it directly, she felt that this was too confrontational for her. Instead, the next time he gave her an assignment, she said, "Let me be clear on what the expectations are here—I don't want to be in the situation again where I show up unprepared as happened last month." She then repeated her understanding of the requirements and added, "If, when I get there, it turns out to be more complex and to require more time than I'm allotting, will I have your support in letting the plant manager know we'll have to reschedule his project?" Perfect! She tactfully let her boss know she didn't like what happened last time and wasn't going to be held responsible for his failure to get the facts straight at the outset. Although she can't control what the boss does in the future, she can make every effort to preclude its happening again.

COACHING TIPS

• Assess the risk against the profit of meeting unreasonable expectations caused by someone else's mistake. There will be times, as in Maria's case, where you'll have no choice but to put in the time needed to meet a customer's needs. But there will also be times when you have the latitude to push back by saying something like "This wasn't what we originally discussed and agreed to. Since I'll have to rethink the plan and put more time into it than I anticipated, I won't be able to have it completed within the initially proposed time frame."

• Before rearranging your life to correct someone else's mistake, try to negotiate a win-win solution. Let the person know you want to provide the best service possible—and that to do so, you may need more time or resources. Ask for what you realistically need to do the job in a reasonable manner.

ACTION ITEM

Mistake 128

Being the Last to Speak

$\mathcal{O}$h, boy. This one is a big problem for women. I've conducted workshops and team-building programs for women as well as mixed groups for more than twenty years. There's a particular exercise I do that involves giving the group a problem and ambiguous instructions for solving it, then observing how participants respond. In all that time, with literally thousands of participants, I can count on one hand the number of times a woman was the first to speak in the exercise when there were both men and women present.

The inclination to hold back when men are present is a huge mistake. Whether it's a small team meeting or a larger group, those who speak early and often are seen as more credible, greater risk-takers, and possessing more leadership potential than those who speak later. Speaking early in meetings shouldn't be confused with being pushy or domineering. Nor should you worry about being accused of talking just to hear your own voice—I'll give you some tips that will make that unlikely. The longer you wait to speak, the more likely it is that someone else will say what you're thinking—and get credit for it.

COACHING TIPS

• In a group, be among the first two or three people to speak, and speak every ten to fifteen minutes thereafter.

• If you can't be among the first to speak, make sure you're not the last.

• You don't always have to give an opinion when you speak. Supporting what someone else has said, asking a legitimate question, or commenting on an emerging theme are equally good ways to make your presence known without appearing as if you like the sound of your own voice.

ACTION ITEM

Mistake 129

Playing the Gender Card

*P*art of my career was spent as an equal employment specialist. In this position my responsibilities included investigating and responding to scores of claims, from sex discrimination to violations of the Rehabilitation Act. The common thread through 90 percent of these cases was not discrimination but poor management. And like it or not, poor management is not illegal. Despite the fact that there are also laws to protect those who file claims of discrimination from retaliation, I never saw a claim that helped anyone's career. It didn't always hurt, but it never helped.

There is no doubt in my mind that sex discrimination is a real part of a woman's employment experience. Except in egregious cases where the discrimination is so blatant it cannot be defended, a company will make every effort to protect its reputation, its management, and its staff. I distinctly remember investigating one case in Texas where a woman said she was discriminated against by her boss because she was a woman. Her claim was that he verbally abused, demeaned, and embarrassed her in front of her peers. Interviews with nearly twenty employees revealed he didn't do this just to her—he did it to everyone. Using this as the defense, the company won the case. When it was over, the manager received no more than a slap on the wrist.

In another case, a woman filed an internal complaint that she was treated differently than her male colleagues when it came to assignments. Despite the fact that my investigation showed she was right— she was treated differently and for no apparent reason other than that she was a woman—the company opted to defend the manager's decisions. She filed a claim with the Equal Employment Opportunity Commission, but before it could be investigated, she was terminated for what I thought was fabricated "cause." It took the commission nearly a year to investigate her claim, find in her favor, and order her to be reinstated with full pay and benefits retroactive to the date of termination. She did come back to work, but, as you might imagine, it was so uncomfortable that she eventually quit voluntarily. She may have won the battle, but she lost the war.

Even if you don't go so far as to file a formal internal or external charge of sex discrimination, there is a stigma attached to women who "make noise" publicly about it—people suddenly become uncomfortable with you. They begin to act differently around you and treat you more carefully. In most cases this is counter to what women want—which is to be treated fairly. These are a few reasons why I strongly urge women to explore every other alternative available to them before playing the gender card.

COACHING TIPS

• Before suggesting there has been sex discrimination, try directly confronting the problem from an objective standpoint. Identify the manifestations of the problem, not the causes. For example, if you think you've been overlooked for a promotion because you're a woman—don't go there at first. Instead, ask your boss or human resources representative why you didn't get the job and what you should do to be considered a better candidate in the future.

• Don't try to change the system alone. You'll wind up being a martyr. If enough other women feel as you do, form a task force to look into the issues, define the problem objectively, and propose solutions.

• Think long and hard before verbalizing concerns about sex discrimination to anyone in your company. It's not something companies take lightly. Many have adopted stringent zero tolerance policies, which means any suggestion of discrimination will be immediately and thoroughly investigated. Once you put the ball in motion, it's often impossible to stop it.

• If gender is a legitimate impediment to success in your current workplace, you have only three options: Put up with it (which I don't recommend—it will only further diminish your self-esteem); pursue the formal internal channels for addressing it (which may or may not yield the desired results); or leave (which is the only option over which you truly have control).

ACTION ITEM

Mistake 130

Tolerating Sexual Harassment

*N*o woman should ever feel she has to tolerate sexual harassment, which is different from sex discrimination. Whereas sex discrimination refers to decisions made on the basis of gender, sexual harassment refers to decisions made based on a woman's willingness or unwillingness to respond to requests for sexual favors or tolerate an intimidating, hostile, or offensive work environment. There isn't quite the same stigma attached to a claim of sexual harassment, because most smart employers know women do not make the charge frequently or frivolously.

A general rule used by many labor lawyers is the "one bite of the apple" theory. A coworker gets one shot at asking you out on a date. Once you say no thanks, the person has had his (or her) one bite of the apple, and further propositions may be construed as sexual harassment. Since it's socially acceptable to date coworkers, one bite of the apple can be defensible. The situation is quite different, however, when the coworker is senior to you. Given the norms around workplace dating, it is incumbent upon you to make your wishes clearly known when you have no interest in the other person.

COACHING TIPS

- In the case of quid pro quo harassment (requests for sexual favors), your first and best recourse is to tell the harasser in no uncertain terms that the behavior is not wanted or welcome. In the case of environmental harassment (making the workplace uncomfortable or intimidating), you should similarly let it be known that you want the jokes, innuendos, or comments to stop. Once you say "No" or "Stop," the behavior moves from being socially acceptable to harassment.

- If the behavior doesn't stop immediately, ask your human resources department for help. If you simply want it to stop and don't want to pursue it further than that, they'll most likely speak with the person and that will be the end of it. It's important that you not tolerate the behavior—allowing it to persist can give the impression you liked it at one time, then changed your mind.

- If, after speaking with human resources, the unwanted behavior continues or if there is retaliation of any kind, consider filing a formal internal charge of sexual harassment. At this point an investigation into your allegations will most likely be conducted. Outcomes can vary from a verbal warning to transfer or termination of the offender.

ACTION ITEM

Mistake 131

Engaging in E-Mail Wars

 $\mathscr{T}$ hank you to Amy Franko of Impact Instruction for suggesting this mistake made by many women who would rather have it out in e-mails or texts than face-to-face. I hate to admit it, but I, too, have gone a few rounds with people in an e-mail war. These types of interactions are rarely satisfying and never productive. A poison-pen e-mail may make you feel better in the moment, but if you're anything like me, you later regret not taking the high road. There are a few exceptions.

Let's go back for a minute to the difference between transactional and personal relationships. The former is one where goods or services are exchanged on a onetime or infrequent basis, whereas the latter are long-term relationships with people I know, like, or want or need to have in my life for one reason or another. You may choose to confront in writing someone with whom you have a transactional relationship. It may serve the purpose of documentation or providing detailed clarity about your concerns. This is certainly acceptable and understandable.

On the other hand, if you do the same thing with people with whom you have a personal relationship, you will most likely escalate the problem and damage the relationship. In this case, you have also given the other person ammunition in writing that can later be used against you if you were inappropriate, vulgar, or mean-spirited in your communications.

COACHING TIPS

- When using written communications to confront an issue, keep it factual, civil, and professional. If you wouldn't make the comment to someone's face, don't say it in an e-mail, text, or letter.
- If two rounds of correspondence don't solve the problem, it's time for a face-to-face. Another reason why you want to remain civil.
- Avoid the inclination to respond in kind to inappropriate correspondence that you receive. Stooping to the level of the other person will ultimately backfire on you.
- Don't copy everyone in your address book on your correspondence where problems or concerns are discussed. It's not about getting people to take sides, it's about resolving the problem.

ACTION ITEM

Mistake 132

Going for the Bait

*A*fter a keynote that I did for Nestlé's women's affinity group where I requested input for the update to this book, Jeanette Rojas, a financial analyst with the firm, came up to me and said she hoped I might touch on being a lesbian in the workplace. At first I struggled to find a place to put it, because I couldn't associate being a lesbian with a mistake per se. I followed up with her by phone to find out more about her thinking and realized she was talking about the way you respond to people in the workplace who are either curious about or uncomfortable with your sexuality.

I asked Jeanette if she felt as if it were her responsibility to educate people who ask inappropriate questions or make inappropriate comments. To her credit, she said she did not. She believes who she is, acting with authenticity in all aspects of her life, speaks for itself. In other words, she doesn't go for the bait. Instead, she chalks it up to the other person's ignorance or discomfort. Nonetheless, it is a challenge she and other lesbians face when they are out of the closet.

You don't have to be a lesbian to be baited. Nice girls get baited in all kinds of ways. People say things that are offensive, off-the-wall, or thoughtless to women of color, differently abled people, pregnant women (married and not), single moms, and women going through a divorce. When that happens, you have to make a decision: Address the comment or ignore it. If you address it, you're sometimes thought of as defensive. If you ignore it, you might feel badly about yourself or internalize a message as true when in fact it's not. The ultimate call about whether or not to go for the bait, particularly when others are making comments of a personal nature, is one that each woman has to make for herself, based on her values. With that said, the following tips might be useful in making that decision.

COACHING TIPS

- Give yourself permission to think about how you want to respond to an inappropriate comment or question. One of the things women tell me is that they have a hard time coming up with a response in the moment, but later they think of something they wish they had said. It's okay to say you want to think about, then circle back and say something like "I was thinking about your comment and realized it made me feel uncomfortable because..."
- Before responding, ask the person where the question is coming from. Oftentimes we realize that what seems inappropriate or baiting is actually coming from a place of wanting to learn more. In this case, you can choose to educate or not.
- Continue to work on developing a sense of confidence and self-comfort. When we're comfortable and have done the work that's needed to feel grounded with who we are, warts and all, we are far less likely to go for the bait. This comfort allows us to be our most authentic selves, rather than feel that we have to explain or defend ourselves.
- Don't feel as if you have to respond at all if a comment or question makes you feel uncomfortable. Instead, let the person know you're not comfortable answering and change the subject.

ACTION ITEM

Mistake 133

Crying

*Y*ou had to know I would get here sooner or later. You don't need a PhD to know many women cry when they're happy, when they're sad, when they're frustrated, when they're angry, when the sun is shining, when it's not—well, you get the point. While most women know they shouldn't do this at work, there are times when you just can't help it. You don't need an example—you've either seen it or done it. Let's cut straight to how you can at least minimize it or recover professionally from it.

COACHING TIPS

• Don't substitute tears for anger. Women often cry because they've been taught being angry isn't ladylike or acceptable. When you feel the tears well up, silently ask yourself the question *What's making me angry?*

• When you do cry at work, immediately ask to be excused. Don't sit there bawling. It only makes people uncomfortable. By removing yourself temporarily from the situation, you let others off the hook (which they'll appreciate) and give yourself time to become composed. Make it a stock response to say, "I hear what you're saying. Give me some time to think about it and get back to you."

• Studio City–based psychotherapist and business coach Susan Picascia provides her clients with these four tips:

    o Put words to the tears and focus on the problem instead of your feelings. Say something like "As you can see, I have strong feelings about this. Why don't we focus on specific outcomes to solve the problem?"

o Don't be seduced by seemingly humanistic organizations (hospitals, nonprofits, and the like) into thinking crying is okay. Crying gives people the impression you're not in control, not competent, and weak. We like to think there is room for these very human, very real emotions in the workplace. But we're not there. People have negative associations with crying in the workplace—and it crosses gender lines. Women are no more compassionate than men in this arena.

o If you find yourself welling up frequently or easily, you may want to look inside with a good friend, coach, or psychotherapist. We cry when we're on overload, angry, anxious, hurt, or for a reason appropriate to a situation. If you're welling up a lot, you may find your thinking is too negative or catastrophic. Few things in the workplace are life-and-death or so dramatic they can't be addressed reasonably well. Keep your emotions from causing you to think the worst. Think positively about what may seem like a very scary experience and you will cry less.

o When someone goes for your jugular in a personal way, don't go for the bait and do set him or her straight. Focus on the content of your conversation by saying something like "Stan, this is not about me overreacting, this is about a workload problem we need to solve."

ACTION ITEM

Appendix

Personal Development Planning and Resources

Until one is committed, there is hesitancy, the chance to draw back. Concerning all acts of initiative (and creation), there is one elementary truth that ignorance of which kills countless ideas and splendid plans: that the moment one definitely commits oneself, then Providence moves too.... Whatever you can do, or dream you can do, begin it. Boldness has genius, power, and magic in it. Begin it now.

Goethe

Now that you've spent time reading this book, it's time to make a commitment and a plan for how you will achieve your goals. This is where the rubber meets the road. You can say you're going to do things differently, but like the story of the pig and the chicken who were both asked to bring something to breakfast, *commitment* makes the difference.

Go back through each of the chapters and take a look at the Action Items you've checked. Before completing the development plan provided, look for commonalities and categorize the items into three to five behaviors you believe will make the most difference for you. Then go ahead and write down what you commit to doing differently as a result of having invested your time and money in this book. You'll find a sample line to use as a model to get you started.

Resist the urge to get carried away with too many commitments. You really can't work successfully on changing more than just a few things at a time. Besides, it's not the number of things you change that's important, but selecting those few behaviors that will make the biggest difference. I once had the opportunity to interview Wimbledon champ Julie Anthony, who now coaches several women players on the tennis pro tour. When I asked her about the secret of creating meaningful change, she told me if you focus on one thing, other change occurs naturally. For example, she would never tell a player to focus on changing her grip, her stance, and her forehand all at once. Anthony pointed out that by just changing the grip, the player will find her stance and forehand changing along with it.

The same holds true for you. You don't have to worry about being more concise, less apologetic, having a stronger handshake, and wearing the right clothes to work all at the same time. Do just one thing—and do that well—and you'll find that over time there will be a subtle shift in many other behaviors. The point of coming up with three to five items for your personal development plan is so that as you master one, you can check it off and move on to the next.

You'll notice there's also a column for "resources." The remainder of this chapter provides you with suggestions in books, courses, articles, and other resources to help you develop the skills that will bring you closer to achieving your professional goals. You don't have to reinvent the wheel; just go through the list and select those that seem most appealing to you and realistic in terms of your actually utilizing them. Don't set yourself up to fail. This isn't a diet. Stretch yourself, but don't make it so difficult that you'll want to abandon your plan after a week.

Finally, remember that growth is a process of two steps forward, one step back. This is what clients report to me all the time. In the beginning it seems as if you'll never quite get the hang of it. Before long, it's second nature—unconscious competence. As the Chinese philosopher Lao-tzu said, "A journey of a thousand miles must begin with a single step."

This is where I leave you. It's been a pleasure sharing my experiences and those of my clients and colleagues with you. I would be delighted to hear from you with your comments, success stories, and areas where you get stuck. I can be reached by e-mail at info@drloisfrankel.com. Every letter I get is answered (although it sometimes takes me a little while), so don't hesitate to write. You deserve to have your questions answered, and I would value your feedback.

PERSONAL DEVELOPMENT PLAN

Action Item	Commitment	Start Date	Resources
Speak more concisely	*Ask for feedback from Roberta after each team meeting*	*March 1*	*Read:* You Are the Message
	Mentally plan what I'm going to say before speaking	*Ongoing*	
	Join Toastmasters	*April 1*	

Coaching

Obviously, I'm a proponent of business coaching. I've seen firsthand how it helps good performers distinguish themselves as great performers in comparison to their peers. Prospective clients often ask for statistics related to the results of coaching. The data collected in my own firm indicates that about 60 percent of the people we coach are promoted within one year. An additional 10 percent choose to leave their current jobs and/or employers as a result of coaching and go on to more satisfying positions or companies that are a better match for them. Ten percent of those coached remain in their jobs doing better than before, but not enough so that they are considered high performers. And in about 10 percent of our clients, we see no change at all due to their lack of commitment to the process or other intervening factors.

A variety of factors contribute to results. Is the client paying for the coaching or is the company? When it's the latter, there may be less sense of urgency about getting the most possible from the process. Is the client in a position that's well suited for him or her? If not, no amount of coaching will enable him or her to achieve maximum potential. What are the goals coming into the process? If the focus is on being promoted, the likelihood of promotion increases. If it's to get better at a current position, then that's what usually happens.

Another factor is the coach himself or herself. During the past decade, the field of coaching has exploded. With so many people entering the field, it's inevitable that some are great coaches, while others haven't had the business experience needed to help clients understand the many nuances of business. Coaching, like any other field, consists of people with a wide variety of experiences, expertise, and credentials. My suggestion is that before investing money in any coach, you ask him or her these questions:

- How long have you been in practice?
- What did you do before you were a coach?
- Do you have any particular credentials or licenses to coach?
- What is your educational experience?
- Are you a member of any professional coaching associations?
- Before I decide to work with you, may I have the names and phone numbers of current or former clients whom I can call for a reference?
- What services are included in your fee?
- In what area do you consider yourself a coaching expert?
- Have you actually worked inside a corporation or have you been a consultant for your entire career?

The answers to these questions will give you an idea of whether you're dealing with a seasoned professional or someone new to the field with little business background. I personally find the business background critical—it's what I look for when hiring coaches. There are many psychologists moving into the field as personal coaches, but they lack the practical experience needed to understand workplace dynamics. They may be well qualified to help you address issues related to stress or relationship issues, but if they haven't experienced the realities of life inside a corporation, they may not be as qualified to assist you with the subtleties that contribute to success.

Because it's impossible for me to know all the reputable coaches currently in practice, I will provide you with a listing of only those with whom I am personally familiar. I've also included the website of a professional association that will enable you to locate other coaches in your area. As with any service—caveat emptor.

Corporate Coaching International
http://www.corporatecoachingintl.com
877-DOC-LOIS

What kind of coach would I be if I told you to market yourself, then left out my own coaching firm? In 1987, after two decades spent working in the field of human resources both inside and outside corporations, I became a pioneer in the field of executive coaching and developed the concept of team-based coaching. This unique approach allows each client the opportunity to work simultaneously or sequentially with several coaches, each with a particular expertise. Our focus is on leadership development, team building, and one-on-one coaching. Although I no longer personally coach, Dr. Pam Erhardt, my handpicked successor, is an ICF-certified coach with expertise in mindful leadership, emotional intelligence, political savvy, and team development. You can learn more about Pam and our other coaches, take a coaching quiz, and find complementary resources on our website.

International Coach Federation
http://www.coachfederation.org

In addition to general information about the coaching process, the website of this professional association of coaches allows you to sort potential matches using a variety of factors including discipline, location, price, and more. Once you've logged on to their site, go to the Coach Referral Service link.

Liz Cornish
First Hundred Days Consulting
707-433-5972
http://www.100days.com
info@100days.com

Liz, author of the book *Hit the Ground Running*, coaches women from middle management through executive levels to manage transitions, achieve their goals, and sustain top performance. She helps leaders who must leverage relationships, deliver results, inspire confidence, jump-start teams, and manage the push to action against the pull to make thoughtful, informed decisions.

Mindy Danna
Minds for Change, LLC
323-839-7335
mindy.danna@gmail.com

Mindy works with people struggling to change their behavior in the face of escalating complexity and an unrelenting pace. Using an approach that reveals how we unintentionally obstruct the very changes we want to make, she helps people get "unstuck" and unleash their potential and achieve results.

Tom Henschel
Essential Communications
818-788-5357
http://www.essentialcomm.com
thenschel@essentialcomm.com

Tom is an internationally recognized expert in the field of workplace communications and self-presentation. He works with professionals at all levels to achieve "the look and sound of leadership." Trained as a classical actor at the Juilliard School, Tom helps clients to learn proven techniques for becoming a valued actor on the corporate stage.

Linda Novack
Novack & Associates
310-454-2886
http://www.Novackandassociates.com

Linda is a results-driven master certified coach. She coaches women leaders to achieve peak performance in their work, balance in all aspects of their lives, and successful navigation through life's transitions. She has extensive experience working with women in senior management in a variety of industries. Her areas of expertise include: (1) leadership development; (2) communication and influencing skills; (3) public speaking skills; (4) executive presence; and (5) team development for a high-performance, collaborative workforce.

Susan Picascia
818-752-1787
SPicascia@earthlink.net

As a business coach, Susan helps individuals overcome obstacles to achieving peak performance, strong professional relationships, and work-life integration. She works with employees and management to minimize workplace conflict and also has a private practice in psychotherapy, where she focuses on work-related issues and career development.

Christine Reiter
Time Strategies
626-795-1800
chrisdr@pacbell.net

Time Strategies coaches clients who are constantly challenged by paper flow and time management. Solutions are customized to meet each client's needs to enable better management of paper, time, and technical resources. Out-of-the-box techniques are used for clients who are frustrated by traditional approaches to time and paper management.

Workshops and Training Programs

As with coaches, the quality of workshops and workshop leaders runs the gamut. If you've ever attended a training program, you're probably already on the mailing lists of many firms who provide public workshops. Other consulting firms conduct only private workshops for the employees of companies that pay their fees. Given the choice, I would advise you to take company-sponsored classes simply because the facilitator should be familiar with your company and its unique requirements for success. There are a few firms, however, that I recommend based on the outstanding programs they offer in specialized areas. You'll find these listed below.

Before signing up for any program, remember that the purpose of training is to increase your skill in a particular area. Here are a few suggestions to maximize participation in training programs:

- Set specific goals or skills you want to take away as a result of attending the program.
- Sit in the front of the room. This will cause you not only to pay closer attention, but also to *get* more attention from the facilitator.
- Fully and actively participate. As a trainer, I know that those who participate the most get the most out of the program.
- Don't be afraid to ask questions—especially ones that relate to you personally. Facilitators appreciate participants who seek practical ways to apply their classroom learning.
- Prepare a summary of the key themes to share at a future team meeting. If you know in advance you're going to do this, you'll participate in a different way than if you're not expected to share the learning experience.
- After the program, thank your boss for the opportunity to attend and discuss with him or her what you learned. There's no better way to assure you'll be allowed to attend future programs.

American Management Association
http://www.amanet.org/seminars/index.htm
800-262-9699

AMA seminars are geared to every organizational level—from chief executive officers to administrative professionals, from senior executives to first-time managers. These small-group, team-learning experiences are dynamic and interactive. Seminar leaders are active business professionals with years of hands-on experience.

Dale Carnegie Training
http://www.dalecarnegietraining.com

Although I've never attended a Dale Carnegie program myself, I'm told by people who have that they're professionally done and can really make a difference in how you see yourself and interact with others. In addition to workshops related to increasing confidence, public speaking, and widening your personal horizons, they offer classes that can be used toward continuing education credits (CEUs) and college credits.

Amy Franko
Impact Instruction Group
www.impactinstruction.com

Amy Franko is a nationally recognized speaker, trainer, and moderator with a focus on developing emerging women leaders. She has worked with many professional organizations and Fortune 500 companies, and her training design has twice received the APEX Award for Publication Excellence. Her website offers a variety of free articles, e-books, and white papers ideal for the emerging woman leader.

The Heim Group
www.heimgroup.com
888-917-7797

Since establishing the Heim Group in 1985, Dr. Pat Heim, CEO and best-selling author, has become recognized internationally as the expert in the area of gender differences in the workplace. The Heim Group, a research-based workplace communication consulting firm, is dedicated to helping organizations identify and solve communication issues, including gender-related issues, and learn how to leverage differences into a competitive advantage. Dr. Heim also provides individual coaching.

NTL
http://www.ntl.org
800-777-5227

I highly recommend NTL to clients who want to gain increased insight into their workplace behavior and how others perceive them. Founded in 1947, it is the premier provider of experiential programs for people at all levels of an organization. I encourage you to visit the NTL website and explore the spectrum of experiential programs it offers.

Toastmasters International
www.toastmasters.org
949-858-8255

Toastmasters is not really a training program, but organized groups of businesspeople who meet weekly for the purpose of improving their skills in conducting meetings, giving impromptu speeches, and preparing more formal presentations. There are more than eighty-five hundred chapters in seventy countries around the globe—and if there's not one convenient for you, the website contains information about how you can start one. One woman I referred to Toastmasters told me it significantly increased her self-confidence and platform skills.

Negotiating Women
866-616-9804
http://www.negotiatingwomen.com

Through live negotiation training, online e-learning courses, and consulting to organizations, this firm provides practical advice to help women at every stage of their careers to claim their value and create conditions for success in business.

The Women's Wilderness Institute
303-938-9191
http://www.womenswilderness.org

The Women's Wilderness Institute offers programs that help women develop their courage, confidence and leadership skills. Learn and practice self-awareness, communication, conflict resolution, and standing your ground in the face of peer pressure in a supportive group of women. Their courses also teach climbing, backpacking, and other wilderness skills.

Recommended Reading

Throughout this book I've mentioned books and articles that I believe will help you to gain greater skills in many of the areas we've touched upon. For your convenience, I've summarized these below as well as included several others that I've found valuable.

Books

Adams, Marilee. *Change Your Questions, Change your Life: 10 Powerful Tools for Life and Work.* San Francisco: Berrett-Koehler, 2009.

Ailes, Roger. *You Are the Message: Getting What You Want By Being Who You Are.* New York: Crown Business, 1989.

Bailey, Deborah. *Think Like an Entrepreneur: Transforming Your Career and Taking Charge of Your Life.* Bright Street Books, 2010.

Bateson, Mary Catherine. *Composing a Life.* New York: Plume, 1990.

Bradberry, Travis, and Jean Greaves. *Emotional Intelligence 2.0.* San Diego: TalentSmart, 2009.

Brandon, Rick, and Marty Seldman. *Survival of the Savvy: High-Integrity Political Tactics for Career and Company Success.* New York: Free Press, 2004.

Brown, Brené. *The Gifts of Imperfection: Let Go of Who You Think You're Supposed to Be and Embrace Who You Are.* Center City, MN: Hazelden, 2010.

————. *I Thought It Was Just Me (But It Isn't): Making the Journey from "What Will People Think?" to "I Am Enough."* New York: Gotham, 2007.

Bundles, A'Lelia. *On Her Own Ground: The Life and Times of Madam C. J. Walker.* New York: Scribner, 2002.

Chamine, Shirzad. *Positive Intelligence: Why Only 20% of Teams and Individuals Achieve Their True Potential and How You Can Achieve Yours.* Austin, TX: Greenleaf, 2012.

Cornish, Liz. *Hit the Ground Running: A Woman's Guide to Success for the First 100 Days on the Job.* New York: McGraw-Hill, 2006.

Edmondson, Ella L. J. *Career GPS: Strategies for Women Navigating the New Corporate Landscape.* New York: Amistad, 2010.

Feldhahn, Shaunti. *The Male Factor: The Unwritten Rules, Misperceptions, and Secret Beliefs of Men in the Workplace.* New York: Broadway Business, 2009.

Fisher, Roger, and Daniel Shapiro. *Beyond Reason: Using Emotions as You Negotiate.* New York: Penguin, 2005.

Fisher, Roger, and William Ury. *Getting to Yes: Negotiating Agreement Without Giving In.* New York: Penguin, 2011.

Frankel, Lois P. *See Jane Lead: 99 Ways for Women to Take Charge at Work.* New York: Warner Business, 2007.

————. *Stop Sabotaging Your Career: 8 Proven Strategies to Succeed—in Spite of Yourself.* New York: Warner Business, 2007.

————. *Women, Anger, and Depression: Strategies for Self-Empowerment.* Deerfield Beach, FL: Health Communications, 1991.

Frankel, Lois P., PhD and Carol Frohlinger, JD. *Nice Girls Just Don't Get It: 99 Ways to Win the Respect You Deserve, the Success You've Earned, and the Life You Want.* New York: Harmony, 2011.

Green, Charles H., and Andrea P. Howe. *The Trusted Advisor Field Book: A Comprehensive Toolkit for Leading with Trust.* Hoboken, NJ: Wiley, 2011.

Heim, Pat, and Susan K. Golant. *Hardball for Women: Winning at the Game of Business.* Rev. ed. New York: Plume, 2005.

Hollands, Jean. *Same Game, Different Rules: How to Get Ahead Without Being a Bully Broad, Ice Queen, or "Ms. Understood."* New York: McGraw-Hill, 2001.

Houston, Phillip, Michael Floyd, and Susan Carnicero. *Spy the Lie: Former CIA Officers Teach You How to Detect Deception.* New York: St. Martin's Press, 2012.

Kayser, Thomas A. *Mining Group Gold: How to Cash in on the Collaborative Brain Power of a Team for Innovation and Results.* 3rd ed. New York: McGraw-Hill, 2010.

Klaus, Peggy. *Brag! The Art of Tooting Your Own Horn Without Blowing It.* New York: Warner, 2003.

Kolb, Deborah M., Judith Williams, and Carol Frohlinger. *Her Place at the Table: A Woman's Guide to Negotiating Five Key Challenges to Leadership Success.* San Francisco: Jossey-Bass, 2010.

Maister, David H., Charles H. Green, and Robert M. Galford. *The Trusted Advisor.* New York: Touchstone, 2001.

Marshall, Lisa B. *Smart Talk: The Public Speaker's Guide to Success in Every Situation.* New York: St. Martin's Griffin, 2012.

McGinty, Sarah Myers. *Power Talk: Using Language to Build Authority and Influence.* New York: Business Plus, 2002.

Mitchell, Pamela. *The 10 Laws of Career Reinvention: Essential Survival Skills for Any Economy.* New York: Dutton, 2010.

Patterson, Kerry, Joseph Grenny, Ron McMillan, and Al Switzler. *Crucial Conversations: Tools for Talking When Stakes Are High.* New York: McGraw-Hill, 2011.

Reardon, Kathleen Kelley. *The Secret Handshake: Mastering the Politics of the Business Inner Circle.* New York: Crown Business, 2002.

Sandberg, Sheryl. *Lean In: Women, Work and the Will to Lead.* New York: Knopf, 2013.

Siegel, Daniel J. *Mindsight: The New Science of Personal Transformation.* New York: Bantam, 2011.

Silver, Susan. *Organized to Be Your Best!: Transforming How You Work.* Los Angeles: Adams-Hall, 2006.

Stone, Douglas, Bruce Patton, Sheila Heen, and Roger Fisher. *Difficult Conversations: How to Discuss What Matters Most.* New York: Penguin, 2000.

Thaler, Linda Kaplan, and Robin Koval. *The Power of Nice: How to Conquer the Business World with Kindness.* New York: Crown Business, 2006.

Ury, William. *Getting Past No: Negotiating in Difficult Situations.* New York: Bantam, 2002.

Weston, Liz. *The 10 Commandments of Money: Survive and Thrive in the New Economy.* New York: Plume, 2011.

Wilson Schaef, Anne. *Women's Reality: An Emerging Female System in a White Male Society.* New York: HarperOne, 1992.

Articles

Barron, Lisa. "Ask and You Shall Receive? Gender Differences in Negotiators' Beliefs About Requests for a Higher Salary." *Human Relations* (June 2003).

Hewlett, Sylvia Ann, Lauren Leader-Chivee, Laura Sherbin, Joanne Gordon, and Fabiola Dieudonne. "Executive Presence." Center for Talent Innovation, 2012.

Ibarra, Herminia, Nancy M. Carter, and Christine Silva. "Why Men Still Get More Promotions Than Women." *Harvard Business Review* (September 2010).

Kotter, John, "What Leaders Really Do." *Harvard Business Review* (December 2001).

Network of Executive Women. "Affinity Networks: Building Organizations Stronger Than Their Parts." 2006.

Slaughter, Anne-Marie. "Why Women Still Can't Have It All." *Atlantic* (July/August 2012).

Book Club Guide

Discussion Questions

1. What does the author mean when she refers to "nice girls"?
2. What were some of the messages you heard in childhood about how girls were supposed to behave? How did those messages differ from those received by your brothers or male cousins?
3. If you received the message that girls could do anything, how was that message reinforced or negated in school and the workplace?
4. How does the media's portrayal of women (in movies, advertising, television, etc.) impact how you see yourself and what others expect from you?
5. How do you think the author uses the term *corner office* as a metaphor?
6. The author talks about the workplace as a playing field with rules, boundaries, and strategies.
   - What are the implications when the boundaries narrow for a particular person or group?
   - How are the rules and boundaries different in your workplace for men and women? How are they the same?
   - How are the rules and boundaries different in your workplace for Caucasians and for women of color? How are they the same?
7. In what area on the self-assessment did you score the lowest? Highest? How do your experiences validate these scores?
8. What three mistakes in the book do you most identify with and why?
9. What would be the hardest coaching tip for you to implement and why? What would be the positive ramifications if you did implement it? What might be the negative ramifications?

10. What are some of the greatest challenges for you personally in achieving your career goals? What can you do to meet the challenges?
11. What can you do to facilitate change that will help make the workplace even more hospitable for the next generation of women?
12. What mistakes do you make in the workplace or do you see others making that the author did not discuss? How would you coach someone to overcome these challenges?
13. What goals will you set for yourself as a result of reading this book? How will you measure success?
14. Whom in your life can you count on to help you achieve your goals? What "naysayers" do you need to sequester?
15. The author believes in the maxim "Each one, teach one." From what you have read, what can you teach others to help them achieve *their* goals?

About the Author

DR. LOIS FRANKEL, president of Corporate Coaching International, a Pasadena, California, consulting firm, literally wrote the book on coaching people to succeed in businesses large and small around the globe. Her books *Nice Girls Don't Get the Corner Office*; *Nice Girls Don't Get Rich*; *Nice Girls Just Don't Get It* (coauthored with Carol Frohlinger); and *See Jane Lead* are international best sellers that have been translated into more than twenty-five languages worldwide. *Stop Sabotaging Your Career*, a book based on her experiences as a pioneer in the field of business coaching working with everyone from CEOs to entry-level professionals, is a must-read for both men and women.

Sought after as a public speaker for her witty, warm, and practical presentations that simultaneously engage, educate, and entertain, Dr. Frankel is among the top names of international speakers. She has appeared on the *Today Show*, *Larry King Live*, CNN, *Tavis Smiley*, and *20/20* and also been featured in *USA Today*, *People* magazine, and the *Wall Street Journal*.

Dr. Frankel can be reached through either of her websites:

www.corporatecoachingintl.com
or
www.drloisfrankel.com
and at
www.facebook.com/drloisfrankel
www.twitter.com/drloisfrankel